RETURN TO BELIEF

Yvonne Lubbock

My Knowledge was Divine, I knew by Intuition
those things which, since my Apostasie,
I collected again by the Highest Reason.

(TRAHERNE)

Collins

ST JAMES'S PLACE · LONDON · 1961

© Yvonne Lubbock, 1961
Printed in Great Britain
Collins Clear-Type Press: London and Glasgow

DEDICATED TO THE MEMORY OF FRANCES CORNFORD

Contents

PREFACE   *page* 9

PART I   HOW IT ALL STARTED   15

PART II ON IMMORTALITY
         1. A future life and the existence of God   29
         2. A future life independent of God   42
         3. Probability and evidence of survival   50

PART III ON VARIOUS IDEAS OF GOD and
         what I learned from them
         1. I reach belief in absolutes   67
         2. I reject the God of Aristotle   80

PART IV THE SAME (continued)
         1. The value of intuition   91
         2. The hollowness of pantheism   101
         3. About original sin   116
         4. The necessity for a subjective approach in
            religion   127
         5. A meaning behind Christian doctrine   136
         6. The significance of ' full Christianity '   145

PART V   FOUR GREAT RELIGIONS:
         What I learned from them and what I rejected
         1. Hinduism   161

Contents

2. Buddhism   page 173
3. Islam   182
4. Judaism   187

PART VI   CHRISTIANITY
1. The Incarnation   195
2. Faith   204
3. Dogma and religion   210
4. At-one-ment   228
5. The Resurrection   236
6. The Church   242

TEXTS RELEVANT TO
PASSAGES DISCUSSED   for details see page 261

INDEX   369

Preface

It has been remarked by Norman Douglas that it is one of the maladies of our age that in trivial things we profess a fanatical loyalty to truth, whilst we consistently refuse to face it in matters of real importance. It is only too easy for us to spend our whole lives in an elaborate system of escape from every question that is vital.

But for those who cannot be content to pursue apparently meaningless existences in an altogether mysterious universe, there is a need to discover some philosophy that will make sense of their world, and according to which they can order their lives. That I was one of those who became aware of this need and undertook such a voyage of discovery the following pages will show. The very nature of this work, however, demands that it should start with an apology. For here is an account of a preliminary search for enlightenment on questions no less tremendous than the existence of God and the possibility of man's survival of death. What qualifications had I for such a search, let alone justification for its recording? Two assets for seeking I did possess: rather dreary streaks of earnestness and love of reclusion.

I had found from as early an age as I can remember, a peculiar satisfaction in solitude. However severe the storms in the adult sphere around me, once I was alone they generally ceased to trouble me. It was not that I had to invent a world of my own in order to cheer myself up; I cannot recall a time when it did not exist as the most important thing in my life. And as I grew

9

older, it was filled with an indefinable wonder about the mystery at the heart of things—a wonder which was at the same time peace and an intense excitement, a balm and yet a stimulant. It was inseparable from a feeling of expectancy—common to most children—and from a sense that there was something far more real and permanent than what appeared to be the trivial, unpredictable and shifting adult world, and which I might discover.

This feeling of expectancy I have never quite lost although for a long time it was overlaid. And it was this sense that I was just on the point of discovering something of peculiar significance that gave me an incurable persistence when in my middle years I spent the leisure of twenty of them in reading some two hundred and fifty works which promised to shed light on these tremendous questions. For I experienced as keen a desire for my quarry as the drunkard feels for the bottle and the lover for his mistress. This desire possessed my earliest waking moments and haunted my pillow before sleep came to interrupt the chase.

Anyone is entitled to seek. But what of the recording of the findings? Against the charge of hubris that may be levelled at any ordinary person daring to write an account of such a journey, it is just my ordinariness that I put forward in extenuation. Persuaded as I always have been—whenever I gave it a thought—that religion must be 'something for all men' rather than a system evolved by the learned whose God is a *Dieu des savants et des philosophes*, I have tried to describe what the unlearned like myself can find of value in the different philosophies I read. And this account I offer, in much diffidence, to other ordinary people who share my inability to rest content until some meaning and purpose in life has been discovered.

It will be immediately obvious in the pages that follow that I am devoid of philosophical training and that I read only as an amateur. It is therefore hardly necessary to disclaim pretensions to even the most elementary scholarship. And further, I looked only for views on God and immortality, and not for philosophical systems as a whole, which would have proved beyond my intellectual grasp. (I have tried, however, not to injure the ideas I quoted by wrenching them from a context necessary to their import.) Above all, I do not pretend that my own reactions to the various philosophies have themselves any value philosophically. This is the story of how, since I could not think in a vacuum, philosophy worked with me as a catalyst. Although individually there is nothing recondite here in the extracts from philosophical works, as a collection the cumulative effect does appear to me to provide an answer to those questions I was asking.

And where else could I have looked for answers? Theology of course was suspect, since it assumed as 'true' so many things I was in no position either to affirm or to deny: it did not start 'far enough back' for such as I. And the physical sciences, although they used a method of thought which was both definite and universally convincing, could not give an answer to those ultimate questions with which I was primarily concerned. Metaphysics it seemed might do so, although the 'evidence' supplied could not, by its very nature, have scientific precision and objectivity.

In spite of these limitations, I took courage from the words of Plotinus to Flaccus:

' I applaud your devotion to philosophy: I rejoice to hear that your soul has yet set sail, like the returning Ulysses, for its native land—that glorious, that only real country— the world of unseen truth.'

I ventured into that strange country to see what I could learn there. And although it cannot be denied that the account of what I found—often indeed pedestrian—has taken the form of a spiritual Odyssey, there are no explicit yearnings after the Infinite to be seen here, no blush-making exposures of a naked soul. All, I trust, is decent and decorous.

And let not the constant reiteration of the pronoun first person singular suggest that my personal opinions are considered to have intrinsic importance. Their significance is acknowledged to be purely relative and to derive wholly from the nature of this work of which they are an essential part.

I will not apologise for examples of my naïvety which occur here and there throughout. I believe, with Dostoievsky, that most men are simpler and more naïve than they know. And although the very object of my search must brand me nowadays as being not only that but 'old-fashioned' as well, in my obstinate concern with fundamental questions my head will remain bloody but for ever unbowed.

Such thanks as cannot adequately be expressed are due to Professor Basil Willey and the late Mrs. Frances Cornford for their most generous giving of time and labour in reading my typescript. But for their inexhaustible patience, their advice and encouragement, I should probably have lacked the courage to bring this work to completion.

I am also much indebted to Professor Broad for his permission to quote from *Mind and its Place in Nature*, Messrs. Routledge & Kegan Paul, and to the literary executors of the following for permission to quote from their respective works, J. McT. E. McTaggart from *Some Dogmas of Religion*, Messrs. Arnold, C. E. M. Joad from *The Recovery of Belief*, Messrs. Faber & Faber, D. H. Lawrence from *Apropos Lady Chatterley's Lover*, Messrs. Heinemann; and to Alexander Dru, David Swanson, and Walter Lowrie, translators of Sören Kierkegaard, for permission to quote from the *Journals*, *For Self-Examination*, *The Point of View*, *Training in Christianity*, *Concluding Unscientific Postscript*, *The Philosophical Fragments*, and *The Sickness Unto Death*, all published by the Oxford University Press; and to the Universities of Oxford and Cambridge for permission to quote from the *Revised Version* of the Bible.

Cambridge,
July, 1960

PART ONE

How it all started

'Nor could I guess,
What kind of thing I long'd for; But that I
Did somewhat lack of Blessedness,
Beside the Earth and Sky
I plainly found.'
                                    TRAHERNE, *Solitude*

Anatole France believed that the root of man's unhappiness and distaste for life lies in the complete ignorance of his purpose. And Camus has made one of his characters declare that loss of life itself is a small matter, but that what is intolerable is to feel the meaning of life being destroyed, to see our reason for living vanish. For man cannot live a life devoid of meaning.

Twenty-five years ago I should not have understood what France and Camus were talking about. I had managed to live happily, if, no doubt, superficially, for what was probably nearly half my allotted span without troubling myself as to the intrinsic meaning or ultimate purpose of life; although, doubtless, I had many semiconscious motives for living; short-term policies which ensured me, as far as man could plan, all the felicity of which I was then capable.

I had been brought up with little religious background, and I certainly knew nothing of the aim and purpose of life as set forth in the Church catechism until I was almost adult. It is perhaps curious, then, that I should twice have experienced theophanies during my childhood. I had heard but little talk of God. What convinced me suddenly of his existence? Surrounded as I was by an atmosphere to which philosophical and metaphysical speculation contributed no part at all, the material, the temporal and the factual alone formed my habitual environment.

These experiences, not surprisingly therefore, soon became overlaid although they were never entirely smothered. In youth,

15

as a result of school habits, I went through all the motions of a practising Anglican; but I was a callow creature and religion failed to impinge upon my slumbering mentality, evoking neither intellectual doubt nor genuine faith.

With adolescence I lapsed into agnosticism far more, as I now see, from mental laziness and indifference than for any worthy reason. I worked hard; I pursued my tiny but all-absorbing career, and, for the rest, the pleasant rhythm of life—the daily routine, eating and sleeping, getting and spending—lulled me into a false sense of purpose which discouraged disruptive questionings. And obviously I had no leisure in which to think, largely because I did not wish to think. Like other ordinary people, I would always have found it easier to be strenuously active than to sit still and reflect about life.

My drift into agnosticism had not been direct. I had made the journey via ill-defined and ill-digested forms of bastard Hinduism and Buddhism. I admired the lofty Hindu thought of Professor Radhakrishnan and was influenced by the breadth of his views—for in those days to be 'broad-minded' was what I considered mattered most—by his scorn of dogma, disparagement of organised religion, dislike of creeds and authority, and his respect for anyone who could think out a religion of his own—a free personal religion.

The last characteristic surprised me as he seemed to overrate the difficulty. But it encouraged me to make a personal religion out of an amorphous and bogus syncretism. The Vedic *Atman* or the *Brahmā* of Brahmanism as an impersonal, supreme, spiritual principle provided me with a vague Deity. To this I joined the Hindu and Buddhist doctrine of *karma* and its necessary corollary *metempsychosis*, the Buddhist disbelief in the efficacy of ritual and its repudiation of the priesthood. But since I neither adopted the Four Noble Truths nor trod the Noble Eightfold Path, my alleged sympathy with Hinduism and Buddhism was more a protest against Christianity as I saw it, than a reasoned belief in

either of the eastern religions. Besides which I continued to hug
pretty tightly the Ten Fetters of the Soul.

I was too immature to see the pitfalls of a subjective syncretism, or to realise the difficulty for a western mind of rightly
understanding eastern doctrines. Such an abortive and hazy
'religion' as I so half-heartedly assembled for myself could not
have held anyone for long, especially as there was no attempt to
deepen or vitalise it. The haze therefore intensified. I ceased to
peer through the fog, and at last I pronounced it impenetrable.
I sank into an agnosticism of the ignoble kind.

But with the approach of middle-age, misgivings arose as to
the complete satisfactoriness of my mental outlook—or perhaps
it would be more correct to say of the absence of any mental outlook. Was it perhaps possible that those pursuits which seemed
to be ends in themselves, might be merely means? But if so,
means to what? Was there conceivably a substance, of which the
things I grasped so energetically were only shadows?—a substance
which eluded me because I had been so easily satisfied with its
counterfeit?

Gradually I came to suspect what I was to read about more
fully later: that the unexamined life might well not be worth
living. But how could life be examined without taking death
fairly into account? It was not a welcome thought, but one that
refused to be dislodged. It was my first taste of the truth of
William James's remark that however jolly the feast, the skull
will inevitably appear at the banquet. Once I had seen its grin
I was unable to shift my gaze from the inevitability of death.

In childhood I had badly cracked my heart, like any other
child, at the death of pet dogs and canaries. But although I knew
then that all men must die, I knew the fact only as an academic
truth, certain that old age was so far ahead as to be almost an
eternity away. Now, with approaching middle-age, I had seemed
to turn a corner and see the grinning skull at the end of the road
—and not such a very long road either. What could a life mean

that ended summarily in annihilation? What could be its purpose?

Cyril Connolly has commented on the absurdity of starting to play a game without first learning the rules; observing that this is in fact what most of us do in the game of life, because we are quite unable to find out what the rules are. In his opinion there could not be more than two kinds of rules, according to whether there is a Deity or not. Cannot it be ascertained decisively if he exists, Connolly asks; have we created him in our imaginations, or does he exist in his own right, distributing clues for the seekers after him throughout the world?[1]

My own quest for meaning and purpose in life, I saw, was none other than a reaching out towards that great decision: did God exist? (And with it was naturally included the question of man's mortality. Was he annihilated with bodily death?) If there were a God, life might have an intrinsic meaning apart from all the different meanings with which different men might choose to endow their lives—something absolute, unchanging and eternal, rather than relative, shifting, and subject to time and fashion and the idiosyncrasies of men.

Aldous Huxley has generously admitted that during the twenties when the philosophy of meaninglessness flourished exceedingly, he, like many of his contemporaries, assumed that there was no meaning in life largely because he did not wish to find any.[2] He points out how easy it is for the artist and scientist to use their work of creation and research respectively as a means of escaping from ultimate questions; such absorbing occupations appear to be ends in themselves, and to justify ignorance of any more fundamental purpose. But Mr. Huxley considers ignorance to be mostly vincible: it is just because we do not want to know that we do in fact not know.[3]

John van Druten, too, has said that in his youth the desire for

---

[1] *Palinurus, The Unquiet Grave*, p. 106 (Hamish Hamilton, rev. ed. 1951).
[2] *Ends and Means*, p. 273 (Chatto & Windus, 1937).   [3] *Ibid*, p. 270.

sexual freedom, together with acquisitiveness, were all-engrossing and left no place for speculation on the ultimate meaning of life. He, like many artists he knew, desired meaninglessness apart from literary and artistic creation.[1]

It seemed unlikely that it was only scientists and creative artists who used their occupations as a kind of drug.[2] The man-in-the-street would have his 'dope' too, although it would be of a lower order. And Clive Bell tells us that Proust recognised as 'drugs' for the ordinary man, the everyday round, some golf, more whisky and, at regular intervals, matter-of-fact sensuality divorced from the emotions; all leading to early senility and an unearned tomb.[3] One can escape life by never being quite alive. And what life we do have, we live, as de Ruggiero says, as if death were not inevitable, ever busy about futile tasks.

I found that it was not only the more ordinary of my companions who were uninterested in the question whether life had a meaning and purpose, whether God existed and whether man had a soul which survived bodily death. Some of the most intellectually gifted of my agnostic friends evidently thought it a pure waste of time and energy to bother about what could never be known. But it seemed to me that most of those who insisted that we could not know the answers to these questions really did not want to know them. They seemed quite satisfied that life should have only such meaning as each individual chose to invest it with—a purely arbitrary and subjective choice. They agreed with Freud that it was 'better' to study the purposes for which men live rather than to ask about life's purpose. They were quite content with the state which was neither belief nor disbelief in God, as if the question of his existence were of rather less moment, one way or the other, than that of the Abominable Snowman. And they appeared undisturbed by the further question of the survival or

---

[1] *Vedanta for the Western World*, ed. C. Isherwood, p. 373 (Allen & Unwin, 1952).

[2] *Ends and Means*, p. 276.   [3] Clive Bell, *Proust*, p. 86 (Hogarth Press).

extinction at death of those they loved. It was not that they were at all lacking in true affection—indeed they were mostly far better at it than I was. But they endured 'their going hence, even as their coming hither' unquestioningly. They appeared to be possessed of an amazing 'negative capability' at which by then I could not but marvel.[1] How did it come so easily to them—no longer lulled by youthful acceptance of things as they seem—to sit down in a quiet ignorance of the rules of the game, content not to seek for clues that might suggest answers to questions so absolutely fundamental to man's life?

I came to see that many 'agnostics' actually overstepped the decent and greatly to be respected bounds of agnosticism. For most of those I knew did positively disbelieve in the supernatural. Even when they did not admit this disbelief, it was obvious that their minds were closed to the possibility of such a sphere's existence. They believed that it was only man's ignorance that led him to posit the supernatural, and that there was nothing which now seemed mysterious that science would not one day make clear.

Such 'agnostics' were only so in name. By their actual disbelief in the supernatural, God and the soul of man were reduced to concepts necessary only to the ignorant and undeveloped mind. I termed most of these friends ordinary honest down-to-earth disbelievers, unworthy of the classification 'agnostic.' Yet not so unworthy as those whose claims to agnosticism were prompted chiefly by a desire to appear intellectually respectable. Their 'honesty' consisted in saying what they thought without having taken the trouble to think.

I came to the conclusion that the true agnostic was not as common as he was generally thought to be. Genuine 'negative capability,' too, appeared to me rare. Be that as it may, most of

[1] ' That is when a man is capable of being in uncertainties, mysteries, doubts, without any irritable reaching after fact and reason.' Keats, *Letters*, No. 32 to G. and T. Keats, 22nd Dec., 1817 (ed. M. B. Forman, 4th edition, p. 71. Cumberlege, O.U.P., 1952).

my friends seemed quite content. Absorbed in their snug pursuits, academic, literary, or artistic, or even by an elaborate unconscious 'escape'-system, they had no incentive to search. But I'd seen the grinning skull and I was not content.

A speech of Simmias in the *Phaedo* gave me the encouragement I needed. He says:

> 'Well, Socrates . . . I will tell you my difficulty. . . . For I daresay that you . . . feel as I do, how hard or almost impossible is the attainment of any certainty about questions such as these [immortality, etc.] in the present life. And yet I should deem him a coward who did not prove what is said about them to the uttermost, or whose heart failed him before he had examined them on every side. For he should persevere until he has achieved one of two things: either he should discover, or be taught the truth about them; or, if this is impossible, I would have him take the best and most irrefragable of human theories, and let this be the raft upon which he sails through life—not without risk, as I admit—if he cannot find some word of God which will more surely and safely carry him.'[1]

It would indeed, I felt, be faint-hearted not to attempt these things. And, mindful as I was of Claude Bernard's saying that it is what we think we know that prevents us from learning, I was convinced that I must 'travel light.' I had not much to jettison, I thought.

Looking back I realised that, as a child, my happiest moments had had their source in nature, and I remembered that on two occasions in this connection I had known experiences totally other than those I usually knew. It can never be easy to describe what will doubtless earn one a place in the category of the absurd or even slightly dotty; but as it is possible that both these experiences had a formative influence on my subsequent beliefs, they must

---

[1] 85 c. and d. Jowett's translation, 1895 edition (O.U.P.).

be honestly recorded, however tenuous and apparently negligible.

On the first occasion I was in the garden, muddling about alone. A cuckoo flew over, calling. Suddenly I experienced a sensation that I can only describe as an effect that might follow the rotating of a mental kaleidoscope. It was a feeling of timelessness, not only that time stood still, that duration had ceased, but that I was myself outside time altogether. Somehow I knew that I was part of eternity. And there was also a feeling of spacelessness. I lost all awareness of my surroundings. With this detachment I felt the intensest joy I had ever known, and yet with so great a longing—for what I did not know—that it was scarcely distinguishable from suffering. The only analogous anguish would be that which one experiences in severe physical thirst on the point of being assuaged.

I have no idea how long this experience lasted—I was quite small—but I have never been able entirely to forget it. Recently I was forcibly reminded of it by Edgar Allan Poe:

' An immortal instinct, deep within the spirit of man is
. . . plainly a sense of the Beautiful. This thirst belongs to
the immortality of man. It is at once a consequence and an
indication of his perennial existence. It is the desire of the
moth for the star. It is no mere appreciation of the Beauty
before us, but a wild effort to reach the Beauty above.
Inspired by an ecstatic prescience of the glories beyond the
grave, we struggle, by multiform combinations among the
things and thoughts of Time, to attain a portion of that
loveliness whose very elements, perhaps, belong to Eternity
alone.'

' Thirst,' ' desire,' ' ecstatic prescience.' Words, empty words, doubtless, to those who had never experienced them in such a context. And as ' Mark Rutherford ' (W. Hale White) said in connection with his own similar experiences, it would not be difficult to prove them absurd. But he added that nothing could now shake his conviction that there was no death.[1]

To return to my own experiences, the second of which occurred a good while after the first. It was an absolutely still day, flooded with sunshine. In the garden everything was shining, breathless, as if waiting, expectant. Quite suddenly I felt convinced of the existence of God; as if I had only to put out my hand to touch him. And at the same time there came again that intensest joy and indescribable longing as of an exile, perhaps, for home. It seemed as if my heart were struggling to leap out of my body.

How long I stood, or would have gone on standing, I do not know; the tea-bell rang, shattering the extra dimension into which I had seemed to be caught up. I returned to earth and went obediently in, speaking to no one of these things.

'Is it not strange that an infant should be heir to the whole world, and see those mysteries which the books of the learned never unfold?'[2] But of course all the rational thinkers have 'let in the chill breath of cleverness upon the garden of beatitude.'[3] They have disposed of all such experiences years ago. 'A child's awakening feelings of sex' would quite sufficiently account for all those emotions and indefinable longings.

Well, they may be right. That is just what I wanted to find out. But there is this to be said: it was my experience, and how are they to judge unless they had a similar one? Perhaps there was something in their very make-up which prevented that. I felt a little sorry for the rationalists with their iconoclastic breath. One cannot be ecstatic and too 'clever' for ecstasy in the same instant.[4]

Anyway, although I had come, in retrospect, to look upon these two isolated 'moments' as possible intimations of the

[1] *More Pages from a Journal*, pp. 181-3, Quoted by Basil Willey, *More Nineteenth Century Studies*, p. 229 (Chatto & Windus 1956).

[2] Traherne, *Centuries of Meditation*, II.   [3] Oriental trope.

[4] A. Quiller-Couch, *On the Art of Reading: On Reading the Bible*, pp. 133-4. (Guild Books, 1947.)

numinous and the eternal, I was willing to discount even that suspicion in the interests of a fair-minded search. And indeed the glimpse of that garden of beatitude had been more than a little obscured by over twenty years of a facile agnosticism which encouraged the belief that here were things I could never know.

But, I now wondered, might there not be different kinds of 'knowledge,' or rather, might there not be a certainty which, although not patient of proof, held firm? And what of the 'surer and safer raft'? If there was a God, was there too a word of God? Revelation was out of fashion, and I had tended to write it off, together with a personal God and Christianity as well. But though I pushed these out of my mind, I never quite banged the door on them. What kind of sense would that be which discarded completely something one had failed to understand, and for no better reason than that so much in them was distasteful? Although at that time I found all three unacceptable, I knew that my examination of these questions had been superficial and unduly influenced by the climate of opinion.

I realised, then, that not only must I venture into the world of philosophy; and, later, explore the four great religions, Judaism, Hinduism, Buddhism and Islam; but that I must thoroughly and dispassionately re-examine Christianity. Even if I subsequently still felt unable to accept it, the question would still remain, 'What think ye of Christ?' That I saw as a challenge which no one with the smallest pretensions to seriousness could neglect. It could not just be ignored.

But I was not nearly ready for all that yet. I was groping in utter darkness, pondering on chance and design. Could the universe all be fortuitous, and life on earth merely the result of coincidence; and man hopelessly astray in seeking to extract a meaning and purpose from a universe that was no outcome of design? Some saw the finger of God; others nothing but blind chance. What a fantastic, almost unbelievable chance that could produce such results! And was it rational to think that intelligence could arise from any system that was not due to a Mind, whether it was called Eternal Substance, the Absolute, or God? Evolution might indeed afford some explanation but must there not be something like a Mind behind it? I felt as George Eliot when she said:

' To me the Development Theory, and all other explanations of processes by which things came to be, produce a feeble impression compared with the mystery that lies under the processes.'[1]

And if all were purely fortuitous, how had man evolved his ideas? How had his idea of perfection arisen to be a perpetual gadfly stinging him out of complacency to ever fresh endeavour in life and art? How account for disinterested love? That old question whence man had derived this and his sense of the Good had never been satisfactorily disposed of by any materialist theory.

But it would not do to use the word 'God' as a simple solution for everything I did not understand. Before long I would be seeing him in electricity or other such phenomenon as I had failed to master, like any other 'savage.' Anything that might be legitimate inference once the existence of God had been established, could not be used in order to make this establishment possible. How difficult though with all these questions to be asked that none should be begged!

What question should I ask first? Where was I to begin? As Plato approved the endeavour to discover the truth concerning human immortality, I would turn first to him for his 'best and most irrefragable theory.'

---

[1] Cross's *Life of George Eliot*, vol. II, p. 148 (letter to Mme. Bodichon, Dec. 5th, 1859). Quoted by B. Willey, *Nineteenth Century Studies*, p. 238 (Chatto & Windus, 1949).

PART TWO

On immortality

'Philosophy can bake no bread; but
she can procure for us God,
freedom and immortality.'

NOVALIS

1. *Through Plato I find the question of a future life inseparable from that of God's existence*

It was almost a new life which Plato offered to my lean and hungry mind; as if I had been reborn and knew the joy of the first days of Creation. Friends long familiar with his thought laughed at my naïve enthusiasm, themselves untouched by its truths beyond an academic interest in them, displaying thereby an astonishing capacity for turning bread into stones.

What drew me most to Plato was his assumption that the question of man's ultimate destiny was one of fundamental importance. So often I had heard the argument that it could not affect behaviour one way or another whether the soul lived on or not after bodily death. But it seemed to me odd that it should not affect a man's thoughts and actions. (Wouldn't anyone contemplating the possibility of living in another country want to learn the language and customs and assemble the right kind of wardrobe in anticipation of such an eventuality?) For if there were this other sphere of being, the meaning of human existence could not be contained in an earthly life alone and could only be understood with reference to the eternal. The acceptance of such meaning might well demand a different kind of earthly sojourn from one which was recognised to be an end in itself and therefore as largely as possible in the nature of a pleasure cruise, however enlightened the pleasures.

Indeed, Plato himself holds that he who lives the best life is the man whose soul is to the greatest extent eternal. And that the object of the training of the soul is to fit it for citizenship in another world.

In the *Symposium*, Socrates speaks of holding converse with the true beauty divine and simple:

' Do you not see that in that communion only, beholding beauty with the life of the mind, he will be enabled to bring forth not images of beauty, but realities (for he has hold not of an image but of reality), and bringing forth and nourishing true virtue, to become the friend of God and be immortal, if mortal man may. Would that be an ignoble life?' (211-12.)[1]

In the *Phaedrus* it is said that the more the soul feeds upon beauty, wisdom, goodness and the like, the more akin to the divine will it become.

And in the *Republic* we read:

' Can a man help imitating that with which he holds reverential converse? And the philosopher holding converse with the divine and immutable, becomes a part of that divine and immutable order, as far as nature allows.' (Book VI, 500.)

' The gods have a care of anyone whose desire is to become just and to be like God, as far as man can attain the divine likeness, by the pursuit of virtue.' (Book X, 613.)

And in the *Laws*, the Athenian Stranger declares that

' He who would be dear to God must, as far as possible, be like him and such as he is. Wherefore the temperate man is the friend of God, for he is like him.' (715.)

' When she [the soul] has communion with divine virtue

---

[1] All translations of Plato are by Benjamin Jowett from the 1895 edition of the *Dialogues* (O.U.P.).

and becomes divine, she is carried into another and better place, which is also divine and perfect in holiness.' (904.)

Socrates, in the *Theaetetus*, says:

' We ought to fly away from earth to heaven as quickly as we can: and to fly away means to become like God, as far as this is possible; and to become like him is to become holy, and just and wise. . . . He is perfect righteousness; and he of us who is the most righteous is most like him.' (176.)

But why then, Socrates asks himself, if a man is better dead, is he not allowed to be his own benefactor but must wait for the hand of another?
To this he answers:

' I admit the appearance of inconsistency in what I am saying; but there may not be any real inconsistency after all. There is a doctrine whispered in secret that man is a prisoner who has no right to open the door of his prison and run away; this is a great mystery which I do not quite understand. Yet I too believe that the gods are our guardians, and that we are a possession of theirs. (62.)
' And if one of your own possessions, an ox or an ass, for example, took the liberty of putting himself out of the way when you had given no intimation of your wish that he should die, would you not be angry with him, and would you not punish him if you could?
' Then there may be reason in saying that a man should wait, and not take his own life until God summons him, as he is now summoning me.' (62c.)

(Years after, I was to find this echoed by Origen: ' It is not fitting that a servant of God should dismiss himself from life, but should wait God's sentence.' Locke too considered that men were

31

God's possessions. 'They are his property, whose workmanship they are, made to last during his, not another's pleasure.')

For myself, I had a strong aversion to the idea of suicide, although I was not sure of the existence of 'the gods,' and could find no more rational basis for its rejection than a vague prejudice against quitting one's post and downing tools before the siren had sounded. But was not the whole question of knocking off work or of escaping from school before the signal had been given inseparable from a tacit belief in a Master of some sort—one who had the prerogative of ringing bells, and who had therefore a right to object if a man took the law of bell-ringing into his own hands? True, in my attitude to suicide I was no more illogical than many agnostics who also rejected the idea, except that I did not advance those lesser arguments whose speciousness could not disguise a hollowness beneath the surface. If there is no Master, what is to forbid the man without attachments from seeking a blessed oblivion when the miseries and anxieties of this life outweigh its joys and pleasures?

It was not oblivion however that Socrates expected after death, according to the *Phaedo*. For he says:

'I am quite ready to acknowledge . . . that I ought to be grieved at death, if I were not persuaded that I am going to other gods who are wise and good (of which I am as certain as I can be of anything of the sort), and to men departed (though I am not so certain of this last) who are better than those whom I leave behind; and therefore I do not grieve as I might have done, for I have good hope that there is yet something remaining for the dead, and as has been said of old, some far better thing for the good than for the evil.' (63b and c.)

This sounded like the system of rewards and retributive justice familiar to me in Christianity: the division of the sheep from the goats which had always troubled me since goats were so much more lovable and intelligent than sheep. And I simply did not believe—supposing there were an after-life—in a Judgement as an external proceeding by which a Potentate granted good things to the sheep and evil to the goats. It seemed more reasonable to suppose that the soul would be self-judged in its very capacities: the soul desiring, and capable of, good would receive it accordingly, whereas the soul unfamiliar with the good would be unable to desire or receive that to which it was not susceptible.

Socrates argues that the true philosopher can but depart this life with joy, since it is the soul alone which can achieve pure knowledge. For him death is nothing but the separation and release of the soul from the body.

> ' The body introduces turmoil and confusion and amazement into the course of speculation, and hinders us from seeing the truth; proving by experience to us that if we would have pure knowledge of anything we must be quit of the body—the soul in herself must behold all things in themselves: and then we shall attain the wisdom which we desire; not while we live, but after death as the argument shows; for if while in company with the body, the soul cannot have pure knowledge, one of two things must seem to follow—either knowledge is not to be attained at all, or, if at all, after death. For then and not till then, the soul will be in herself alone and without the body.' (66c-67.)

It was clear that knowledge of reality was not attainable in an earthly life; man's limitations were sufficiently obvious. But what was not so immediately clear was that there was another mode of being in which man might be able to attain to this knowledge. And it had, surprisingly perhaps, never occurred to me in my unawakened state that man might therefore perish completely without knowing just those things which were the most worth knowing (and according to Plato, the only ones about which we could have knowledge as opposed to opinion). This was an argument that I now felt in the pit of my stomach. Life would indeed be meaningless, senseless, an idiot's tale if reality were obtainable only in another sphere to which man could not reach. What, then, would be the purpose of an existence for ever denied the hope of a true satisfaction? What its meaning if man had to 'settle for less' from the word 'go'?

What too, was the cause of this craving for ultimates and absolutes—for the eternal—in a life which, however shot through with glimpses of transitory beauty, could offer no permanent attainment of the real? And was such a life, by its very finiteness, a promise of a greater infinite, or a perpetual snub to man for daring to be dissatisfied with the finite and the transient? Was there any reason to assume that the presence of certain needs of the soul argued for their ultimate satisfaction? Might they not be merely a manifestation of man's inordinate *hubris*?

These were all questions on which I hoped that my search would give light. I saw already, however, why some men desired another life. It was not that their own insignificant little personalities might be preserved (who in their senses could be sufficiently in love with their egos to care about *that*?) Rather was it that they felt the whole consummation of an earthly life to reside in that knowledge which must lie, if anywhere, beyond this life: that knowledge of the Supreme Good of which all intimations here were but the veriest shadows.

Yet, inevitably, to speak of knowledge implies some kind of 'personality' which will know; and it seemed necessary for a personal enjoyment of absolutes and ultimates that there should be some survival of memory, and of some faculty which made man susceptible to their significance.

But I was going too fast. Memory and consciousness would have to survive apart from the brain. The brain-mind problem in its immensity overwhelmed me with a sense of my own inadequacy. Was truth on so fundamental a matter attainable

only by the specialists? And why was it that so few of these
bothered their heads about a matter that was literally one of life
and death? And, too, there was the question of the relationship
between knowing and being. How was anyone lacking philosophical training to form any opinion on that? I thought it best
merely to register these difficulties for the moment and to refuse
to be deterred by them at the starting-post.

Plato's (or rather the Pythagorean) doctrine of reminiscence—
the theory that all learning is the re-acquaintance of the soul with
knowledge it has brought with it but has forgotten that it
possessed, the recapturing of inborn knowledge, had something
about it that made it impossible to reject it out of hand however
fanciful its implications.[1] Such a doctrine would account particularly well for intuitions and for all æsthetic experience; for
man's response to beauty, his soul lifted up by unconscious
memory to those scenes which the visible, material image evokes.
It reminded me of Forrest Reid's assumption, implicit in all I had
read of his, of a vision engraved upon the soul before a man's
eyes are ever opened on earth. At times I thought something not
unlike this might be allegorically true; but more often I dismissed
it as fantastic. Plato, to my mind, moreover, fails to establish the
doctrine. And I had therefore to reject the argument for immortality which he hangs upon it. (72e-77d.)

In fact, the only argument for man's survival which I found
at all promising was that which makes the soul's immortality
dependent upon the perfection of the divine nature; that, and the
idea that the soul being uncompounded cannot perish, since it is
only combinations which are dissoluble.[2] The case for the former
has been stated in modern phraseology as, ' If God exists then the
souls of men are immortal; but if there is no God neither are
the souls of men immortal.'[3]

[1] This pre-existence is illustrated in the *Phaedrus*. See also the *Meno*.
[2] See Text I, p. 263 for some of the argument; 78b-84c.
[3] Benjamin Jowett, Introduction to the *Phaedo*.

On Immortality

As yet I believed in neither God nor immortality, but in reading Plato I had come to suspect that their existence might be inseparable. And it is really the divinity of the soul which Plato seeks to establish; the mere fact of the soul's being uncompounded is a natural corollary. Only because the soul resembles the divine is it beyond the possibility of decomposition; its simplicity guarantees its permanence, and in virtue of its deiformity the soul is immortal. It is the master whilst the body is the servant. But the compounded must be mutable and liable to decomposition in the same manner as it was composed.

The two great deterrents to belief in immortality I found to be epiphenomenalism—the postulate that the self or soul is a product of the body, that mind cannot function independently of bodily causation—and the mechanical theory of nature. These I felt to be the most important battles fought in the *Phaedo*; and although my sympathies were with Simmias, I was annoyed with him for crumpling so easily and choosing the doctrine of reminiscence in preference to that of epiphenomenalism—since the two were obviously incompatible. For although somehow I did not believe that anything in the nature of a soul could be an epiphenomenon—either there was no soul or it was not an epiphenomenon —there appeared to be little evidence for believing that the theory was false, whilst there was none for believing that the doctrine of reminiscence was true.[1] And although Socrates entirely persuades his listeners that the mechanical interpretation of Nature cannot adequately explain a single process in Nature, it was clear that both this and epiphenomenalism, denounced by Plato in the *Laws*, retain their influence to this day.

Throughout all the dozen *Dialogues* I had so far read, I found the existence of an Absolute, whether called the Forms, measure, the Creator or God, presupposed. I suspected that I had made an ingenuous blunder in supposing that the question of the immortality of the soul could be considered apart from the existence

[1] For the argument against epiphenomenalism see Text I, p. 265.

of God. For of all the arguments for an after-life advanced in the *Dialogues*, the one which to me, as I said, appeared most reasonable was that which made immortality dependent upon the divine perfection.

I had never reflected on what kind of an existence survival of bodily death would entail if there were no God. From my early and not entirely ungodly childhood, I had vivid memories of what I imagined 'heaven' ruled by the God of the Christians to be. And it may have been symptomatic of a lingering subconscious belief in a Deity that I had never contemplated an atheistic after-life.

I now wondered how such a godless 'heaven' would compare with an earthly paradise if, indeed, either could be imagined. Doubtless no atheist could believe in the resurrection of the body. What, then would a godless after-life offer in the way of joys to the disembodied?

Valéry has expressed the opinion that just to have a soul and never to be anything any more than just that soul is a peculiarly pallid wish when set beside the possession of a body and the experience of duration.[1] But an unreasoning conviction seemed to persist generally that such a future disembodied life must be 'better,' 'happier' for the participators than any earthly one could be. But, search as I did, I found nothing in my imagination that could suggest any manner in which this could be so. Certainly the possibility of meeting lost friends in some recognisable form pointed to a source of great joy. And I could even believe in what Keats called one of the grandeurs of immortality—what he saw as a direct communication between spirits. This, I imagined, would be more complete than the ordinary earthly communication could be where words so often proved inadequate to express the deepest emotions.

But what else would there be? Even if there were no longer

[1] Biancani, *Le Mystère de la Vie* quoted by Jean Guitton, *The Problem of Jesus*, p. 139 (Burns, Oates, 1955).

the illusion of time, would there not be some feeling of duration? And with no bodies to feed or clothe or house, no disease or dirt to fight, with no money to be made or spent; no books to be read or written; no travelling, since there would be no space and no bodies to be transported; no sex; no blessed sleep, no night, no day, no seasons; well, what would one *do* 'all day'? With no eyes to see beauty, no ears to hear music, no palate to savour any nectar or ambrosia, what would life consist of? Was there not more than just a faint possibility that one might be bored, and that one might remember nostalgically—if memory could still function—even Monday mornings and the return to office life or the weekly washing, the daily round and common task, according to one's erstwhile class and sex? I could imagine no occupation for the disembodied other than this direct communication between spirits. But would their 'material' be sufficient for all eternity? And how could the 'club bore' be circumvented if he gained admittance?

I wondered, too, how heaven would be ruled. Presumably by a Republic since there was no monarchy. But would there not be something hollow at the heart of things—a lack of Blessedness? It was impossible, I found, to imagine that everlasting joys not mediated through the senses could have their origin in anything but a God; for all finite bliss must fade and perish. Thus I could form no conception of an after-life which could be enjoyed by the disembodied spirit apart from him. And would not even that 'grandeur of immortality,' that kind of extra-sensory perception functioning between spirits of another world be dependent on 'minds'? Further, what constituted a mind, and could it be in any way independent of the brain, I continued to wonder.

It seemed to me that an earthly paradise—provided good weather and perpetual youth could be guaranteed—offered incomparably greater facilities for enjoyment than a heavenly one in which spirits dwelt under conditions pertaining to the worst of both worlds, with joys neither of God nor of bodies.

When I was a child, I imagined that heaven was ruled by someone resembling our favourite Uncle Arthur, and whose main occupation would be playing in the gardens with all the children gathered there. Directly he appeared, everything would break out in glory. Flowers would open, the trees burst their buds, the sun become more golden, the light more lovely; the morning stars would sing together, and all the sons of God shout for joy. The lions, too, would roar, the elephants trumpet and yet above all the noise of the larger animals, the song of the birds would rise clear and plangent, like the first violins in an orchestra. Every note would be necessary and right, and fit into the orchestral pattern. And the angels would circle round and there would be a great sound of beating of wings like that of a flight of swans. And a cry go up, 'Hosanna,' from every throat. Then there would be dancing, and laughter, and joy would be everywhere running like wildfire. 'Oh, how did all their lovely faces shine!'

Alas! 'I sent my God away.' When I ceased to be a child, I sought to put childish things away. I doubted that God could be like Uncle Arthur apotheosised. Clever people spoke of beliefs that were wish-fulfilments, of the foolishness of anthropomorphism, of the incredibility of human immortality.

'The first Light which shined in my Infancy in its Primitive and Innocent Clarity was totally Eclypsed: insomuch that I was fain to learn all again. If you ask me how it was Eclypsed? Truly by the customs and manners of men, which like contrary Winds blew it out. All Men's thoughts and Words were about other matters. . . . I was little and reverenced their Authority; I was weak, and easily guided by their example: Ambitious also and Desirous to approve myself unto them. And finding no one Syllable in any man's Mouth of these Things, by

Degrees they vanished. My Thoughts (as indeed what is more fleeting than a Thought?) were blotted out; and at last all the Celestial, Great and Stable Treasures to which I was born, as wholly forgotten, as if they had never been.'[1]

Having rejected what I then considered to be the anthropomorphic God of the Christians, I had nothing to put in its place except a nebulous and equally old-fashioned trinity of the Good, the Beautiful and the True. These I visualised as three enormous candles in a two branched candlestick; the Good in the centre, all cold and pure and immobile, their wicks unlit. I could not feel that they were quite the living God.

Yet Plato supposed an after-life spent in contemplation of the Form of the Good by souls freed from their bodies. His doctrine of the soul and its immortality, I now saw, could not be divorced from his theory of the Forms—the argument for man's immortality from the perfection of the divine nature which Plato implies throughout the *Dialogues*. This Jowett interprets as, ' If the ideas of men are eternal, their souls are eternal; and if not the ideas, then not the souls'; which has its modern equivalent in, ' If God exists then the soul exists after death; and if there is no God, there is no existence of the soul after death.'

Yet I wondered what there could be in the human soul of sufficient value to make its survival even arguable. I felt like Simmias that the subject was so great and human nature so weak and fallible, that I could not avoid having doubts. And for myself, I found literally nothing that could be accounted worthy of preservation, unless it were the desire I felt for my three candles.

And if the soul did survive, whence did it get its indestructibility? How did it alone come to be uncompounded when everything else appeared to be a compound and therefore destructible? The only possible argument could be that it was

[1] Traherne, *Centuries of Meditation*.

the divine afflatus that made it so—uncompounded and therefore indestructible; indestructible and therefore immortal. I saw no other argument which could make the soul's immortality probable or even faintly possible.

Provided it could be established that there was a benevolent Creator, then Jowett's reading of the problem seemed to me entirely acceptable. But Simmias and Cebes were more convinced of the existence of the Forms (God) than of the immortality of the soul. I wondered, was the contrary situation possible? McTaggart was reputed to be an atheist, yet he evolved a whole theory to disprove the impossibility of man's survival of bodily death.[1]

I was curious to know what his arguments for such disproof could be, since he dispensed with the only one which, for me, carried much weight. Negative as disproof of the impossibility of survival would be, it might perhaps clear the ground for more positive arguments for or against man's immortality.

[1] J. McT. E. McTaggart, sometime lecturer in Moral Sciences at Trinity College, Cambridge.

2. McTaggart and his belief in a future life independent of God. His views on the primacy of love and Spirit

McTaggart proves the impossibility of epiphenomenalism by demolishing the materialistic theory on which it is based. If, he says, the self were merely the behaviour of matter under varying circumstances, it would then be possible to explain the self adequately in terms of matter alone. But to consider matter as existing independently of consciousness, he finds absurd. Matter for him is explicable only in terms of a conscious self.[1]

This I found rather a large Berkleian camel to swallow—the Berkeley who could say:

> ' Some truths there are so near and obvious that a man need only open his eyes to see them. Such I take this important one to be, *viz.*, that all the choir of heaven and furniture of the earth, in a word all those bodies which compose the mighty frame of the world, have not any subsistence without a mind—that their *being* is to be *perceived* or *known*.'

In my simple ignorance I did not reject dualism and think it necessary to deny the separate existence of matter in order to be assured of the reality of spirit. It was trying reason rather hard

[1] *Some Dogmas of Religion*, pp. 77-111 (E. Arnold & Co., 1930). See Text II, p. 267.

to suppose that things suddenly sprang into existence whenever anyone perceived them, but did not trouble to exist when no one was looking. And G. E. Moore, I had read, suggested that, logically, idealists must believe that trains have wheels only when drawn up at platforms, since travellers cannot perceive the wheels unless they get out of the train.[1] I supposed, however, that it might be said that, since God was 'always about in the Quad' observing the tree, he would also frequent railway lines, perceiving the wheels of trains.[2]

McTaggart's arguments against the independent existence of matter did not appear to me conclusive. I could not therefore find in them a basis for my belief that the self was not merely an activity of its own body. Epiphenomenalism in which, influenced by Plato, I did not believe, would have to be disproved on other grounds.

Discussing the question whether a body is necessary to the existence of a self, McTaggart observes that whilst the self has a body, that body is necessary to mental life. But it need not follow that a self without a body would be unable to obtain material in some other way. And he argues that, even should the brain be indispensable to thought whilst the self has a body, it would not follow that with the cessation of the body we should be unable to think without brains. It may well be that our present failure to think otherwise than in connection with the body is a limitation inherent in the presence of that body, and disappears with it.[3] Later when I read Bergson's view of the brain, this theory no longer seemed as fantastic as it sounds.[4]

McTaggart states that a thing perishes only through the separation of its constituents (as I had learnt from Plato). But

---

[1] See Bertrand Russell, *History of Western Philosophy*, pp. 682-3 (Allen & Unwin, 1947).

[2] From Ronald Knox's rhyme on why the tree exists even when there is no one in the Quad to observe it.

[3] *Op. cit.*, p. 105. [4] See Text III, p. 273.

he finds that the self is a complex and not a combination and it cannot therefore perish through the separation of its parts.[1]

Despite the above arguments, however, the idea constantly recurs to us that the self cannot be immortal. Reflection may dispel our doubts but more often habit reassumes its sway. Our smallness contrasted with the greatness of the transitory makes it hard to believe that the self can be a permanent element when planets and realms are but ephemeral shapes.[2]

McTaggart suggests one argument against belief in immortality which I found impressive. It might be considered, he says, that some anomaly in the idea of the self forbids our recognising in it a satisfactory expression of reality, and that therefore the belief that there is any particular self to participate in the eternity of true reality is without foundation.[3]

And the ordinary believers in immortality, as I found, make the belief even more incredible, for many believe in it blindly, without judgment, because they wish it to be so. But it is wrong, he holds, to conclude that a belief must necessarily be untrue because it has most often been held for invalid reasons; although in practice it is never easy to keep our incredulity from extending from these reasons to the belief itself. He observes that whilst the arguments in this chapter would not justify a positive belief in immortality, he considers that reasons for belief in this may be discovered of sufficient cogency to overcome all difficulties.[4]

Moreover, in another work, he expresses the opinion that once we have established to our satisfaction the existence of a harmony in a universe which is in all essentials moral and rational, we are justified in arguing that such and such a thing is because it is fitting, or conversely that it is fitting because it is. Therefore

[1] *Op. cit.*, pp. 108-9.
[2] *Ibid.*, p. 110.   [3] *Ibid.*, pp. 109-10.   [4] *Ibid.*, pp. 110-111.
I am painfully conscious of how much McTaggart's arguments lose in plausibility in such a severely truncated form and divorced from his own delightful philosophical prose.

those who believe in a benevolent Creator are perfectly correct in inferring that man must be immortal because the lack of immortality would make of life a farce of the most hideous kind. But such an argument is wholly invalid until such harmony has been established.[1]

Besides McTaggart's refutation of epiphenomenalism, I found here, too, one suggestion to answer my question as to the possibility of the survival of thought and mind apart from the brain, although I had no reason to suppose it to be more than a possible theory which other philosophers might, and scientists certainly would, seek to demolish.

But how right he undoubtedly was about the difficulties of belief in immortality! The bare idea I thought would amount to mad arrogance were it not part of the question of the existence of God. It seemed to be an almost outrageous conception that the human soul alone remained indestructible whilst whole systems perished; man, such a latecomer in the scheme of things assuming such importance in so vast a universe. Yet I remembered Coleridge's saying: ' My mind had been habituated to the Vast, and I never regarded my senses as the criteria of my belief.'[2] Was vastness the criterion of value?

There was something, I thought, in Lotze's idea—always assuming the existence of a Deity—that finite individuals might exist only in order to fulfil some divine plan, and that the individual ceased to exist if he became unnecessary to it. But how to find out about this plan, there was the rub. Why was God, if he existed, so inexplicit, so silent? Many people, of course did not find him so. To them he had spoken in no uncertain terms, 'through the mouth of the prophets which have been since the world began,' through the Church by means of that extraordinary proceeding 'revelation.' But I could not accept as from God such very odd 'revelations' as his triune personality, his

---

[1] *Philosophical Studies*, pp. 231-2 (Arnold, 1934).
[2] *Letters*, ed. E. H. Coleridge, Vol. 1 (1895), p. 16.

Incarnation and so on, and all that talk about the Lamb, water and blood and that kind of thing. If that were 'revelation' this God endowed with personality did not speak a language that man could understand. A God who wished to be believed would have done better than that, I felt sure.

But this did not mean that because I rejected revelation I disbelieved in God. I was still in no-man's-land where the visibility was poor, where only Plato shed a ray of light, a bright beam of hope that if God existed, knowledge of his existence and even of his purpose might not be entirely beyond the reach of man's apprehension. Moreover, Plato's idea that the only reality in the soul of man was that which derived from the divine might have a distinct bearing on the theory McTaggart mentions that unless the self can be recognised as a satisfactory expression of reality, there can be no possibility of its participation in the eternity characteristic of true reality.

Most of us, I thought, could not be recognised as satisfactory expressions of reality. And the more facile believers in immortality who had never sounded the depths of the difficulties inherent in the belief, brought the whole question into disrepute. But although I marvelled how unreflecting Christians assumed unquestioningly that at death they would be snatched away to beatitude; and how neither the problem of the *modus operandi*, nor even the more fundamental question of what exactly survived seemed ever to disturb them, yet I saw that it must in fairness be admitted that their belief was founded on that conviction of the existence of a benevolent Creator to which McTaggart refers, and that, therefore, such belief was neither illogical nor unjustifiable. Just a shred of recognition, however, of the difficulties involved would make all believers so much more palatable I thought. And what assured them, I wondered, of the existence of a benevolent Creator? Nothing but revelation, I supposed.

Yet, I was already persuaded that unless there were such a God this so-called heaven had little to offer. I wondered why

McTaggart, as an atheist, had been so set on it. But then I remembered that Professor Broad has told us that by no philosopher other than Plato has love been so seriously treated, so attentively examined and so persuasively written of as by McTaggart. Professor Broad points out, however, the deep and essential difference between the two thinkers in this. In the case of Plato, love between humans is but a rung on the ladder towards the love of the Form of the Good. In McTaggart's case, love is the one thing of supreme value in the universe; it can lead to nothing better for there is nothing better than the best.[1]

For anyone who loved deeply it must be an anomaly I now saw not to wish that death brought no final separation. I recalled that some Georgian poet had written:

> ' methinks the love I bear you
> will make you not to die ';

which I had thought whimsical, rather pathetic nonsense when I had read it, perhaps because I was so deficient myself in love. Now I understood another reason why some people might desire a life after death, although I doubted that there were many who would willingly embark on this even for the sake of love. Would not most of us choose annihilation, assured and lasting oblivion — if a choice were offered—rather than the hazards of another life, a doubtful future?

Perhaps it is just that which is wrong with most of us. We do not want to love and live with all our being even here and now; or rather we want love and life on our own terms, which maybe give us only synthetic substitutes of both. Perhaps that was why we could not be recognised as 'satisfactory expressions of reality.' Here, I was the chief of sinners, wanting only as much—which

---

[1] C. D. Broad, sometime Professor of Moral Philosophy in the University of Cambridge. See his Introduction to McTaggart's *Some Dogmas of Religion*, p. xlii.

really meant as little—of either as would still allow me a certain 'undisturbedness' and mental comfort, a stoic invulnerability. So I, like many others, preferred those things which deadened rather than quickened life. And when I was young, on thinking of the inevitable death of anyone I ' loved,' I consoled myself with the thought that perhaps by that time I would not greatly care for him or her. I had a childish desire for felicity at all costs; and if I had been offered the choice I would then have chosen to cease from loving rather than endure a sense of loss. This was to turn from reality in a denial of life and love. But most of us, I now thought, inclined to a similar 'deadening' in our preference for epicureanism. How, then, could we want eternal life which, it appeared to me, must be of an unimaginable intensity? I saw it as far easier and therefore more natural to wish for death. But to McTaggart it appears the very reverse.

His beliefs on spirit seem to invest it with a quality and power suggesting the divine: it is the fundamental reality of the universe, and it is hardly possible that the world could contain any thing sufficiently potent to destroy it. If, he says, the nature of spirit is one of ultimate reality, spirit cannot be merely in time and therefore cannot cease to exist, and since merging would entail quantity —a conception inapplicable to spirit—spirits can no more be merged than they can be extinguished.[1]

Here were strong words. For McTaggart, although an atheist, was a convinced believer in immortality.[2] But his arguments against the impossibility of human survival were those of Absolute Idealism. How would they stand up to those of philosophers who rejected such a system?

Professor Broad, I knew, had been a pupil of McTaggart and had, I understood, demolished the McTaggartian system as such, as Aristotle had destroyed his teacher's, Plato's, theory of Forms. It was not, however, with philosophies as a whole

[1] *Philosophical Studies*, pp. 216-17.
[2] Introduction to *Some Dogmas of Religion*, p. xlviii.

that I was concerned; indeed, they would have been beyond my understanding. What interested me passionately here was to know what was believed concerning the possibility of survival.

The next step, then, required the finding of some work of Professor Broad relevant to the questions discussed above.

3. Probability and survival:
Professor Broad and the work of the
Society for Psychical Research

Professor Broad agrees that Idealism favours the antecedent probability of survival. But, in his opinion, the question is of such a nature that it has to be decided before we can choose between metaphysical systems. It must be discussed on data which are common to all people whatever rival systems of thought they may uphold. He finds that metaphysical arguments for the immortality of the soul convince few men apart from their authors.

On what grounds, then, did people believe in their survival of bodily death, I wondered. And were there any grounds on which I should be so persuaded?

Undoubtedly, belief in divine revelation was one of the reasons, as Professor Broad observes.[1] But obviously that was useless for me since I did not believe in this; or that immortality was immediately manifest. Far from it.

For the third reason that he gives—that it would follow inevitably from premisses of an ethical nature—there was, I thought, much to be said. And he has stated elsewhere that it appears to him, as it did to Sidgwick, that without survival of death for at least some members of the human species, the life of the individual as well as that of the race is devoid of meaning. He finds it incomprehensible that anyone with some knowledge

[1] *Mind and its Place in Nature*, p. 481 (Routledge & Kegan Paul, 1925).

50

of history and psychology, on the one hand, and biology and physics on the other, can consider mankind as a whole capable of attaining and maintaining indefinitely a paradise on earth. It is not suggested that survival *per se* is an all-sufficient good, but that it is a condition necessary to human life if this is to be other than an absurdity. This opinion it seems cannot be attributed to wishful thinking since Professor Broad does not desire survival for himself, and avows an insufficient concern for the fate of the human race after his decease.[1]

With his opinion I could now wholeheartedly agree. Life on earth would provide only a dusty answer to men's questionings if there were no survival of death, and if, as Plato believed, it were only in another sphere that reality could be attained. But no argument of an ethical character could, I thought, bear any weight unless the existence of a benevolent creator had been established. Without such a being I saw no reason why the answer should not be very dusty indeed.

It is Professor Broad's last suggestion why people believe in immortality—that it is warranted by evidence of an empirical nature—that alone holds any promise for him. And he states that if human survival could be shown to be at all probable, this could be done solely through arguments of an empirical nature arising from phenomena treated by the Society for Psychical Research[2]

The S.P.R., I found, had collected a mass of facts which can be considered 'supernormal' inasmuch as the usual explanations of science and commonsense fail to meet these cases. Professor Broad, who was trained in physics before he became a philosopher, assumes as genuine a large number of these cases which attain the very severe standards of evidence which the Society requires. And he takes human survival to be, amongst others, one hypothesis which would explain some accepted supernormal phenomena.[3]

[1] S.P.R. *Proceedings*, Vol. 45, 1938-9 (*Henry Sidgwick & Psychical Research*).
[2] *Op. cit.*, p. 486.   [3] *Ibid.*, pp. 514-15.

He suggests that what we recognise as 'mind'—or one might say a person—may be a compound of two things, a psychic factor and a bodily factor neither of which independently has the properties characteristic of a mind. This psychic factor, he considers, may persist for some time after death, and much of the phenomena believed to indicate survival of some particular mind, appears to him only as a persistence of some factor which was a constituent of a living mind.[1]

I had often, when young, attended meetings in friends' houses where amateur mediums displayed their unusual powers, my incentive being nothing worthier than an idle curiosity and a desire to annoy my family. And if I had hoped for information about another sphere of being I would have been quickly disappointed. For little or no information about a present life and *milieu* was ever given by any communicator; and what was recounted was generally quite embarrassingly silly. Yet at the same time I was aware of special characteristics of the supposed communicators. And, moreover, they often gave information about their past lives on earth which was usually verifiable. This, it appears, is consistent with the *Compound Theory* of Professor Broad.

Since these youthful meetings I had become inclined to think that telepathy must be the explanation of most of those communications. And after reading Professor Broad's theories I began again to attend a medium's private séances, but with a curiosity which was now much less idle. Over a period of two years I obtained a great deal of evidence—surprising to myself— of what seemed to me the power of a goodish medium to tap the subconscious of the sitter; but none that I could accept for belief in communication from the deceased. Even when the matter contained in such 'messages' was unknown to the medium and the only other sitter, I could not rule out the probability that my

[1] *Ibid.*, pp. 535-6. For further views of Professor Broad, see Text III, p. 270.

own subconscious was contributing to, or controlling, such communications.

But admittedly my investigations had been of the most elementary and amateurish kind. Now I was content to leave such examinations to the experts and to read about the results in the publications of the Society for Psychical Research. Indeed, my main purpose in joining this body was to have access to its library. My great interest was the question of the establishment or refutation of telepathy and extra-sensory perception generally; for it was thus that belief in epiphenomenalism could be demolished or increased. If it could be demonstrated that mind was not dependent for its existence solely on an organism, this would be to destroy the chief antecedent improbability of survival. Whether survival itself were desirable or not did not for the moment concern me. The first question was its possibility.

Since that time, many years ago, when I read Professor Broad's views on man's possible survival of death, in *Mind and its Place in Nature*, we have been told that although as recently as 1954 it appeared to him unlikely that a *psi* factor which persisted after death could have any experiences at all,[1] by 1957 he was inclined to think that a very few of the *psi* phenomena do argue for something more than a mere persistence of the *psi* factor. Some of Mrs. Willett's scripts, for example, make it hard, he says, to reject a conviction that a mind has survived and is actually thinking and planning.[2] Disembodied existence he finds factually possible and not necessarily inconsistent with our knowledge of physiology, physics and psychology.[3] (His view of the brain appears to be that of Bergson and Professor Habberley Price.)

[1] Rosalind Heywood, *The Sixth Sense*, p. 210 (Chatto & Windus, 1959). She refers here to his lecture, *Human Personality & the Possibility of its Survival*, given at the University of California, 1954.

[2] *Ibid.*, pp. 210-11. A broadcast is given as context of this. We are also referred to his *Personal Identity & Survival*, the thirteenth *Myers Memorial Lecture*, where these ideas are developed (Pub. S.P.R.).

[3] *Ibid.*, p. 209.

This, and much more, I learnt only recently from *The Sixth Sense*. I had read some fifteen years before what was then published by the S.P.R., in their *Proceedings* of the Willett scripts; but I was baffled as to their true explanation, knowing myself incompetent to judge of such matters. Now I found that those competent to do so and yet to whom the idea of their survival of death was distasteful, such as Mr. J. E. Piddington (ex-Hon. Sec. of the S.P.R.) and Professor Broad, were increasingly driven towards belief in the authorship claimed for these scripts as the least extravagant explanation.[1] And according to Professor Gardner Murphy the most reliable evidence for survival is of the type supplied through the mediumship of Mrs. Willett in the *Ear of Dionysius* case where communications appear to be the joint expression of a surviving interpersonal relationship between Dr. Verrall and Professor Henry Butcher, and to be intelligible as a plan devised by them after death.[2]

It astonished me that educated people could look askance on a Society which, founded and conducted by men and women of generally acknowledged first-rate intellect and integrity of character, had done work of a genuinely scientific nature for over seventy years. But prejudice as well as ignorance of the aims of the Society and the nature of its investigations I knew still to exist. The S.P.R. I found often confused with Spiritualism (although Spiritualists have the greatest dislike for the Society's investigations); and I noticed that wherever I mentioned the S.P.R., there was an uncomfortable hush, followed by a quick change of subject as if I had said something indecent.

What astounded me even more than people's prejudice against the S.P.R. was their complete lack of interest in those things which it was investigating. Lord Balfour, it is said, wrote in 1894 that no event in the structure of the physical sciences should cause as much intellectual curiosity as the fact of communication by extra-sensory means.[3] And although it is undeniable, as Mrs.

[1] *Ibid.*, p. 88.   [2] *Ibid.*, pp. 199-200.   [3] *Ibid.*, pp. 10-11.

Heywood observes, that there is little of practical usefulness in a faculty which is unpredictable and unreliable, to any reflecting mind the most vital of questions must concern the nature of life. Here, in ESP (extra-sensory perception) she finds a new glimmer of light on a faculty owned by living human beings.[1]

Many people I found did not wish to have their neatly stacked little apple-carts upset. On these ESP could have nothing but a disruptive effect. And Alexis Carrel has pointed out the fundamental tendency of the human mind to reject those things which cannot be fitted into the general framework of the philosophical and scientific findings of the time; so that even scientists are not unwilling to state that things which they cannot explain do not in fact exist.[2] It is frequently quoted that Helmholtz said, 'neither the testimony of all the Fellows of the Royal Society nor even the evidence of my own senses could lead me to believe in the transmission of thoughts from one person to another independently of the recognised channels of sensation.' For such an attitude, the term *scotomisation* (the bringing about of a blind spot) has been introduced by psycho-analysis.

It has several times been recorded that Freud—a member of the S.P.R.—had gradually become persuaded of the existence of ESP through finding strong evidence of its workings between analyst and patient. But although his acceptance of this occurred as early as 1924, he was prevailed upon not to disclose this publicly for fear of the menace it would prove to psycho-analysis.[3]

I found it was not only people of the calibre of Helmholtz

[1] *Ibid.*, p. 11.
[2] *Man the Unknown*, pp. 48-9 (Hamish Hamilton, 14th imp., 1954). (Professor Sir Alister Hardy, F.R.S., believes that telepathy has been established and that it is a revolutionary discovery; whilst Sir George Thomson considers it to be of immense importance and that not sufficient work is being done on it.) See *The Sixth Sense* (pp. 13 and 167).
[3] Laurence J. Bendit, *Paranormal Psychology*, p. 26 (Faber, 1944), quoting Ehrenwald. Also H. Habberley Price, S.P.R. *Proceedings*, Vol. xlvi. And R. Heywood, *op. cit.*, p. 193.

that were subject to *scotomisation*. As Jung has pointed out, to minds of a certain intellectual mediocrity the overweening faith which they place in orthodox science sets their conscience at rest and absolves them from researching into those things which have been adversely reported upon by orthodoxy.[1] Such faith provides an excellent means of defence behind which prejudice and laziness may flourish. T. H. Huxley in his hatred of blind subservience to any unlimited authority, may I thought have had such minds in view when he prophesied that the following generation would live to see all the *stupidity* approving of science, adding that that might well be harder to suffer than the then existing state of things.[2]

Prejudiced minds seemed to overlook the fact that one of the most important obligations of science was to correct its conclusions continually in accordance with fresh knowledge derived from new experiments. There was never any finality about its pronouncements; that was its essence. And it was this fact that gave the work of the unprejudiced S.P.R. so much importance, I thought. It was breaking new ground, and ground of the utmost significance in the life of man. For, under rigorously scientific conditions, experiments sought for fresh knowledge on man's latent powers however inexplicable by orthodoxy.

Moreover, it could help to establish or demolish theories which had an immediate bearing on the possibility of man's survival of bodily death. And from what I had learned at spirit-ualistic meetings and from various works that I had read, together with some of the *Proceedings* of the S.P.R., I had come to think that the existence of ESP generally could not be denied. The result of my acceptance of this was to reduce for me the antecedent improbability of man's survival. (Incidentally, we are told that Lord Rayleigh, Crookes, Myers, Mrs. Sidgwick, Gurney, Lodge

[1] *Psychology and Religion*, pp. 55-6 (Yale University Press, 9th printing 1955).
[2] Cyril Bibby, *T. H. Huxley*, p. 168 (Watts, 1959).

and William James, members of the S.P.R., all, in the end, believed in survival; but that Sidgwick and Podmore remained unconvinced although they accepted ESP.[1])

And yet to Sidgwick, survival was the prime essential of the value of human life. He longed to believe in both God and immortality. But because of this he was always inclined, we are told, to weight the balance against the *prima facie* evidence for survival which many found in the experiments of the S.P.R.[2] He is reported as saying of stanza cxiii in *In Memoriam* beginning, ' No, like a child in doubt and fear:' that he could never read it without tears, feeling in these lines the inextinguishable and inalienable minimum of faith which men cannot part with because it is essential to their life; and which he knew, in so far as the human in him was stronger than the systematic thinker, he could not abandon.[3] And in a letter, he writes of the indestructible conviction that humanity neither will nor can acquiesce in a godless world.[4]

Tennyson himself desired immortality with an almost fierce intensity. After acknowledging his faith in a chief intelligence and in immortality, he adds that if he did not believe in these he would jump off Richmond Bridge without delay. At another time he says if a God has put in man this passion for immortality it cannot but be the truth. And if it is not, then a mocking fiend must have created us. Tennyson would curse him to his almighty face, plunge his own in a chloroform rag and make an end of it all.[5]

And Tennyson was no religious ostrich. He read eagerly

[1] Rosalind Heywood, *op. cit.*, p. 55.

[2] *Henry Sidgwick and Psychical Research* by C. D. Broad, S.P.R. *Proceedings*, Vol. 45.

[3] See *Henry Sidgwick, a Memoir*, by A. S. and E. M. S. (1906) pp. 538 ff. Quoted by B. Willey, *More Nineteenth Century Studies*, p. 103.

[4] *Ibid.*, pp. 538. Quoted by B. Willey, *More Nineteenth Century Studies*, p. 102.

[5] Sir Charles Tennyson, *Life of Tennyson.*

current scientific works; and it has been pointed out that he actually anticipated Darwin in stating (in *In Memoriam*) Natural Selection as a fact.[1] All new truths were examined and no religious assurance was acceptable to him if it were incompatible with these, even though he strongly desired such assurance.

But I doubted whether that 'hope and passion' for immortality were at the present time as general as Tennyson implies it was in his day. The result of a poll taken recently amongst Church of England members shows that nearly 50 per cent actually disbelieve in man's survival of death. And if such a percentage is found amongst Church members it is reasonable to suppose that amongst those professing no allegiance to either Christianity or Judaism the proportion of disbelief will be vastly greater. Emerson has said that 'the blazing evidence of immortality is our dissatisfaction with any other solution.' But most of us nowadays it seemed did not contribute at all to the ' blazing evidence.' An odd spark here and there alone showed that the fires of desire were not completely extinct. Man had for the most part rejected the idea of immortality because he had no use for it.

I thought the Church as the strongest upholder of immortality was largely responsible for the general decrease of man's belief in his survival. It had continued in our day to speak of immortality in terms that no longer aroused any desire for such a state, in language that modern man had ceased to understand. And although few now went to Church, belief in an after-life was indelibly dyed by those colours in which organised Christianity had dipped it. Few attempted to separate it from the doctrines of the Church which they had rejected. But if preachers and religious writers had brought home to man the more fundamental implications of belief or disbelief in immortality, I thought that the possibility of survival might not so commonly be rejected

[1] *Essays and Studies* by Members of the English Ass., 1940. Quoted by B. Willey, *More Nineteenth Century Studies*, p. 87.

without much reflection, especially by those who yet believed in God.

For if there were no world of being to which he might attain, then man, according to Plato (for whom perfection is the only reality), could never know that Supreme Good of which here, in an earthly life, every man had a presentiment. Thus, if his aspirations and his desire for this Good were never to be fulfilled, faculties in his nature never to be expressed, life would thereby be fundamentally irrational. Moreover, if there were no sphere of Absolutes existing as the source of all becoming, man would by his very conception of these prove himself greater than anything that did exist—even greater than whatever it was that made the world tick.

And although it is often said that man has no justification for thinking that the universe is adapted to his emotions and desires, I thought that he could reasonably consider that life was not fundamentally irrational. Even if man were merely a product of this stupendous process called evolution, it was hard to believe that his development into a being who recognised the rational as the norm and the irrational as an aberration, could arise in a system which was itself inconsequent and independent of reason. And I knew that McTaggart went further in saying that if we can establish the existence of a harmony in the universe we are justified in arguing that such and such a thing is because it is fitting, or conversely that it is fitting because it is. (I saw no reason to pre-suppose that a belief in such a harmony would be any more emotionally engendered than the opposite disbelief. The positive in such cases is bound to appear 'farther-fetched' than the negative which is an easier proposition, avoiding the onus of proof.) McTaggart, I remembered, even endorses for those who believe in a benevolent Creator, their inference that man must be immortal because the lack of immortality would make of life a farce of the most hideous kind.

Leigh Hunt has asked:

'. . . why . . . so much half beauty here, and such need for completing it, if completed it is not to be? . . . As to the fulfilment of these yearnings on earth to be made entire in a future state, I can no more believe in the existence of regions in space whose God has made half orbs in their heavens . . . than I can believe he will fail to make these anxious half-satisfied natures of ours which thus crave for completeness, as entire and rounded in that which they crave for as any other fruit of his hands.'

It now no longer surprised me that people who had abandoned belief in an after-life so often ceased at last to believe in God. And I saw it as a short step from disbelief in the possibility of man's attainment to a sphere of being, to disbelief in the existence of such a sphere. As we are constituted, to accept that knowledge of the Supreme Good is unattainable is no far cry from admitting the non-existence of the Supreme Good.

Although, for the moment, I saw clearly only the inseparability of the two ideas—that of another life and of the existence of a benevolent Creator (I was not convinced of either)—I had come to doubt that the source of man's vision and aspirations lay within himself. There was something greater than man, I thought, some Mind or Spirit. But although it did not seem reasonable to suppose that man could have developed intelligence in a system that was not the result of the work of a mind, was this original mind necessarily benevolent? I found it impossible to believe that it could be malevolent, for one at all proficient in male-volence would hardly allow man a blessed release in death; a 'mocking fiend' at all worthy of the name would not kill flies for sport but prefer to torture them unendingly. Moreover, a male-volent God could be no God for he would necessarily be inferior to man on whose nature it was indelibly written that the good alone was the true and the highest of all desires.

Was there, then, a power at work which was something other than a conscious Mind? Something that was therefore indifferent to the men and the universe it was creating? It did not seem that whatever underlay the process of evolution could be distinguished in its results from what would be the effects of planning. And to call this power 'law' instead of mind did nothing to explain its origin. If the whole of the process were mindless, whence did it derive its plan and its original impetus? If there was no mind, then it seemed that we were still, like the pre-Socratics, seeking a Primary Substance.

Pliny said that ' God, if God there be, is outside the world and could not be expected to care for it.' I was to find plenty of support for that view throughout my wanderings. But the very fact of an evolutionary process, of what seemed like a purpose—even if it were unconscious—argued, I thought, against indifference. However impersonal what we called 'law' must be, it demonstrated something like a determination that things should act in such and such a manner and in no other. It was only a state of anarchy which would suggest indifference.

Years later I was to read in *Man on His Nature* the extraordinarily vivid description of the growth of the human fœtus from the microscopic speck of granular jelly to the fully formed infant. Each of the cells, without senses and blind, yet shapes itself and takes up its correct position in the total collection of cells according to the stage at which this has arrived. It is, says Sir Charles Sherrington, as if in each cell there was immanent a principle of knowledge which enables the fulfilling of a design— as if there were prescience and purpose.[1]

Knowledge, design, prescience, purpose; all these did indeed suggest an underlying mind. And, in fact, Sir Charles Sherrington goes on to ask himself whether the evolution of the brain could produce mind out of no mind, since it is clear that evolution does not create. All it can do is to construct something further from

[1] Charles Sherrington. *Man on His Nature*, pp. 100-101 (Pelican, 1955).

something that already was.[1] And what did it have from which mind could evolve? In the case of the embryo, again mind appears to come from no mind, and at death to merge again into no mind. But the devolution into nothing he finds as hard to accept as the evolution from nothing.[2] Mind is without material confirmation and will always be so; and the idea of 'energy,' as it is now understood, is quite incapable of accounting for mind.[3]

Elsewhere in the same work, he speaks of the change that slowly came about in man as originally pitiless in his sub-human state. And he asks from where has man derived his 'values,' and were they his own inventions?[4] These were questions to which I was continually returning.

It was clear that only a Creator who was benevolent could be associated with a Creation which he maintained in existence; and also with the idea of another life for man after death. But it has been suggested that

> ' all doctrines are to be suspected which are favoured by our passions and the hopes and fears which give rise to this doctrine [immortality] are very obvious.'[5]

I did not believe that this doctrine could now be said to be 'favoured by our passions.' And were these fears so obvious? If death were really complete annihilation, what was there to fear (unless you happened to be like Baudelaire with his ' J'ai peur du sommeil comme on a peur d'un grand trou')? For my part I felt it was the 'perchance to dream' that alone engendered fear. Yet it was true that the belief in immortality was generally accompanied by hopes. With a few there was the passionate desire that death should not be the final separation from those they loved; whilst with others, perhaps equally few, there was a need inalienable from our very natures, that there should be a world

---

[1] *Ibid.*, p. 219.   [2] *Ibid.*, pp. 219-20.   [3]*Ibid.*, p. 266.
[4] *Ibid.*, p. 287.   [5] *Essay on Immortality* ascribed to David Hume, 1783.

of being, of reality, in which we could find what can best be expressed in old-fashioned language as the holy trinity of the good, the beautiful and the true, existing in all their glory undiminished by the puny conceptions of men.

But how few of us cared enough either for those we loved or for this blessed trinity to hope that immortality might indeed be true. I saw with something of a jolt, that it might be the whole meaning of life that we grew to care so much for them that immortality might seem the one thing desirable. But death is so tempting in its easiness, so comforting in its finality. And so fitting too to our generally pleasant life of epicureanism where everything is so nicely 'taped': an averagely decent life with as much pleasure as can be got without harming others, and after a good run for our money, a sound sleep with no nonsense about a possible awakening. What would most of us 'do' with another life? What has it to offer? Nothing that the majority really want; nothing that, unfortunately, we can't quite well do without. So I saw that although life on earth would be a farce without the possibility of survival for some men, there were very few of us who had the courage to desire it.

But as to proof in ultimate questions what hope was there of any? I thought that the most one could expect would be an attitude of mind derived from collecting the *pros* and *cons* as faggots. No isolated argument could convince one way or another, but when taken all together the various clues might form a bundle of sufficient strength to support either belief or disbelief.

Which way would the game go for me? I found it far easier to imagine the everlasting night than the eternal day. In fact, life in another sphere was so impossible to imagine that I was often inclined to dismiss even the bare possibility. But at other times I was influenced by Plato and by the ethical arguments in its favour.

Since, however, no ethical argument could have complete

force for me unless the existence of a benevolent Creator could be established, I had now to leave my direct search into the question of immortality, and explore the possibilities of the existence of such a God. Before returning to Plato and his theory of Forms, I would try to get some idea of the Greek thought that preceded Socrates.

PART THREE

On various ideas of God, and what I learned from them—1

1. *Through Plato, I reach belief in absolutes*

' Man hath still either toyes, or Care,
He hath no root, nor to one place is ty'd,
But ever restless and Irregular
About this Earth doth run and ride,
He knows he hath a home, but scarce knows where,
He sayes it is so far
That he hath quite forgot how to go there.
He knocks at all doors, strays and roams,
Nay hath not so much wit as some stones have
Which in the darkest nights point to their homes,
By some hid sense their Maker gave;
Man is the shuttle, to whose winding quest
And passage through these looms
God order'd motion, but ordain'd no rest.'

HENRY VAUGHAN, *Man*

Although I spent many months with the Pre-Socratics, I did not gain much that advanced me directly in my search. For with my inclination to agree with Plotinus that 'the most irrational theory of all is that elements without intelligence should produce intelligence,' I was hoping to find a primary substance or a God that was mind or some kind of spiritual force.

When I reached Anaxagoras with his startling words: ' The mind that made the universe is God ' I thought I had reached this idea of deity. And Edward Caird finds here 'the idea of a pure spiritual principle, which subdues the necessity of nature and uses it as its own instrument.'[1] But Lord Russell intervenes between

[1] Edward Caird, *Evolution of Religion*, Vol. I, p. 368. (Maclehose & Sons, 1893.)

us and our subjectivity—what I recognised as man's tendency to fill the unfamiliar with a familiar content—telling us that Anaxagoras thought but little about religion and ethics and that he was probably an atheist.[1] Indeed I remembered Socrates' disappointment that Anaxagoras made no use of intelligence nor assigned any real causes for the ordering of things, but spoke only of 'air and water and ether and such-like absurdities.' There was no mind which ordered things 'for the best.'[2]

And as, according to Cornford, it was Socrates and Plato who took this further step, and through them appeared for the first time in Greek thought, the belief in a benevolent and provident father and fashioner of the universe—presumably a mind which ordered things 'for the best'—I returned to the *Republic* without delay.[3]

Whether the existence of the Forms and the world of being had been well established logically or no was not my only concern.[4] There was the question of the antecedent improbability to be faced. In spite of my refusal to be satisfied that the finite was all, how was it possible to believe in absolutes like Plato's Forms existing independently of the human mind? For such would require not only a sphere beyond the finite, like Plato's world of being, but—or so it seemed to me—that they should exist as ideas in a divine Mind. (And much later I was to learn Abelard's belief that these are indeed God's concepts, existing in the divine Mind as patterns of creation.)

For years, from adolescence onwards, I had slithered about in a world where everything was assumed to be relative, and my mind had grown accustomed to an unexamined rejection of absolutes and ultimates. Reality and unreality were not facts external to the human mind. Truth was man-made. Things were 'true' if they were 'true for me.' This I had absorbed unreflect-

---

[1] *Op. cit.*, p. 82.   [2] *Phaedo* 97c.
[3] *Greek Religious Thought*, p. xxii.
[4] For Plato's theory of the Forms, see Text IV, p. 278.

ingly from the prevailing climate of opinion which also encouraged the belief that any idea which was modern must *ipso facto* be more enlightened than one which was not. And the current disbelief in a supernatural sphere amongst those most affected by this climate, made the presumption that this world is all inevitable. Whence, then, were standards of reality, thought and conduct to be derived if not from the human mind?

I was never quite happy about the dismissal of a supernatural sphere. It seemed to me a trifle hasty as a definite conclusion. How could anyone be so certain? And in the same way I could not rejoice in the disappearance and then the death of God as did many of my friends who evidently made of him an all too human old ogre only kept alive by nursemaids as a cautionary tale. True, I had humanised him myself as a child into all that was good and desirable. That, however, might well have been in another life, so long ago and so far away was the memory, eclipsed too 'by the customs and manners of men.' And, anyway, to suggest that there could be anything agreeable about God now merely earned one —in a certain circle—the label 'sentimental,' and the inevitable discourse on Freud and the ' Father-figure.'

It was odd, I thought, how angry many then were with God, how much they hated him. What had he done to them? Deprived them of years of enjoyment with his Mrs. Grundyism, I gathered. But if he existed would he remotely resemble anything that this conception suggested? And since they had decided now for atheism, it was puzzling how they could be so angry with something that did not exist. If they had turned their fury upon the Church for the idea of God it presented, that would have been understandable. But their attitude savoured rather of revenge, almost as if they exulted in a denial of his existence as the supreme insult to a deity who might not after all be quite dead and who had better learn pretty quick that he was no longer required in any capacity anywhere. They didn't want his heaven, and they no longer believed in his hell. Freud had shown—it was always Freud that they read, never Jung—that religion was 'nothing but a neurosis.' They attacked it with vituperative scorn. Angry young men and women are nothing new; but why the bitterness here? Could it have been that deep down they had a desire for God and could not forgive him that there was no evidence of his existence (although we never even looked for it) and certainly none of his love; and hence the almost hysterical hatred of religion?

I was in no better case than these angry ones. Diffident and vacillating as I was, my attitude to these matters was ambivalent. I thought I simply had not enough data to make up my mind one way or another. I think I was then a genuine agnostic; yet I could neither forget nor dismiss the world of my childhood theophanies, its unearthly beauty. I was a poor mutt wandering between two worlds, the one perhaps moribund, the other perhaps 'powerless to be born.' It would have been far more comfortable to be like most of my friends an ardent disbeliever, especially as it was much more 'advanced' in those circles to be a disbeliever than a mere agnostic. And I got the worst of both these worlds. Since I could not any more wholeheartedly believe than I could disbelieve in God, I was without the support that such belief would bring, and at the same time I could not experience that tremendous feeling of emancipation and relief—of having shaken off the bogeys and the kill-joys and having got rid of fear and 'superstition.' For in my naïvety, it had never occurred to me that God was primarily an encumbrance. Nor could I find it anything but odd how every unpopular theory had, almost overnight, become a superstition, every popular one an indisputable 'fact' endorsed by psychology if not actually by science. Odd, too, that such elements in life which had seemed to require explanations other than those which a purely materialistic answer could supply, simply no longer existed. They had been so thoroughly explained by Freudian psychology that they had been explained away.

I Reach Belief in Absolutes

So with God dead, and no soul and certainly no after-life to bother about, it should have been for these disbelievers 'bliss to be alive.' And there was a vast amount of enjoyment in one kind of circle which I frequented—mostly unlicensed since there was no point in tearing up the divine D.O.R.A. if you did not profit by its destruction, no sense in the cat's being away if mice did not play. But there was little real joy. And this extravagant emancipation was not freedom. There was absolute enslavement to the gospel of enjoyment, and to the doctrine of 'meaninglessness': the only certain thing about life was that it had no intrinsic meaning and that we were annihilated at the end of it—a negative creed which, once it had established the complete independence and self-sufficiency of man, offered little sustenance. And with a disbelief in any absolutes outside ourselves we had to seek the perfection still necessary to us in the finite and the transitory. Any ideals we retained had to be achieved through our own self-sufficiency since there was no supernatural sphere, no world of being to give meaning and direction to the world of becoming.

If I personally had been too vacillating actually to deny God, I had at least relegated him to the lumber room of my mind, where he remained dustily shrouded until with approaching middle-age my thoughts turned to the question of life's meaning and purpose, and the search into God's existence was 'on.'

And now this search had brought me up against the problem of the Forms. I knew that to believe in absolutes and ultimates that were independent of and not derived solely from the human mind would be in a sense to believe in another world, the world of being. And I inclined now to the belief that there was something that existed that was higher than man, and something that was the source of his aspirations, and that this must be in the nature of a mind or spirit. But it was one thing to see the implications attaching to a belief, one thing to 'incline' towards such a belief, and quite another to take a stand on it.

Thus Plato's Forms were a challenge to my ideas to pass from

71

the notional to the real. But I saw that to grant reality to absolutes somewhere 'out there' would be the thin end of a wedge which if driven home to its full extent would arrive at something which could not rightly be isolated from the real existence of a God of some kind.

It was the conviction that this world is all that made it impossible to believe in Plato's Forms, and therefore caused us to see ideal beauty, truth and goodness and so on as existing only in the human mind. And yet that now seemed to me an unsatisfactory alternative; for that would grant them no reality. They would cease to be absolutes and would become merely relative standards, subject to men's temperaments, and slaves to time and fashion—what Plato called 'opinions.' Whereas the very definition of 'absolute' demanded that it should be unchanging and static, with complete self-existence and independence. The more I thought about it the more was I persuaded that absolutes did exist in reality, somewhere, somehow.

Plato holds that it is only of the Forms that we can have knowledge since they are the only reality. A man who knows must know something that exists, something that is real; of particulars we can have opinion only, since they are deficient in reality.

> Socrates says: 'Then those who see the many beautiful, and yet neither see nor can be taught to see, absolute beauty; who see the many just, and not absolute justice, and the like, such persons may be said to have opinion but not knowledge. But those who see the absolute and eternal and immutable may be said to know, and not to have opinion only. The one love and embrace the subjects of knowledge, the other those of opinion.' (*Republic*, Book V, 479e-480.)

These Forms of Plato had all the unchangingness, the unmovedness demanded by an absolute; they existed through themselves alone, independently of the human mind. But it was not until I reached the Form of the Good that I began to be profoundly stirred. Absorbed, disturbed and elated at the same time, I realised that I was at a decisive point. If I accepted the existence of Plato's Form of the Good, his absolute beauty and so on as fundamentally true, I would have crossed the Rubicon from the farther side of which I might never find my way back again.

The knowledge of the Good, Socrates declares to be the end of life, and although he will not define it, the Form of the Good has a unique position. It is the supreme principle of which every man has a presentiment and upon which all things depend.

> 'You have often been told that the idea of good is the highest knowledge, and that all other things become useful and advantageous only by their use of this. Do you think that the possession of the whole world is of any value without the good? or of all knowledge without the beautiful and the good?' (*Republic*, Book VI, 505.)

This was almost like the Christian gospel in sentiment; the supreme principle resembling the Light that lighteth every man which cometh into the world, and the last sentence recalling the saying of Christ; 'for what is a man profited, if he shall gain the whole world, and lose his own soul?'

And certainly this idea of the Good was like the idea of God in being hard to attain.

Socrates says:

> 'My opinion is that in the world of knowledge the idea of good appears last of all, and is seen only with an effort; and when seen, is also inferred to be the universal author of all things beautiful and right, parent of right and of the lord of light in this world, source of truth and reason in the other; and is the power upon which he who would act

rationally either in public or private life must have his eye fixed.' (*Republic*, Book VI, 508.)

Moreover, the Form of the Good is seen to be not only the source of being of all other Forms, but a single, comprehensive and sufficient explanation of the source of all knowledge—a fundamental unifying principle. And we are told that whether called the supreme nature, or the ideal beauty of the *Symposium* or *Phaedrus*, or as here in the *Republic* the ideal good, all are the absolute and unapproachable being.[1]

I could now understand Plato's belief that the perfection of these absolutes was the only reality, and that the whole creation groaned and travailed towards realisation of that perfection. This was similar to much of which I had heard tell in Christianity, but divorced as it now was from the rest of Christian theology which I had found so factitious and repugnant, the idea translated into terms of the particulars' striving towards the perfection of the universal by seeking to 'realise' themselves, was one that I could not dismiss.

In the *Timaeus* I found the tendency to personify mind or God increased. He is the supreme nature, the Form of the Good personified and called God: a God with personal attributes.

I thought something like this was bound to happen sooner or later. What I saw as the thin end of the wedge—the existence of the Forms as absolutes in their own right, independent of the human mind—had been driven home to its full extent and had arrived, as I had foreseen it must, at the real existence of a kind of deity. And once the idea of the reality of the Absolute was accepted, the way was opened to the world of being—to what in Christian terms are God and the supernatural. But since I had already been inclined to believe that a mind or spirit must underlie nature and the process of evolution, why was I so much disturbed? I was often to experience later the truth of the saying

[1] See Jowett's Introduction to the *Republic*.

that it is one thing to seek the truth and quite another not to run away from it once it is found.

For me Plato's Forms had the merit, at the outset, of not being anthropomorphic; and the gradual blending of the impersonal with the personal, of the passing of the Form of the Good into God himself in the later Dialogues, took place so gently, so vaguely, and remained so nebulous an Absolute, so undefined, that I felt none of the antagonism I had experienced towards the God of the Christians. There, what I had rejected so violently was the definiteness of the teaching about him; his 'domestication' by the Church, his 'super-humanity,' his smallness, almost his nearness. Even as I could not believe anyone who was prepared to tell me about the climate of heaven, the exact temperature of hell, so I mistrusted any definite statements about God. I thought that did he exist—'to speak his nature to all men is impossible.'

Timaeus says:

' Was the world always in existence and without beginning? or created, and had it a beginning? Created, I reply. Now, that which is created must . . . of necessity be created by a cause. But how can we find out the father and maker of all this universe? And when found, to speak his nature to all men is impossible.' (28.)

' Let me tell you then why the creator created and made the universe. He was good and no goodness can ever have any jealousy of anything. And being free from jealousy, he desired that all things should be as like himself as possible. This is the true beginning of creation and of the world, as we shall do well in believing on the testimony of wise men.' (29.)

In the *Laws*, I found the power of the good taking the form of an intelligence or person. The will of God, together with the standard of the legislator and the dignity of the soul here fill the place of the doctrine of the Forms. Mind now becomes prior to chaos, whereas in the *Timaeus* God had made the world out of pre-existing materials. Plato goes beyond Anaxagoras whom he criticises in the *Phaedo* for not giving any power to this Mind and accords it both power and priority (eternity). It is not only prior to chaos but everlasting, the source of order and intelligence in all things.[1]

It was to Plato that I owed the recognition that there was nothing that was not intellectually respectable in the idea that God, if he existed, might indeed be a Shepherd of sheep, a God who cared for his creatures and kept providential watch over them. But for all that the tendency to personify mind or God I saw only as a manner of speaking. If I could believe in God it would be as a sort of divine necessity which ordered all things for the best as the Form of the Good towards the realisation of which creation groaned and travailed; something in the nature of Whitehead's figurative conception of process as a tender concern that nothing shall be destroyed.[2] But to endow this with personal attributes could be for me but a figure of speech.

In my youth I had rejected anything that might in the slightest degree associate me with Christianity. And if Plato had now opened for me a window that had long been almost shut, this was not to say that he brought me any nearer to the religion I had rejected. For though my hitherto almost complete ignorance of Plato allowed me room for large-scale surprise at the similarities existing between Platonism and Christian teaching, I yet thought Christianity was Platonism spoiled.

[1] See Jowett's Introduction to the *Laws*. For extracts from the *Laws*, see Text IV, p. 279.

[2] See *Process and Reality*, p. 490 (C.U.P., 1929). On page 209 of the same work the meaning of *process* is given as the growth and attainment of a final end. It is the progressive history of the Universe, Nature, *phusis*—the very essence of the utterly real. And since no actual thing is to be understood as just its static self, nothing is accidental. See *Adventures of Ideas*, pp. 146, 262-3 (Pelican, 1942). Also *Nature and Life*, pp. 59-60 and 93 (C.U.P., 1934).

I Reach Belief in Absolutes

It is said that in the *Laws* Plato, 'from meditating on the priority of the human soul to the body, has learnt the nature of soul absolutely. He has discarded these fancies' concerning the recovery of ideas from a former state of existence.[1] For me, however, there was something about the theory of reminiscence, allegorically, which still made me unable to dismiss it completely however fanciful any literal implications might be. It could account for much that was otherwise unaccountable, (although that was no proof of its truth); not only for all æsthetic experience and for intuitions—those sudden convictions which arrive in the mind and leave an ineradicable mark—but also for such things as my theophanies when I was a child.

I was reminded of Vaughan's *The Retreat*:

> Happy those early dayes! when I
> Shin'd in my Angell-infancy.
> Before I understood this place
> Appointed for my second race,
> Or taught my soul to fancy ought
> But a white, Celestiall thought,
> When yet I had not walkte above
> A mile, or two, from my first love,
> And looking back (at that short space,)
> Could see a glimpse of his bright-face;
> When on some *gilded Cloud,* or *flowre*
> My gazing soul would dwell an houre,
> And in those weaker glories spy,
> Some shadows of eternity; . . .

I had in my childhood often felt 'those bright shootes of everlastingness.' And perhaps that sharp pain mingled with joy, so often experienced in the presence of 'the *gilded Cloud* or *flowre*' was none other than a stab of home-sickness. Had I once

[1] See Jowett's Introduction to the *Laws*.

known the heavenly pattern of which these were but the weaker glories?

I was now convinced of a reality behind the glory and splendour of nature and art which were but manifestations of this something perfect and immutable. And I believed that it was in this reality that lay the power to evoke an emotional response, and not in the manifestations alone. All æsthetic emotion I now recognised as having something other-worldly about it; for it was not explicable in terms of this world, scarcely even analysable. After years of wandering in a world of doubt and negation, I knew myself reorientated. As Plato would say, the eye of the soul had been turned.

I believed, then, rather nebulously, in a divine order and a soul in man; the possibility—not yet the probability—of this soul's survival of bodily death. Since I saw this as entirely dependent upon the existence of a benevolent God, I now wanted to learn more about this divine order and this soul in man; and with that knowledge either to promote the possibility of the soul's survival into a probability, or else to demote it as advised 'to that suspicious rank of largely wishful thought.' But although I was constantly being told that belief in man's survival of death was founded on nothing but wishful thinking, I was not aware of such a wish within myself. For all the reasons I have already stated, I found it more 'natural' to wish for mortality. True indeed, I had a great curiosity about those 'perfect rounds' of Browning, surrounded as we were by 'broken arcs.' But, independent as no doubt truth was of man's curiosity, I felt that I should have to know a good deal more about the divine order and the heavenly set-up before I could decide if I would ever want to commit myself to it for all eternity.

In spite of accepting with both hands most of what Plato offered me—actually or allegorically—I could not but see the occasional anomalies and confusions in the theory of the Forms. But, perhaps because I was untrained in philosophical thinking, it did not at the moment worry me greatly, for example, how matter could exist without form or how there could have been motion in the chaos when as yet time was not, and how chaos came into existence, and so on. I was on the whole content not to count the spots upon my sun and, with gratitude to follow Jowett's advice not to ask for consistency.

Although in the *Parmenides*, Plato criticises his own doctrine of the Forms, I preferred to leave his works with constructive ideas pre-eminent in my mind, and to turn to Aristotle for these criticisms, learning at the same time what he would put in the place of Plato's doctrine.

2. *I reject the God of Aristotle*

Of all the manifold criticisms which Aristotle advances against Plato's theories, the motionlessness of the Forms, I learned, provides the most serious objection.[1] If the sensible world imitates these Forms, it should be as static and unchanging as they. Whence then does it derive that principle of change and decay which does in fact characterise it? Plato strenuously denies that there is any principle of motion in the Forms, and partly because of this Aristotle introduces an Unmoved Mover.

For the powerless Forms of Plato which fail to account for the continuous ebb and flow of life, Aristotle considers that a being must be substituted which is itself without matter and therefore devoid of potentiality. Clearly an object of desire imparts movement without itself being moved; so also does an object of thought. And the highest object of both thought and desire could only be a Mind, a living being.

God therefore, according to Aristotle, is the supreme, immutable and eternal, immaterial being, indispensable to the world's existence, since it is the desire of the world for God which is its motive force. He is the lodestone which draws the world, the cause of the cosmic process by which form develops in matter from potentiality to actuality. He initiates this by his presence, for he is pure activity, a wholly immaterial being, an Unmoved Mover.

[1] See Aristotle, *Metaphysics*, I, ix. For other important objections see also *Met.* XII iv and v, and II., ii.

I Reject the God of Aristotle

But this Unmoved Mover is not the Creator of the world although he educes form from already existing matter (for the origin of which Aristotle does not account). He is immaterial activity and, as such, pure Form without matter; pure actuality, the cause of eternal circular motion. He transcends the visible world, incapable of any passions, desiring nothing, living an eternal life of contemplation of himself (since no other object would be adequate for God's contemplation). His being consists in a thinking of thought; his happiness in this contemplation. He does not operate upon the world by directing thought and volition towards it, since he does not know of its existence. His mere being, as the greatest good, the highest perfection, is the cause of every striving and movement; on that alone depend all order, cohesion and the life of the world.

It interested me that although Aristotle denied the independent existence of the Forms (and his many arguments against this did make the theory appear like the sieve in which the Jumblies went to sea), he retained the belief in God as indispensable to a satisfactory explanation of the existence and cause of change. And as Professor D. J. Allan states, he held not only that physical science demanded a supreme being other than a physical substance, but that psychology was unable to account satisfactorily for human intelligence apart from the hypothesis that a perfect example of intelligence existed somewhere in the universe.[1]

But although I had instinctively been groping my way towards a deity that would be mind or spirit, this God of Aristotle created a very different outlook from that arising out of Plato's philosophy. I proceeded from a warm and sunny country, over which a good and righteous God who cared for all creatures kept providential watch; from a climate where the spirit of man could thrive, to a cold and alien land where the Unmoved Mover,

[1] *The Philosophy of Aristotle*, pp. 114-15 (Home University Library, O.U.P. G. Cumberlege, 1952).

ignorant of the existence of the world, was Supreme Mind, a *Dieu des savants et des philosophes.*

Not being remotely either a *savant* or a *philosophe*, and in spite of my strong reaction against the anthropomorphic God of the Christians, could I find this utter aloofness of the Supreme Mind credible? What I found unconvincing about Aristotle's God was the factitious combination in him of mind and unconscious mechanical force. If he were to be the perfect example of intelligence (*nous*) it was not credible that he should be unaware of the existence of the world; and if he were to be an unconscious magnetic force it was again incredible that he should be thinking reason or absolute spirit. The agnostic view was that any power there was behind evolution could not but be indifferent to the world and its inhabitants since this power would certainly be impersonal and thus as incapable of feeling as any other purely mechanical force. And although I did not think the certainty compatible with true agnosticism, and I was unable to conceive what else that force could be but a mind since it appeared to plan, yet this agnostic theory seemed to me hardly more untenable than one which made God at the same time an example of perfect *nous* and almost perfect nescience. Different as the spheres of reasoning intellect and knowledge might be, to deny omniscience to the divine was, I thought, to make him something less than a God.

I found in myself a profound dissatisfaction with this Unmoved Mover who drew us all as a magnet draws pins whilst being unconscious of the world's distress and of its need of him. I did not think that it was just arrogance that made me resent being demoted to the status of a pin from what in Plato amounted almost to being a child of God. Rather was it due to what appeared as a limitation in this deity. It was not enough that he should be supreme, immutable, eternal and indispensable to the world's existence. Primarily, I rejected this pure actuality because I could no longer separate the role of the divine Absolute from that of a conscious Creator. However many æons evolution might have taken—or be taking, since creation might well be a continuous process—I now found it impossible not to believe that there was a supernatural Power; and moreover, one which was a conscious mind responsible not only for this process but for the creation of original matter from which form was educed. Merely to bring order to chaos as God does in the Platonic dialogues before the *Laws*, and the Unmoved Mover does through his initiating the development of form in matter from potentiality to actuality, was to leave the creation of matter itself unaccounted for and to suggest another creation before God took charge.

And if I attributed mind, will and consciousness to this Creator behind evolution, it was not to attribute to him personality as we knew it. What that could be which possessed such attributes in a manner totally other than when possessed by men was, I thought, beyond human understanding. So, too, the process of his concern that nothing shall be lost. Indeed, in the *Eudemian Ethics*, Aristotle himself speaks of the ruler whose part, if it ever could be to love, would be to love in another way from that of man. Indifference was not compatible, I thought, with such a process any more than with a creation by a divine Mind. Although there had been a time when I had embraced the ideas of vastness, distance and indifference as essentials to Godhead, as being far more reasonable and probable than those presented by the too small, the too near, the too humanised God of the Christians, now I had come to have a different view of these essentials. And I saw that it might be alone in the divine order that vastness could be of such an all-embracing nature that consciousness could comprehend the fall of the leaf no less than the fall of the star.

But the Unmoved Mover is no Creator and, endowed with an almost incredible degree of nescience, he cannot be expected to care about the work for which he is not responsible and of which he knows nothing. Somehow he had for me the character of a hireling. Aristotle had hired him and had installed him as an absentee landlord.

This absenteeism, however, I saw was what might recommend him to many—to those who do not like expressly to deny God and are well content with one who makes no demands and offers only an unrealisable goal. God would be 'there' for anyone who wanted sometimes to think vague, uplifting thoughts, and yet there would be no duty that men would be conscious of owing to him. The divine would not interfere with the human, and the human would not trouble the divine with cries and lamentations. It would be a proper gentlemen's agreement. But as William James has said, 'The prince of darkness may be a gentleman, as we are told he is, but whatever the God of earth and heaven is, he can surely be no gentleman.' And for my part, whilst I had felt that I could without difficulty have made a not unsatisfactory religion of Plato's Forms, I knew that from Aristotle's Unmoved Mover I could manufacture for myself only an artificial and insufficient philosophy. I could not believe in his perfection which is merely posited and never demonstrated in his dealings with men. There was about him something of the elderly and ultra-academic don divorced from reality, which I did not associate with the true nature of deity.

The question whether Aristotle believed in the possibility of some men's survival of death occupied me a great deal. From the *Nicomachean Ethics* it appears that he did believe in an anæmic kind of survival, certainly scarcely desirable.[1] And in *de Anima* we are told that reason is incapable of being destroyed, and that although we have not yet any certain evidence it appears that it alone is able to exist in a state of separation from the body as the eternal is separable from the mortal.

Lord Russell interprets Aristotle's statements on this question as implying that it is only in so far as men become rational and have something divine present in them that they may share in

See Text V for extracts from these *Ethics* and from *de Anima*.

God's immortality. He sees no evidence that Aristotle believed in a personal immortality as taught by Plato and later by Christianity. Individuality would seem to be connected with the irrational soul; and whatever is irrational separates us. But the divine and impersonal is the mind or rational soul; and whatever is rational unites us. Man may indeed increase in his nature that which is divine, and it is clear that to do this must be accounted the highest virtue. But, as Lord Russell points out, where a man succeeds completely in this he thereby ceases to be an individual person.[1]

This sounded a little bleak when I thought of the vast majority of people who 'do not have the power of reason.' But yet there was something here that could not airily be dismissed. Aristotle was, I thought, expressing a profound truth when he stated that it is only through the presence of something divine in the rational soul that men can share in God's immortality; and that God can only love what is 'best and most akin' to himself. Therefore we are urged to increase in ourselves that which is divine, 'whatever . . . will best promote the contemplation of God, that is the best mode'; we are 'so far as we can to make ourselves like immortals, and do all with a view to living in accordance with the highest principle in us.'[2] This was very like Plato's exhortation on the nurture of the soul by the imitation of God. And it followed naturally that the more there was of the divine in the rational soul the less there would be of the irrational 'ego.'

Jung, however, differentiates carefully between the 'self' and the 'ego.' The former he sees as the centre of the human personality, immortal and timeless, existing before any birth: the self which must be enabled to displace the ego as the principle directing the whole psyche.[3] This 'self' might well, I thought, have affinities with what Aristotle terms divine reason and Plato speaks of as the divine part of the soul. There was obviously

[1] *op. cit.*, p. 194.   [2] *Nic. Ethics*, 1178 c., trans. D. P. Chase.
[3] Quoted by R. C. Zaehner, *At Sundry Times*, p. 42 (Faber & Faber, 1958).

85

something which all three thinkers believed could survive death. Of this I hoped to learn more later.

Meanwhile, the more I thought about Aristotle's God, the more he appeared to me as an abstraction, the *deus ex machina* of a scientist, and the less I believed in him. I could not but regret all that gradual, natural growth of Plato's Forms, their flowering into the idea of the Good in the *Republic*, and the identification of the power of this Good with an intelligence in the *Laws*; and I resented this chill blast from Stagyrus which suddenly cut them all off: God banished beyond reach in outer space, the Forms denied true existence, and man left with only the cause of eternal circular motion to love and an unrealisable goal to pursue. What meaning for man could be wrested from such a metaphysic? With a God whom it was humanly-speaking impossible to love and in whom man evoked not only no charity but no glimmer even of recognition, Aristotle had dealt man a poor hand in the game of life. No divine concern for creation, no Beatific Vision hereafter, and possibly no Islands of the Blest.

Coleridge has said that everyone at heart is born either a Platonist or an Aristotelian. Certainly all my heart was with Plato whilst Aristotle had only a small corner of my head. And although I was not of sufficient intellectual stature to dare to pronounce judgment on the world's great thinkers, I could yet enjoy Luther's opinion that Aristotle was a 'damned heathen' whom God had 'sent as a plague for our sins.' For Aristotle's hireling was no God.

It amazed me then that the Medieval Church should have picked on Aristotle as a basis for its theology, with his severely intellectual God unaware of the world and the creatures inhabiting it, that cold and smugly noble Mind, aloof and ever beyond the realisation of man's aspirations; when the Church could have chosen Plato with his God as Father and Fashioner of the world he cared for.[1] And although so much Platonism was incorporated

[1] Some reasons for this choice are suggested in Text V, p. 284.

86

into Christianity it appeared to be done with surprisingly little acknowledgment, and more was always heard of the less attractive Aristotle than of Plato.

I marvelled too that in Christianity so little fuss was made of Socrates. When his character and life and death were considered, I thought it must be admitted that in these no one had so nearly approached Jesus Christ. And I wondered that Christians did not revere him in the same way as they did John the Baptist. Both Socrates and Plato must have been Forerunners of immense importance.

I was interested to find, however, that Lord Russell, whilst admitting the eminent merits of Socrates, charges him with serious shortcomings. He finds him specious and false in argument, dishonest in his private thinking, aiming to prove those things agreeable to him rather than seeking scientifically and disinterestedly for the truth. In this Lord Russell finds the most heinous of sins, a perfidy to truth.[1]

But it was difficult to believe that anyone dishonest in his private thinking and for the sake of a 'lie in the soul' could face death with the absolute serenity of Socrates. And since Lord Russell admits that Socrates cares more for what he believes to be the truth than for all else, I supposed that the perfidy consisted in his believing more than he could prove. That for a modern philosopher would be hard to stomach.

It was clear that Socrates had a deep seated assurance in ultimate questions which he derived from a source other than reason.[2] That there was another source of assurance I could no longer doubt. Keats was right, I thought, in marvelling 'how anything can be *known* for truth by a process of abstract reasoning.'[3] And like him I was not to be dissuaded from a need to feel every truth 'upon the pulses.'[4]   Certainly, the theories that I had

[1] *Op. cit.*, p. 164.
[2] See Plato's *Symposium* for Alcibiades's account of Socrates at Potidaea.
[3] Letter No. 31 to Benjamin Bailey, Nov. 22nd, 1817. *Op. cit.*, p. 67.
[4] Letter No. 64 to A. H. Reynolds, May 3rd, 1818. *Op. cit.*, p. 141.

accepted from Plato were not always those which had been logically the best demonstrated. Some of these—and not only those which were familiar to me—evoked an immediate assent, whilst others more rigorously demonstrated failed to persuade. Much of his language was often mystical rather than philosophical, and dispensed with logical argument altogether.

This was the way of the poet as well as the mystic. And it seemed that the heightened sensibility of the poet might give vision denied to the professional thinker. The poet's logic could be at fault, perhaps, but his immediate perceptions, I suspected, were often sound. Whereas with the philosopher, his logic could be faultless but his premises barren. His gifts did not lie in intuitions, nor would he wish to claim that they did. In fact, intuition I found considered by most philosophers to be a dangerous self-indulgence, amounting pretty well to a *carte blanche* for believing what one wished to believe.

And although Keats said too that 'philosophy will clip an angel's wings,'[1] I thought that it might well be its task to be a trimmer of wings. I should have to see how my assurances fared at the hands of later philosophers.

I would turn next to 'the father of modern philosophy'—Descartes.

[1] *Lamia*, 229.

PART FOUR

On various ideas of God
and what I learned
from them—2

1. *Through Descartes indirectly I recognise the value of intuition*

'It is absolutely necessary to conclude . . . that God exists.'
Meditation III

Descartes's *Discourse on Method* and his *Meditations*, I found full of surprises. But the first one I met with caused me acute disappointment. For here I read:

'I revered our theology, and aspired as much as anyone to reach heaven: but being given assuredly to understand that the way is not less open to the most ignorant than to the most learned, and that the revealed truths which lead to heaven are above our comprehension, I did not presume to subject them to the impotency of my reason: and I thought in order competently to undertake their examination, there was need of some special help from heaven, and of being more than man.'[1]

It was hard to meet a devout Christian of the intellectual calibre of Descartes only to find that his reason appeared to him impotent to examine 'revealed truths.' There might have been here an opportunity to learn what they conveyed to the mind of a philosopher. And my sense of frustration was increased by the fact that I so often met anti-Christians of lesser gifts than Descartes who assumed these revelations to be entirely within man's

[1] *Discourse on Method*, Part I, translated by John Veitch, p. 9 (Blackwood, 1880).

comprehension, and then proceeded to show by their talk that they understood them as little as I did. It seemed that those who should be able to expound them would not, and that it was only those who obviously could not that did.

That was always assuming that these 'revealed truths' had an inner meaning to which I had failed to penetrate. It was useless for me to be referred to revelation apart from that, since I neither understood nor believed it at its surface level. Moreover, I suspected anything that absolved one from reflection and sold a whole lot of ready-made beliefs with a label of 'guaranteed true' attached. And, far from revering Christian theology, I found its claustral character suffocating.

In the *Principles of Philosophy* Descartes remarks that 'the chief cause of our errors is to be found in the prejudices of our childhood'; and that 'we experience a difficulty in expunging them from our memory and, as long as they remain there, they give rise to various errors.'[1]

It is clear that he suspected no possible connection between such prejudices and the beliefs which he accepted without subjecting them to the 'impotency of reason.' He says, 'What God has revealed is incomparably more certain than anything else. We ought to prefer the Divine authority to our perceptions.'[2]

That, I thought, would be true enough if there were valid assurance that the source of any authority were indeed divine. But my antagonism to the idea of revelation derived mainly from my profound distrust and dislike of the Church as the claimant of a monopoly in receiving and interpreting these 'revealed truths.'

Later in the *Discourse*, Descartes tells us:

' I formed three or four maxims. The first was to obey the laws and customs of my country, adhering firmly in the

[1] LXXI, p. 226 (Blackwood).   [2] LXXVI, p. 231 (Blackwood).

faith in which, by the grace of God, I had been educated
from my childhood.'[1]

' Never to accept anything for true which I did not
clearly know to be such; that is to say, carefully to avoid
precipitancy and prejudice, and to comprise nothing more
in my judgment than what was presented to my mind so
clearly and distinctly as to exclude all grounds of doubt.'[2]

There were things, I believed, which, being neither pure
prejudice nor merely familiar ideas, were 'presented to the mind
so clearly and distinctly as to exclude all grounds of doubt.' I did
not of course attribute these to orthodox revelation, but I saw
that just because I disliked his orthodoxy I could not rightly
dismiss as an unreasonable pre-conception Descartes's idea of
God's existence which was to him 'very clear and distinct,' when
I accepted even more far reaching unsupported pronouncements
on God by Socrates.

For Socrates does not trouble to give reasons for his beliefs.
And in the *Republic* he adopts, as Rudolf Otto has pointed out,
an apparently dogmatic tone for his statement that God is true
and that he neither changes nor deceives. What I had found
equally surprising was that Plato portrays Adeimantus as moved
to an immediate assent through realising distinctly, for himself,
the truth of this idea.

This combination of events is for Otto a characteristic of all
a priori knowledge: immediately an affirmation has been
distinctly stated and grasped, recognition of its truth appears in
the mind with the conviction of direct insight.[3] Examples of this
conjuncture, he states, are found continually throughout the
history of religions; and he believes that in the human spirit there
exist *a priori* factors universally and necessarily latent.[4]

These *a priori* factors appeared to be responsible also for

[1] Part III, p. 23.   [2] Part II, p. 19.
[3] *The Idea of the Holy*, p. 154 (Pelican, 1959).   [4] *Ibid.*, p. 157.

Plato's knowledge of the Form of the Good 'the supreme principle of which every man has a presentiment.' And I found the same idea expressed by Luther:

> ' That God is, all men know by the guidance of nature alone, without any knowledge of the arts and disciplines, and this is divinely imprinted on the minds of all men. There never was a race so wild and savage as not to believe in a certain divinity which created all things. . . . All the Gentiles knew that there was a God, however much they were Epicureans, however much they argued that there was no God. Did they not in denying him at the same time confess that there is a God? For no one can deny that of which he has no knowledge. . . . And although the conscience has been crushed for a time by evil and perverse opinions, yet it returns and convicts them in their life's last breath.'[1]

The first sentences reminded me of the argument for the existence of God which Descartes derives from his own idea of perfection, especially when he says in the *Meditations*:

> '. . . as to the way in which I received this idea from God; I have not drawn it in from the senses; it is innate in the same way as is the idea of myself. . . . God, at my creation, implanted this idea in me, that it might serve . . . for the mark of the workman impressed on his work. . . .'

Being himself imperfect and finite, Descartes finds it absolutely necessary to conclude that there is a Being who is perfect and infinite who has placed in him the notion of perfection and infinity.[2] I had really no right to quarrel with this if I was prepared to accept the same sort of argument—fundamentally ontological since it dealt with the abstract essence of being and

---

[1] *Table Talk*, Wei. V 5820.
[2] The text of this argument is given in Text VI, p. 285.

things—which Plato uses to establish the existence of his Forms. Locke, too, I read, held that 'we know ourselves by internal perception and God by inference; we infer from the fact of finite existence, and from the existence of thinking beings (and at least our own thinking is indubitably certain to us) that there exists a primitive and an eternal thinking being. We thus know our own and God's existence with complete clearness.'[1]

Although the fact that the self was imperfect and limited did not prove the existence of a not-self which was perfect, and the statement therefore that the idea of God 'had been placed in me by a nature which was in reality more perfect than mine,' namely, by God, did not follow logically, I was unable to reject Descartes's conclusions. And I experienced a sudden revulsion against the idea of abstract reasoning as alone able to assure us of the truth. As Locke once said about metaphysics, ' You and I have had enough of this kind of fiddling,' so I now felt the bloodlessness and unreality of verbal arguments. To hell, I thought, with logic and all my niggardly searching for proofs. There was something far greater than mere logical consistency and metaphysical demonstrations. That something I had already experienced when my own fumblings, from the very outset of my search, had inclined me to a belief in God as alone able to account for man's sense of the Good; and later to accept Plato's knowledge of the Good as the 'supreme principle of which every man has a presentiment.' It was that kind of instinct which though not patient of proof could hold firm. It spoke with the voice of absolute authenticity, from a region far more profound than those surface levels where the toying with words and meanings took place and where the very impersonality of approach made the pursuit of truth a lifeless game of skill which cost one nothing.

And it was because I now suspected that man, with his desire for the good, was made in God's image, that I found it no longer

[1] Quoted by Friederich Ueberweg, *History of Philosophy*, Vol. II, p. 87 (Hodder & Stoughton, 1874).

possible to believe that there would not be some fundamental correspondence between this human instinct and the nature of reality. Without such an agreement human life would be a farce of incredible magnitude and malignity. For that would force us to the conclusion—which I understood was that of Nietzsche—that man must live without the Truth.

That idea had the quality of a nightmare from which there could be no awakening; where everything was meaningless, mad, without purpose, and where man was doomed for ever to illusion and unreality. But the nature of reality—or God—I was already persuaded was not malicious and I could not attribute to it such a perverted sense of humour. I did not believe that the creation of man after æons of evolutionary process was an elaborate practical joke. As Descartes had echoed Plato in thinking, God was true and no deceiver. And there was some basic agreement between man's instinct that such a God existed and the nature of reality itself.

Yet I burned to know more about Descartes's conception of him other than as the God of a mathematician, introduced to account for psycho-physical parallelism—that God who arranged the faultless synchronisation between mental and bodily events, the perfect accord of which (since there is no interaction between them) is evidence of their creation by him. He has wound and set them in such a manner that without causal connection every tick in the one is accompanied by a tick in the other: and so they will continue for the whole of their association.

Such a God had for me only the unreality of any *deus ex machina*. And I had some sympathy with Pascal when he wrote:

'Je ne puis pardonner à Descartes; il aurait bien voulu, dans toute sa philosophie, se pouvoir passer de Dieu; mais il n'a pu s'empêcher de lui faire donner une chiquenaude, pour mettre le monde en mouvement; après cela, il n'a plus que faire de Dieu.'

' Il faut dire en gros: Cela se fait par figure et mouvement, car cela est vrai; mais de dire quels et composer la
machine, cela est ridicule; car cela est inutile, et incertain
et pénible. Et quand cela serait vrai, nous n'estimons pas
que toute la philosophie vaille une heure de peine.'[1]

But Descartes's views about philosophy in general, and his
humility about his own are a little unusual for a philosopher. For
he says:

' Of philosophy I will say nothing, except that when I saw
that it had been cultivated for many ages by the most distinguished men, and that yet there is not a single matter
within its sphere which is not still in dispute, and nothing
therefore which is above doubt, I did not presume to
anticipate that my success would be greater in it than that
of others; and further, when I considered the number of
conflicting opinions touching a single matter that may be
upheld by learned men, while there can be but one true,
I reckoned as well nigh false all that was only probable.'[2]

(That reminded me of Varro's having said that amongst the
ancient philosophers there were over eight hundred ideas of the
Summum Bonum but that not one hit the right.)[3] Further Descartes
says:

' I had become aware, even so early as during my college
days, that no opinion, however absurd or incredible, can
be imagined, which has not been maintained by some one
of the philosophers.'[4]

And even more surprisingly he writes:

' On pourrait trouver étonnant que les grandes pensées se

[1] *Pensées*, Article XCVI, *Pensées Diverses sur la Religion*,
[2] *Discourse*, Part I, p. 9.
[3] Quoted by Jeremy Taylor, in Coleridge's *The Friend*.
[4] *Discourse*, Part I, pp. 16-17.

rencontrent plutôt dans les ouvrages des poètes que dans ceux des philosophes. C'est que les poètes écrivent par enthousiasme et par force d'imagination. Il y a en nous des germes de science commes des germes de feu dans le caillou. Les philosophes les en tirent par le raisonnement; les poètes les font étinceler par l'imagination; ils brillent davantage.'[1]

It was surprising to me that a philosopher should speak so warmly of the poetic imagination; for it appeared to be rare, as Pascal said, that mathematicians were intuitive and that men of intuition were mathematicians. But it did indeed seem that Descartes, the mathematician, combined intuition with philosophy. Of course this led to inconsistencies, and one of these is said to lie in his attitude to the use of the imagination. Mr. Stuart Hampshire suggests that Descartes's most critical indecision may have been as to whether the idea of God can be one of unmixed intellect or whether it must be partly of the imagination.[2] Can the nature of God be conceived in any way unless his attributes can be described in terms whose meaning is derived from human experience? If the use of such terms is necessary to our comprehension, it follows that our conception of the divine nature cannot but be partly anthropomorphic. But if all such images and therefore anthropomorphism are set aside, nothing but an impersonal and entirely abstract God remains.

This shook me considerably, although it was a truth I was realising increasingly. For now I reflected that perhaps I had been indiscriminate in my rage against the anthropomorphism of Christianity. Maybe the fault had lain partly in my own failure to understand the problem involved. Indeed, my juiciest bone of contention with the Christian seemed to be becoming gradually less succulent.

[1] *Olympica*, p. 13 of *Œuvres Inédites de Descartes* (Durand, 1859).
[2] *Spinoza*, p. 23 (Pelican, 1956).

The Value of Intuition

Another fertile idea which I found in Descartes concerned the falsity of considering a thing unbelievable because it is unimaginable. And I realised that in fact this was an error which most of us commit all the time. I saw, too, how my own inability to imagine another sphere of existence certainly influenced me against belief in man's survival of death.

Descartes's own attempt to find one single thing beyond the possibility of doubt and on which he could base his philosophy, led me to the question of freeing the mind honestly from all prejudices and biased thinking. But I believed that prejudices and grounds for assumptions varied according to the conditioning of the mind, and that purely unbiased thought was not possible. Things could not be viewed entirely objectively, for one of the limitations of man's finite nature was that *quidquid recipitur, recipitur ad modum recipientis.* According to Goethe man can hear only that which he understands. And in this understanding I saw that the conditioning of the mind must inevitably play a part. It was impossible, therefore, that the self should not contribute something in all knowledge. As Bacon has said, 'the human understanding is like an unequal mirror to the rays of things; which, combining its own figure with the figures of the objects it represents, distorts and perverts them.'[1] It seemed therefore that man must accept his human nature humbly and not expect to achieve a hundred per cent Olympian objectivity and detachment; nor flatter himself that any knowledge he had could ever be pure and undistorted.

And though it was Swift's pessimistic dictum that 'happiness is a perpetual possession of being well deceived,'[2] I thought that in aiming to avoid this self-deception (man's powers of which appeared to be very great), there was always a danger in trying to keep an objective balance, of falling over backwards like Thurber's bear, and refusing to believe a thing merely because it was desirable, even when the balance of probability was on its

[1] *Idola*, from *Novum Organum*.   [2] *Tale of a Tub*.

side. And that as Proust has pointed out, we err as often through an exaggerated fear of being influenced by our own desires, as through the tendency to believe what is agreeable to us.[1]

That did not excuse one from examining 'those doctrines which are favoured by our passions,' whether such passions were those of belief or unbelief. But if no logical reasoning could prove or disprove God's existence, by what light were these arguments to be examined? Certainly Descartes's attempt to prove it on a scale as imposing as his psycho-physical parallelism advanced one not at all. Rather was it his instinct behind the faulty reasoning and inconclusiveness of the argument from perfection that had the ring of truth. And the lesson I had learned from him—indirectly —was that the intuitive certainty of God's existence such as I had sometimes felt as a child was not to be regained by metaphysical arguments divorced from human instincts, however suspect to the philosopher such instincts might be.

Yet I was anxious to see if Spinoza had something better than psycho-physical parallelism by which to establish metaphysically the existence of God.

---

[1] Quoted by Denis Saurat, *History of Religions*, p. 314 (Cape, 1934).

2. *What remained after the rejection of pantheism*

'We act by the behests of God alone, and are participators in
his Divine nature; wherefore the more excellent, the more
perfect the acts we do, the more and more do we know God.
Besides conferring entire peace of mind, our doctrine . . .
teaches us wherein our true happiness or beatitude consists,
viz., in the knowledge of God alone, whereby we are led to
do those things only that persuade to piety and love.'
SPINOZA *Ethics*, Part II, from *Scholium* to Prop. XLIX

To understand anything about Spinoza's 'most perfect Being'
required, I found, that all ideas of anthropomorphism should be
rejected. Earlier I should have rejoiced in such a pre-requisite,
believing that at last I might be 'getting somewhere'; but now I
wondered how I could advance at all in learning about a God
whose attributes were not to be described in terms of which the
meaning is derived from human experience. For I had come to
see that the use of such terms as analogies might be necessary to our
understanding, and that if all images and therefore anthropomorphism were to be ruled out, what remained would be an
entirely abstract God.

And Spinoza's Deity—stemming from the monism of
Parmenides with his 'Only Being is'—was certainly very difficult
to grasp. Here, God and Nature are not to be differentiated. He
is *Natura naturata* as well as *Natura naturans*.[1] If I wanted a deity
who was no personal God, here was one as impersonal as the

[1] See Text VII for a short account of Spinoza's philosophy.

Primary Substance of most of the Pre-Socratics. But was this Being credible?

'Oh me, oh me, how I love the earth, and the seasons, and weather, and all things that deal with it, all that grows out of it,' wrote William Morris.[1] I, too, had assumed unreflectingly that because I passionately loved some of her manifestations I was a devotee of Nature as a whole. But now I began to wonder, how deep did all her fairness go? Aristotle found that evil was 'more plentiful than good,' and what was hateful 'more plentiful than what was fair.' Everywhere, inextricably bound up with her splendours, there was conflict, suffering, predacity, insecurity. Man was surrounded by hostility and indifference. 'Nature is cruel; man is sick of blood: Nature and man can never be fast friends,' wrote Matthew Arnold.[2]

It was impossible to love anything with such a terrifying unconscious inexorability. One could love in her that which has been subdued by man. Left to herself, as in the primeval forest, she was malignant, horrifying, terrible. Like some immense machine geared to a maximum productivity, she could not stop herself, but advanced, proliferating, until every inch of earth was covered with teeming life. Her own law seemed a blind necessity, herself amoral and without mind or reason.

I did not find it credible that ' Deity is only Nature ' as Pliny thought. And to believe with Spinoza that God was identical with his creation, one with the world, or completely immanent in it, was to rob him of all supernatural power. For the fate of the universe, whether ultimately it perished by cold or by heat, would, on a pantheistic view, be shared by a Deity for whom it was impossible to free himself from his creation.

It might seem an inspiring thought, that of a Creator whose love for his creation prescribed the voluntary sharing of its fate—the Captain going down with his ship. But in Pantheism God did not appear to have any will or choice, for the Captain was the

[1] Quoted by C. Sherrington, *op. cit.*, p. 283.   [2] Quoted *ibid.*, p. 281.

ship. And the sharing of a fate which one is impotent to avoid inspires compassion rather than veneration. There could be no morality without freedom; it cannot consist in a mere obedience to natural law where no other course of behaviour is possible. Moreover, the concept of the dying God, certainly in the Christian mythos, was inseparable from the idea of sacrifice with a purpose: a death in order that others might live. But nothing of that nature obtained in Pantheism. And certainly the God of Spinoza may not be considered as a God of love. The logical fate of such a non-omnipotent Deity thus deprived the Godhead not only of any meaning but of everything that man might worship.

I had already met a good deal of Pantheism in my youth, amongst people who had rejected Christianity as I had done because it was too narrow, too definite and altogether alien to our mentalities. It had appeared then that Pantheism was much more respectable intellectually, for the vaguer and more amorphous a belief, the higher it seemed to us. We felt we were being very profound in seeing God equally present in good and evil, and in believing that everything is God. But these were mere catchwords never thought out to a logical conclusion.

Before long, however, I began to wonder whether this immense, formless Everything might not equally well be the gigantic Nothing. What could that thing be which had no particularity ever, anywhere, and about which everything could be said to be true? To make a thing 'All that is' appeared to rob it of everything and to make it equivalent to nothing. And to find God as much present in evil as in good was to find him indifferent to both. And what kind of a God would that be? If God were to be 'impersonal' to that degree it was easy to see how little such an abstract Deity could impinge upon man's consciousness. It was clear, too, that Pantheism did not ever really come to grips with the problem of evil.

Indeed, the thing that hit me hardest in Spinoza's philosophy was the absence of any meaning in the universe. This followed naturally from the purposelessness of his Substance which appears to be a blind and more or less mechanical process. And with no meaning and purpose in this gigantic system, terms of moral value could not be more than arbitrarily attached to anything. According to Plato, I remembered, a thing was 'good' in so far as it fulfilled the purpose for which it had been made. But if, as Spinoza holds, man and all natural objects had been created without any end in view, it was obviously impossible to decide what was 'good' and what failed to attain to goodness. To Spinoza everything is God, and the terms 'good' and 'evil' are not applicable to creation which is God himself (*Deus sive Natura*).

But although man has been designed with no end in view, he is urged to find his sole significance and freedom in identifying himself with the sum and system of all that is—with the only thing possible since nothing can be otherwise than as it is. It is in knowledge of this Being that men learn that their minds are at one with and part of the universal order. In this realisation their happiness consists.

It was undoubtedly true, I thought, that men's happiness could only be found in an identification of themselves with something higher than purely personal desires and aims, something greater than themselves. That was no pious poppycock. But I could not believe that the majority of ordinary men of good will would find their sole significance in embracing any system that was essentially purposeless, nor that they could live a life devoid of meaning. The self could only be identified with something believed to have some purpose, however difficult to fathom, and from which the meaning of life derived. Man's joy arose from being part of a purpose however small that part might be. But to love this 'creating creation' which was without aim, will or choice was a very different matter from submission to a necessity that was inseparable from a belief in a divine will emanating from Absolute Mind.

And although truth was independent of its effect upon human

nature, why should men believe in the kind of deity that appeared to be a blind force? For Spinoza nowhere proves the nature of this Being, nor, therefore, the state of determinism which follows. Most of his propositions I found to be based on *a priori* knowledge and although one could not quarrel with their perfect mutual agreement they assumed those very things which they were intended to prove. And I was not led to believe either in this purposelessness or that God and Nature could not be differentiated.

If God is immanent in the world, or if he *is* the world, then there is only one order of reality. Either the world is raised to the level of divinity or God is reduced to the level of the world. This classless society where a democratic God is 'one of us' undoubtedly makes a strong appeal to men with a natural distaste for the supernatural, as I well knew. But now I no longer believed in only one order of reality and that God was identical with his creation. That would be to make man part of God; and this I utterly rejected. For such a God would be no divine being, and such a man no human.

Indeed, the philosophy of Spinoza appeared to remove essentials from both God and man, with meaning and purpose in the universe denied and freedom replaced by determinism. I did not doubt that there was some absence of freedom in men's lives. We were always to some extent 'victims of circumstances' in the web that we continually and inevitably create for ourselves and others. That was the fundamental characteristic of human life: it could not be lived in isolation. There was an ineluctable solidarity which limited freedom for us as individuals. And it was fitting I thought that it should be so. But to believe in a thorough-going determinism would be to remove all incentive from human struggles and invite a general apathy and despondency. Man had to believe in his freedom to choose good or evil.

Yet with Spinoza's idea that God was not a judge inflicting punishment I could not but agree. It was only in such punishment as sin carried with it of itself that I believed. So, too, would virtue be its own reward by making a man susceptible to greater good. But when Spinoza says that God never forgives transgression but extracts to the uttermost farthing the penalties he has imposed for every infringement of his eternal decrees, it was clear that the idea of forgiveness as distinct from a remission of penalties was one which could find no place in a deity who was *Deus sive Natura* and knew no will or choice in the course of necessity. And here I saw Spinoza's God as inferior to the Christian Deity. The concept of forgiveness had something so sublime that I found myself—suddenly and surprisedly—unable to believe that it was just another attribute that man had foisted upon God. It was, I thought, part of the divine essence—something that man could never have invented alone. But, oh dear! how was it possible to imagine anything but a Person forgiving?

Spinoza's statement that everything tends to conceive of God after the fashion of its own nature, and that were a triangle gifted with imagination it would conceive of God as triangular, was of course true. Like the fish in Rupert Brooke's poem who conceived of his Deity as piscine in form and face, so man thought of God by analogy in terms of human personality. And what else could either fish or man do? We had to think through the minds we possessed, whether fishy or human. And there was this at least to say on man's behalf: he was the most highly evolved of God's creatures and capable of the reflection that no anthropomorphism could ever contain the Deity. Moreover, it now seemed to me that if man attempted to escape his own human limitations by trying to conceive of God as without purpose, choice, will and so on just because we knew such attributes only as human manifestations, any alternative conception of Deity was likely to be so alien as to fall abysmally short of anything that could inform man's life or inspire his worship.

For myself, I found it impossible to think of God otherwise than as possessing these attributes. Yet I did not believe that personality as we knew it could be attributed to him. And the

fact that this conception of mine appeared little different from that
of a 'personal' God arose, I thought, from man's finite limitations,
because he could not think except as a human, and because it was
not in the nature of the finite to understand the infinite. And in
his *Cogitata Metaphysica*, Spinoza says:

> 'How the Essence, the Intellect, and the Will of God are
> distinguished I set down as among the things which we
> wait to know. And here I do not forget the word
> *Personality* which theologians use to explain this difficulty;
> but though I am not ignorant of the word, I am ignorant
> of its meaning, nor can I form a conception of what it is,
> although I firmly believe that in the blessed vision of God,
> which is promised to the faithful, God will reveal this to
> his own.'[1]

Spinoza holds—rightly I thought—that errors arise from our
viewing things in relation to our own being instead of observing
the nature of things themselves. Our hatreds and our desires, it
is obvious, are determined by our own conditioning and not by
the true properties of the objects. Some things appear evil—as
liver-flukes do because of the harm they bring to man—yet are
not evil in themselves. And it seemed that Heraclitus might be
right in assuming a unity of opposites inasmuch that each
necessitated the other. Could evil exist without good any more
than dark without light, cold without heat?

But now I surmised that it was only in the Divine Mind that a
real unity could be effected, and this only through transmutation.
The nature of the Divine, since it was the Form of the Good,
would be to bring good out of its opposite. And it might be
argued that but for one particular evil another particular good
might not be brought into being. Indeed, Professor Dodd, as I
was to learn later, holds that evil must inevitably be conquered

[1] Quoted by R. D. Willis, *Spinoza: Life, Correspondence and Ethics*, p. 202
(Trubner, 1870).

in the end, because the worse its endeavour the greater the calling forth of a counter power creative of good which will more than prevail.[1] Reflecting on the general state of humanity and of the world, this seemed to me at first far too optimistic a theory to accept. To believe anything else, however, I came to see, would be to disbelieve in the ultimate power of the Good—the divine working of grace through finite causes.

If, in his description of the wise man, Spinoza pours scorn upon the hopes and fears of anthropomorphic religions, he speaks of Christ himself with love and reverence. And although, Semite as he was, he could not conceive God as particularly incarnate in any individual man, he says:

> ' God, I opine, revealed himself immediately by the mind of Christ to the Apostles, as he had formerly mediately made himself known to Moses by articulate sounds. The voice of Christ therefore, even as the voice which Moses is said to have heard, may be called the voice of God. And in this sense also may we say that the wisdom of God, in other words, the wisdom which is more than human, put on humanity in Christ, and that Christ consequently is the way of life to man . . . Christ, it must be maintained, communed with God immediately in the way of mind with mind.'

> ' Christ is not a prophet in the same precise sense as are the other prophets. They only attained to a knowledge of divine things by intermediate means and the aid of imagination, whilst Christ knew them without utterance and without imagery. Christ may be said to be the wisdom of God enshrined in humanity.'[2]

Clearly, Christ possessed a greater measure of the Divine

---

[1] *The Bible Today*, p. 139 (Cambridge University Press, 1946).
[2] Willis, *op. cit.*, p. 62.

Essence than other men. And Spinoza adds: ' Christ perceived things truly and adequately. For Christ was not so much a prophet as the mouth of God '(*Os Dei*). It could not be otherwise, for he was sent to the whole human race.[1]

The *Ethics* themselves had to be understood, I found, in the light of Spinoza's correspondence. And yet there did appear to be discrepancies. For instance, how in a system that is without purpose and where men have been created to no end, is it possible to speak of Christ as having been 'sent'? And in one letter Spinoza even speaks of prayer as 'useful.' He can only have been referring to the psychological effects on the one who prays when he says:

> '. . . as intelligent beings we can submit ourselves, mind and body, without a show of superstition to God, and without denying that prayer may be extremely useful to us; for my understanding is too limited to take in all the means that God has provided whereby men may be brought to the love of him, in other words, to salvation.'[2]

I despaired of ever really understanding Spinoza. And indeed, Jacobi said that, ' To understand Spinoza requires too long and

---

[1] Of Mohammed he speaks quite differently:
' From all I say of Mohammed I plainly show that I regard him as an impostor, inasmuch as he denies throughout the Koran that liberty which the universal religion, the religion which is revealed by natural as well as by prophetic light, allows—the right to worship God in spirit and in truth, a right which I have maintained must under all circumstances be conceded to mankind.

' As regards the Turks and other people not included in the pale of Christianity, I am free to confess that I believe if they worship God in love and truth and do justly by their neighbour they have within them that which is equivalent to the Spirit of Christ, and that their salvation is assured, whatever notions they, in their ignorance may entertain of Mohammed and his revelations.'
(It is clear that his indictment of Mohammed springs from Islam's condemnation of natural religion.)
See Willis, *op. cit.* Letter from Spinoza to Isaac Orobio pp. 357-8.
[2] *Ibid.*, p. 308.

too laborious an effort of mind; and no one has understood
Spinoza to whom a single line of the *Ethics* remains obscure.'
But although that dictum doomed pretty well everyone to
failure, the attempt to understand was, I thought, an experience
of the greatest value.

Although to many Spinoza would appear to be an atheist, for
me the greatness of his philosophy lay in its theocentricity, and
in the passionate necessity it attaches to man's striving to transcend
his finite condition, subordinating all personal desires to the higher
desire to know and understand things as they are. This to Spinoza
is love of God.[1] Every day I grew more persuaded of the truth
not only of Plato's conclusion that it was only by ' holding
converse with the divine ' that men were able to ' bring forth
realities ' and ' become a part of that divine and immutable order,
as far as nature allows,' but also of Aristotle's exhortation to them
to ' play the immortal ' by increasing in themselves their highest
quality which alone can share in the divine nature. These ideas
were fundamentally the same as Spinoza's statement that ' the
intellectual love of the mind towards God is part of the infinite
love wherewith God loves himself.' In all three thinkers different
as they were, the same paramount idea was to be found: that
' he who would be dear to God must, as far as possible, be like
him and such as he is.' In all there was the same belief in the
necessity for men to strive to transcend all that is finite in their
nature.

Perhaps it was this conception of the love of God that was
the most important thing I learnt from Spinoza. It was no vague
emotion, soft and pleasurable, but rather a consuming passion.
That it would bring happiness, however, is suggested in the
Ethics:

' From this we clearly understand wherein our salvation,

[1] See Text VII, p. 291 for extracts from the *Ethics* on this subject. Also on
the possible eternity of the mind.

our true felicity, our liberty consists. It is in this, unswerving and eternal love of God, or the eternal love of God for us.'[1]

'... how much they are mistaken in their estimate of virtue who for virtue and good works expect to be richly rewarded and especially regarded by God as for some great service done, as if virtue and the service of God were not of themselves no slavery, but supreme felicity and most perfect freedom.'

(How similar to the words I had heard as a child: the allusion to God 'whose service is perfect freedom'). And we are told that in his *Ethics*, Spinoza sought that which would give him joy eternal.[2]

I loved and revered Spinoza whilst rejecting his Pantheism. The failure of his system to make God Absolute Mind rendered it impossible for me to believe as a whole; his God appeared to be a force guided by no will or choice but only by 'free necessity,' and in that sense to be not unlike the God of Anaxagoras whose mind had no power to order things. But I was convinced now that a divine Mind underlay the whole process of evolution, and that there was a meaning and purpose behind creation however hard to understand. The whole evolutionary process, I thought, cried out for belief in this.

And although I realised the appeal Spinoza's philosophy might hold for those who deplored the idea of man's being at the centre of a world created for his special satisfaction, I thought it might be argued that without the mind of man there could be no science, no interpretation of the universe. And, in fact, Sir James Jeans has said that we can no longer consider Mind as intruding accidentally into the realm of matter and that there is reason to

[1] *Scholium* to Prop. XXXVI, Part V.
[2] From the *Tractatus de Emendatione*. Quoted by William Hale White, *Spinoza*, pp. xxxi and xli (Frowde, 1910).

believe it should be hailed as creator and ruler of this realm. There is evidence in the universe of a power that designs or controls, and which has some property shared with men's individual minds.[1]

Again, Sir Julian Huxley has recently stated that the primacy of human personality which in Christianity is a *postulate*, in evolution is a *fact*. The highest product of evolution, by any objective standard, is the properly developed human personality.[2]

I had no longer any doubt that it was the capacity for love of God that was the highest thing in man: that alone enabled him to transcend the ego. It was the divine spark in him, the leaven. And I was suddenly aware that, in spite of Spinoza's caveats, love must after all be the essence of the divine Nature. Moreover, I refused to blush for what might seem to many to be a naïve and old-fashioned conclusion.

In my so called Christian days I had grown to hate the word because so much woolly waffling had hidden what I thought must be its true and intensely virile nature. If indeed it were the essence of the divine, it could have little relation to the mawkish sentimentality that was generally associated with the texts picked out in pokerwork or pansy-heads over the lodging-house bed. Rather was it something inexorable that made almost unbearable demands upon man. It was nothing easy or weakly indulgent that he could either pooh-pooh or luxuriate in according to his mentality, but a stark reality from which he might be tempted to flee. I now understood how it could be considered a terrible thing to fall into the hands of the living God.

How perverse, how irrational that such a surmise should take possession of my mind after months spent with Spinoza's idea of God! And the deduction that because love was the highest of

[1] *The Mysterious Universe*, p. 137.
[2] *Evolution in Action*, quoted by C. A. Coulson, *Science and Christian Belief*, p. 104 (O.U.P., 1954).

man's capacities it must therefore be the essence of the divine, was like Descartes's assumption that because he had the idea of God it must have been placed in him by God himself. Yet, my own conviction was not to be shaken. And although this had seemed to leap fully armed like Minerva from my head, I realised that it had been gestating not only during those long months when I struggled with Spinoza's thought, but in all those years since I set out upon my search.

But how was it possible to believe in love as the divine essence in view of the overwhelming wretchedness and misery in the world? It was certainly not for me, especially as a newcomer in the field, to seek to justify the ways of God to other men. But I had to face the problem for myself. And through all the years of searching since Plato had led me to belief in the Supreme Good, I had had to recognise that God hid himself very effectively from his world.

I had come to see the truth of Plato's conclusion that the divine persuasion as the foundation of the order of the world, could effect only that degree of harmony such as it was possible to accomplish amid brute forces (and which Whitehead saw as a clear anticipation by Plato of a doctrine of Grace, seven hundred years before the time of Augustine and Pelagius.[1]) And I believed what I was to find much later in the philosophy of Jaspers: that the manifestation of God is always indirect and only through man's own concern for man. This idea is even more forcibly expressed by Simone Weil when she says that the good which God effects in humanity and the world as a whole over any period must be in direct proportion to the co-operation of men.[2] (This was not unlike Spinoza's view that God works only through finite causes.) To her there is no possibility of there being a shred more good than is afforded through this co-operation. Moreover, it now seemed to me that men's lives were neces-

---

[1] *Adventures of Ideas*, p. 156 (Pelican, 1942).
[2] *Notebooks*, Vol. 1, p. 273 (Routledge, Kegan Paul, 1956).

sarily the place of conjunction of good and evil, and that but for evil, good could not here exist. In that sense there was a unity.

Free-will appeared to bear on the problem with the withdrawal of God from his creation. For there could be no intervention between cause and effect. God had bestowed free-will on men and he abided by their use of it. It was not God who sent tribulations and trials to mankind. All followed through necessity. And even in Nature, this necessity took its course. It was perhaps a distorted idea of God as a divine Santa Claus, that caused unreflecting men to blame him for not interfering between cause and effect.

But although I was able to believe in love as the divine essence and manifest in all that was eternal in man, the exercise of this highest human faculty was impossibly hard for me: to recognise in experience that 'no man is an island' instead of merely acknowledging it as an academic truth whilst continuing to pursue a snug invulnerability, a stoic undisturbedness. The truth that only by losing one's life could one save it was the same as that which I had accepted in the fairy stories of my childhood (so often mythological accounts of fundamental realities)—that man can possess only that which he renounces. All this I believed although I knew myself to be a copper-bottomed egoist, incapable of such renunciation.

It seemed like the Red Queen's logic too, that only by becoming something else could one retain something of what one was. If anything could survive death, I thought it would be only that which was permeated by this love of God. It might be the divine 'reason' of Aristotle, the 'eternal part' in man's soul of Plato, the 'fundamental reality' of McTaggart, the 'self' of Jung. And I was to read later Professor Gabriel Marcel's idea that in the next world it is the survival of the loving link that is vital, and not of an isolated entity shut in upon itself. This is the meaning of faith in immortality. For it is inconceivable that a God of love should reject and destroy love.[1]

The conviction that love was the essence of the divine nature was one which ill-fitted with my own make-up. And the recognition that if anything could survive death, the capacity to love was equally the capacity to receive eternal life, brought also the realisation that such a life was never likely to be mine. For if I was not completely an island, I had at any rate done my best to be a peninsula.

Leibniz, I learned, had attempted to exonerate God from all the evil in the world. I would turn next to the *Theodicy* and to the *Monadology* where the idea of God as necessary substance appeared to have been taken over from Spinoza. Would Leibniz, I wondered, establish the existence of this substance as necessary to anything but his own individual system of thought.

---

[1] *The Mystery of Being*, Vol. II, pp. 155-6 (Harvill Press, 1951).

3. *Leibniz leads me to consider the doctrine of original sin*

'The final reason of things must be found in a necessary substance. And this substance we call God.'
'Creatures have their perfections from the influence of God, but they have their imperfections from their own nature which is incapable of existing without limits. For it is by this that they are distinguished from God.'

Monadology 38 and 42

I found that Leibniz, whilst rejecting Descartes's dualism between mind and matter, retains the belief in the impossibility of interaction between different substances (which he calls monads). There is an infinite number of these, and since he believes that any and every event in one substance is accompanied by exactly corresponding events in all the others, he, like Descartes, is obliged to introduce the benevolent intervention of God; and he attributes this correspondence to a divine institution called Pre-established Harmony.

So, instead of a continual miracle as in the system of Descartes's occasional causes, Leibniz introduces one comprehensive miracle. The Two Clocks theory implicit in Descartes is now enlarged to include an infinite number of clocks all functioning simultaneously because all wound and regulated by God. And to those who considered this theory somewhat peculiar, Leibniz merely remarked on the excellence of the evidence it provided for God's existence. 'Dieu seul fait la liaison et communication des substances.'

About Original Sin

The monad is an ultimate spiritual unit or atom; its active force consisting in ideas. Of these monads (simple and unextended substances, each of which is an immortal soul, and of which a human body is entirely composed), the dominant monad is *the* soul of the man of whose body it forms a part. And all changes in this body take place in respect of this dominant soul, the guiding monad. These monads form a hierarchy according to their mental development and their superiority in the reflecting of the universe; less developed ones mirror obscurely, the more highly developed ones clearly. But God alone has none but adequate ideas. He is the Supreme Monad, and all other monads are fulgurations of this primitive substance.[1]

The most interesting thought I found in Leibniz concerned the limited freedom of God. Although God invariably acts for the best, he is under no compulsion to do so. Moreover, he is not free to behave contrary to the laws of logic. According to Mr. Stuart Hampshire, Leibniz used this argument to demonstrate that in the creation of the world, God was not absolutely free, but only relatively free to decide upon the best of all logically possible worlds. The compromise was effected, we are told, from motives of expediency. The doctrine appeared to reconcile rationalistic science with orthodox theology, inasmuch as the Creation might be understood by the use of reason, and yet the belief might still be held that the world was created by God's free choice and will.[2]

And in the *Theodicy* I read that

' imperfections and faults . . . arise from the original limitation which the creature was bound to receive with the first beginning of its being, by virtue of the ideal reasons which restrict it. For God could not give it all things, without making of it a God.' (31.)

[1] For extracts from the *Monadology*, etc., see Text VIII, p. 292.
[2] *Op. cit.*, p. 52.

In this view Leibniz is said to follow St Augustine.

Did this 'original limitation' constitute a fatal flaw? Could man then be entirely responsible for his actions? If God was only relatively free, then how much less free was man? The *Theodicy*, as an attempt to exonerate God from all the evil in his Creation, argues that as the work of his hands the world must be the best amongst all possible worlds; for were a better one possible, his goodness, will and omnipotence would have brought it into being (although Leibniz nowhere shows what it means to God that other worlds should be possible but not actual).[1] If there was to be any world at all it was necessary that it should consist of finite beings, so the evil in the world arises inevitably from its very existence. And he goes on to argue that pain is beneficial as a corrective and a means of instruction. Further, it would not be possible to remove evil without taking away man's power of self-determination and with it morality itself. This power is of man's very essence; he is free to decide for himself according to known law.

> ' He (God) has allowed evil, because it is contained in the best plan existing in the region of what is possible, which plan supreme wisdom could not fail to choose.' (335.)

What, then, of the theory of the Fall?

I gathered that through this doctrine Christians believed that in men's pristine state it was natural for them to centre their lives upon God in an almost effortless love and adoration. Obedience was a joyful self-surrender. But that at some time, someone or something suggested that men could know for themselves what was good without reference to the God for whom they were made. As John the Scot holds, sin arose because men turned towards the self instead of towards God. They became their own

---

[1] See H. W. B. Joseph, *The Philosophy of Leibniz*, p. 188, on this subject (Oxford, Clarendon Press, 1949).

principle, living a life ruled by self-will, rejecting their creaturely status.

Thus, pride and ambition grew naturally from self-will and self-love. And although the spirit in man could still turn to God it was now a movement requiring effort and involving cost. For what should have been man's original nature fell into that merely natural state from which it had been lifted at his soul's creation. Man who could have been spiritual in body became carnal in mind—a spoiled species.

The beautiful account of Creation, in the language of myth and poetry tells us that God saw that everything he had made was very good. But can the world really have been good before the Fall of man? Was nature ever not red in tooth and claw, with animals preying upon each other in an uncomprehending natural 'cruelty'? And was man, in fact, created free when his whole ancestry was predatory and ruthless, however necessarily, in the struggle for existence? How could he avoid inheriting genes of savagery and starting with an overwhelming disadvantage? (Perhaps these were the imperfections and faults to which Leibniz refers in the *Theodicy*.)

It seemed that the world could not have been good for some time before the Fall of man, and that a case could be made out for the theory that the Fall had affected the whole of creation, that some malign power had been at work on this planet even before the higher apes had evolved into man. Something appeared to have corrupted the animal world. For I found it utterly unbelievable that beasts should have been created by a benevolent Creator with no other means of preserving and sustaining their lives than by destroying each other.

Leibniz argues that the Author of things has found it necessary that one animal should frequently serve as food for another. And that this arrangement inflicts no undue distress on the victim since death by disease is generally even more painful than death by violence. Further that, having no capacity for anxiety or reflection on the future, animals are not disturbed by the fact that they are preyed upon except when they are actually in danger.[1]

That was all very well as far as it went. But why had God found it necessary? Animals were certainly no worse off than men who were subject to even greater menaces in life, since they were capable of infinite anxiety. But if it is argued that the human condition is a result of the fall of man, it seemed only logical to suppose that the afflictions of the animal kingdom derived also from a fallen state which reduced it to the level of the vegetable world designed as a means of sustenance. Leibniz appears to view with unruffled complacency God's apparent inability to arrange things better. And I sympathised with Voltaire's having said, ' Si c'est ici le meilleur des mondes possibles, que sont donc les autres? '[2]

How could the world have been 'good' before man's Fall? For the animal creation to be adjudged good would seem to demand at least the practicability of the lamb lying down with the lion (if it ever entered the silly little mutton head to wish to do so presumptuous a thing), and that the king of beasts should so condescend to the most succulent of his subjects. Maybe animals, too, had had allegorically their forbidden fruit, and perhaps if they had never tasted their brothers' blood they would have remained content with an innocent vegetarian diet. And in fact, *Genesis* expressly states that God has given to the beasts 'every green herb for meat.' In my naïvety I thought that had they stuck to this, their sexual impulses might have been reduced; so that there would perhaps have been enough of the green herbs to go round without beasts having to resort to carnivorousness as a means of sustenance.

It is often assumed that Godhead could not know or care

[1] See *Observations on the Book, ' The Origin of Evil,'* from *Theodicy*, p. 414, ed. Austin Farrer (Routledge, 1952).

[2] *Candide*, Chapter VI.

about such details as the suffering of animals; and if those who assume this do remember the 'fall of the sparrow,' the saying merely furnishes them with an example of Christ's ignorance; obviously he didn't know anything about God. God if he exists, is too great for such consciousness.

But I could not dismiss Christ's remark with such ease and temerity. And it seemed to me at least worth considering that divine omniscience might be as penetrating as the full tide which floods into every diminutive crevice, touching the tiniest plant, the minutest insect. Much as it would offend our intelligence, because we cannot grasp the *modus operandi*, God might be a God of detail.

But to return to the imperfections of creation and its problems. Of course it might be argued that the very fact that animals had this propensity to prey upon one another was evidence that the Creator, or this mysterious evolutionary force, was in no wise benevolent. But if there were no fundamental goodness and rightness in whatever Power there was, how did man come to recognise goodness as the positive norm and to feel all evil as contradiction, as a negation of this? Precepts of childhood, heredity, Platonism, Christianity all transmitted this recognition. But for its origin, I was persuaded, we had to go farther back in regress to man's very creation when God had invested him, evolved from his ape-like ancestors, with a different kind of consciousness, making him capable of knowing God and reflecting on the self.

Whitehead has spoken of the unprovable supposition of a constancy and order within Nature but for which the efforts of the scientist would be meaningless.[1] And Einstein has declared that although God the Creator may be very difficult to understand, he is neither capricious nor malicious.[2] So I saw in this Power underlying the evolutionary process an essential goodness and rightness. Moreover, I was persuaded that man could not be in

[1] Quoted by C. A. Coulson, *op. cit.*, p. 57.   [2] *Ibid.*, p. 61.

any way superior to such a Power, and that therefore it was extravagant to deny to it a consciousness of the Good whilst imputing this to man. I did not believe that such a Power could be a blind force or that intelligence in man could arise in any system that was not due to Mind, whatever we chose to call that Power.

But although speculation on the doctrine of the Fall on mythical and poetic lines was enjoyable and to me inescapable, it was obviously impossible to apprehend more than a few of its implications. Not only was there the extremely tricky matter of reconciling poetic with scientific truth, of interpreting myth in a language that preserved its essential meaning, but we were further handicapped by being without comprehension of time with which all such questions were inextricably bound up. St Augustine held that time is in the human mind which expects, examines, and remembers. Thus, there can be no time apart from created beings. It is useless to try to understand either time or space before the world was made, since there was no time before the Creation and no place where the world was not.[1]

Origen believed that the world had been created as a means of disciplinary correction for fallen man; but this was to place the Fall outside space and time as we knew them. Conditioned, however, as my mind was to thinking in terms of geography and chronology I could not but wonder where, then, did it occur and when—questions which according to St Augustine are meaningless.

But was it after all necessary to have recourse to the theory of the Fall in order to find an explanation for the presence of evil and sin in the world of men and animals? Was retrogression the explanation? Would it not be simpler to attribute man's present imperfection to the fact that he has been such a comparatively short time on earth and that his advance along the road of evolution is insufficient to attain a more perfect state? Simpler

[1] See St Augustine's *Confessions*, Book X.

certainly, if one is able to project the germ of all our sins upon ignorance and immaturity, upon our animal ancestors. But I, for one, was no longer able. What animal suffered from pride, which is man's fundamental sin? And on the theory of an inadequate evolution would a man's vision always so far outrun his performance? How would one account for the consciousness of the 'grandeur et misère' of his state so ably described, I remembered, by Pascal: ' Car qui se trouve malheureux de n'être pas roi, sinon un roi dépossédé ? '[1]

' La grandeur de l'homme est grande en ce qui'l se connaît misérable.'[2]

Neither was I now able to think that it was purely a question of incomplete evolution that 'the good that I would, I do not; but the evil which I would not, that I do.' ' I see what is good and approve it, but pursue what is bad '—the cry of both St Paul and Ovid.[3]

Again, Pascal writes:

' Car enfin, si l'homme n'avait jamais été corrompu, il jouirait dans son innocence et de la vérité et de la félicité avec assurance. Et si l'homme n'avait jamais été que corrompu, il n'aurait aucune idée ni de la vérité, ni de la béatitude. Mais, malheureux que nous sommes, et plus que s'il n'y avait point de grandeur dans notre condition, nous avons une idée du bonheur, et nous ne pouvons y arriver; nous sentons une image de la vérité, et ne possédons que le mensonge, incapables d'ignorer absolument et de savoir certainement, tant il est manifeste que nous avons été dans un degré de perfection dont nous sommes malheureusement déchus.'[4]

And finally:

[1] *Pensées* Article XVIII, v, *Grandeur de l'Homme.*
[2] *Ibid.*, Article XVIII, vii.   [3] Ovid, *Metamorphoses*, vii, 20.
[4] *Pensées*, Article XXII, i, *Contrariétés dans la Nature de l'Homme.*

'. . . une preuve admirable de la misère et de la corruption de l'homme et en même temps de sa grandeur, puisque l'homme s'ennuie de tout, et ne cherche cette multitude d'occupations que parce qu'il a l'idée du bonheur qu'il a perdu, lequel ne trouvant point en soi, il le cherche inutilement dans les choses extérieures, sans pouvoir jamais se contenter, parce qu'il n'est ni dans nous ni dans les créatures, mais en Dieu seul.'[1]

Foolish as Pascal saw that the doctrine of original sin must appear to the wise of this world, it seemed to him to be indispensable to any true understanding of man's present condition.

But the fact that I was inclined to think there was something in the doctrine of the Fall did not mean that this brought me any nearer to belief in Christianity as a whole. It was inevitable, however, that it should contribute something towards my ever growing belief in a God who created man in his image.

In the *Monadology*, the idea of the monads as substances between which no inter-communication is possible, when applied to the dominant monads or souls was one which quarrelled with my increasing sense of human souls as being members one of another. Moreover, the windowlessness of these monads seems to be postulated in order that Pre-established Harmony might prove the existence of God. Yet the most valuable idea I found in Leibniz was that this God was a self-determining Monad who revealed himself to the other monads (generated by continual fulgurations of his divinity), and was manifest in them according to their receptivity.

As to the other interesting suggestion that God might not be entirely free and therefore not omnipotent, I found that opinions varied considerably on what constituted omnipotence. Thus,

[1] *Ibid.*, Article XXI xiv, *Misère de l' Homme.*

McTaggart, we are told, insisted unlike Leibniz that it must not exclude the power of acting contrary to the laws of logic. For him a God who could not perform contradictions could not be omnipotent.[1] If God's omnipotence, however, were thus, there could be no constancy and order within Nature such as Whitehead has spoken of, and the efforts of the scientist would then be meaningless. So capricious a deity would be the spirit of anarchy. And it seemed more reasonable to believe with Abelard that God cannot will things impossible in themselves, and that he cannot make a contradiction true.

So far, except for the God of Plato's later *Dialogues*, I had met no deity in philosophy who had awakened any responsive emotion in me. I had been offered by the Pre-Socratics: Water, Air, Fire, a sentient Soul of the World, a Sphere, Being, a powerless Mind, all as Primary Substance. Then a kind of magnet or eternal circular motion; and the most perfect of clock-makers, all as God. Now the Supreme Monad of Leibniz suggested, from the role he played in the *Monadology*, a kind of telephone-operator whose purpose was to effect indirect communication between the subscribers, the monads.

How useful God appeared to be; so far necessary to every system of philosophy since the Pre-Socratics' search for a Primary Substance, but nowhere proven to exist even as a *deus ex machina*. I should have liked to meet a God existing in his own right (certainly Leibniz had made a step in that direction); but in philosophy generally God had to be fitted into the system so that he earned his lodging in the capacity and position where he could be most useful. God is made by man for man, and not man for God. And for me with my old-fashioned views of what God was, this seemed to give him an artificiality which made him quite incredible. Moreover, I no longer believed that it was the function of philosophy to attempt to prove God's existence or

[1] C. D. Broad in his Introduction to McTaggart's *Some Dogmas of Religion*, p. xxxviii.

man's immortality; although I thought it could demonstrate that neither was beyond the bounds of possibility (much as McTaggart had done in the case of immortality).

Disappointed as I had been in my reading of Descartes and Leibniz, I was still eager to know what arguments Kant might use in such a demonstration.

4. *From Kant I learn the necessity of the subjective approach in religion*

> ' In this case [the Three Postulates] we have a *want* of reason,
> springing not from the subjective ground of our wishes,
> but from an objective ground of the will, which binds every
> rational being, and thence authorises him *a priori* to
> presuppose in nature the conditions necessary for its
> satisfaction.'
>
> *Critique of Pure Reason*

According to Kant, sense-knowledge is incapable of reaching to reality; and therefore as far as knowledge is concerned, God must remain a transcendental ideal. Pure Reason cannot establish the existence of a Supreme Being, and all proofs of this are fallacious when approached by speculative philosophy, as he shows in the arguments dismissing them all.[1]

But the ideas of God's existence and man's immortality, he finds defensible once these can be positively established on the principle of practical reason. On the purely impersonal grounds of this reason, Kant claims that since man is required absolutely to seek and foster the supreme good, the presupposition of a felicity proportionate with virtue is a legitimate demand. And the union of felicity with virtue cannot be conceived as caused otherwise than by God—the only adequate cause. Therefore his existence is postulated.

That did appear to me as putting the cart before the horse.

[1] For the proofs of God's existence and their dismissal by Kant, see Text IX. pp. 300-301.

And that these arguments could have no force except for those who already believed in a benevolent deity on other grounds. Further he says:

'The righteous man may say: I *will* that there should be a God: I *will* that, though in this world of natural necessity, I should not be of it, but should also belong to a purely intelligible world of freedom: finally, I *will* that my duration should be endless. On this faith I insist and will not let it be taken from me.'

To Professor Wizenmann, who brought against these statements the objections of inconclusiveness and subjectivity, Kant replies:

'I quite agree with Professor Wizenmann in all cases where the feeling of want is due to mere inclination. Such a want cannot postulate the existence of the object desired, even for him who feels it: still less can it be the ground of a postulate which is universal. In this case, however, we have a *want* of reason, springing not from the subjective ground of our wishes, but from an objective ground of the will, which binds every rational being, and thence authorises him *a priori* to presuppose in nature the conditions necessary for its satisfaction.'[1]

The postulates of pure practical reason of immortality, freedom and the existence of God derive, Kant believes, from man as a moral agent. (1) Reason demands that the supreme good should be realisable, and this can only be fulfilled if man as a free agent is immortal. (2) Reason postulates that man as a free agent is capable of determining his will independently of his desires, and in conformity with moral obligation. (3) Reason postulates a Supreme Being, moral and intelligent, as the *sine qua non* of the realisation of the highest good.

[1] *Critique of Practical Reason*, quoted by E. Caird, *op. cit.*, Vol. II, pp. 339-40.

Jacobi, I read, attacked these postulates as self-destructive, since holding a thing to be true for merely practical reasons—believing only because one needs to believe—could have no force at all. But he himself finds that men do have an immediate conviction of the supra-sensible, to which Kant's postulates of the practical reason relate, as well as of the existence of sensible objects. This conviction he calls faith.

And Kant himself said:

' Providence has not willed that those convictions which are most necessary for our happiness should be at the mercy of subtle and finely spun reasonings, but has delivered them directly to the natural, vulgar understanding.'[1]

Moreover:

' it is altogether necessary that we should be convinced of God's existence, but not so necessary that we should be able to demonstrate it.'[2]

This idea that the will must play a part in matters of belief was a new one to me. And the importance which Kant attaches to the experiencing subject appeared to take the matter out of the realm of a purely objective search and to place the needs of man's conscience and moral nature above all the facts of his experience. Was it not, I wondered, against just such an argument that the objection might be raised that the universe was not designed in conformity with man's needs and desires? But although at first I found Kant's *Critique of Practical Reason* inordinately tendentious, later, when I had recovered from the initial surprise of finding such arguments in philosophy, it occurred to me that all that Kant might be saying was that the good is the true, and that the spirit in man knows this beyond need of proof.

It was now more than ever clear that there could be no

[1] Ueberweg, *op. cit.*, Vol. II, p. 200.   [2] *Ibid.*, p. 200.

satisfactory proof of God's existence. The arguments for this which Kant dismisses, although they might provide evidence of this existence for one who already believed in God, could do nothing to show an incontrovertible reason for that initial belief.

And that evidence was what I had been seeking. But I found that I was two people, one of whom could not forget the childhood's theophanies and who held fast to those sudden Archimedian thoughts which dropped into the mind unsought (those which Locke found frequently to be the most valuable), and insisting on the counsel ' Be still and know that I am God,' consigned to hell all need for proofs.

That was all right when I could be still. But the trouble was that the other person made such a noise, clamouring for 'metaphysical backing,' 'purely rational conclusions,' shouting about 'subjective bias,' 'psychological beliefs' and God knows what besides. I felt much as Jacobi when he said:

> ' There is a light in my heart, but when I seek to bring it into the understanding, it is extinguished. Which illumination is the true one, that of the understanding, which discloses indeed well-defined and fixed shapes, but behind them an abyss, or that of the heart, which, while indeed it sends rays of promise upwards, is unable to supply the want of definite knowledge ? '[1]

' He believed that there lives in men a spirit coming immediately from God and which constitutes their most intimate essence. God himself is present to them through the heart, as nature is through their senses. No sensible object can so move our spirits or so demonstrate itself as a true object, as do those absolutes, the true, good, beautiful and sublime which can be seen with the eye of the mind. It is a jewel in the crown of our race, the distinguishing mark of humanity, that these objects reveal themselves to the rational soul. We may even assert boldly that

[1] Ueberweg, *op. cit.*, Vol. II. p. 200.

we believe in God because we see him, although not with the eyes of the body'.[1]

I now realised that to go on seeking for philosophical 'proofs' for what I believed was no longer vital to me; that it would be almost like a game which I played with the peripheral part of my mind. The whole of me would not be involved as it was in the actual beliefs themselves—those I felt in the pit of the stomach. I knew that this was a region very suspect in philosophy and I had made an honest attempt to take the matter out of the region of diaphragms and to listen humbly to what the great philosophers, X, Y and Z said about God's existence. But the trouble was that X, Y and Z, had none of them said anything that could settle the matter beyond dispute. And indeed, how could they? My hope that they would be able to do so had been merely a sign of my retarded development.

There would be nothing but straws in the wind for those clues as to a divine Being which Connolly asks if God may have scattered about the world for seekers after him.[2] The process of belief for me intellectually so far appeared to work in accordance with the faggot theory; clues and arguments when taken separately did not carry the weight of conviction but when assembled into a bundle, they had the power to educe belief. Kant's clue was the affirmation that 'morality is the nature of things'; seeing in the demands of our moral nature not mere subjective wishes but a realisation of the nature not only of the universe but also of the divine principle from which it derives.

To Fichte also, God is the moral order of the world. And Coleridge, too, has said:

' I became convinced that religion, as both the corner-stone and the key-stone of morality must have a *moral* origin; so far at least, that the evidences of its doctrine could not,

---

[1] *Ibid.*, p. 200.   [2] *Op. cit.*, p. 106.

like the truths of abstract science, be wholly independent of the will.[1]

The Will must be in harmony with the intuitions of Reason —that Reason which he understood as 'the source and substance of truths above sense' as contrasted with the Understanding which can judge only 'according to sense.' Like Kant, he found the postulates of moral life to be God, freedom of man's will, and the immortality of his soul. To these he added the fact of man's fallen nature. He removes from the intellect to the conscience the authority to find reality in the postulates, saying that God gave us conscience, that law of conscience which 'unconditionally commands us to attribute reality and actual existence to those ideas and those only, without which the conscience itself would be baseless and contradictory: to the ideas of soul, of free-will, of immortality, of God.'[2]

With Kant the importance of the experiencing subject is stressed. And I had myself found that no argument *per se*, no 'evidence' even could be proof positive. Alone it was impotent. It was what the evidence compelled a man to believe that gave it life. And to every man this compulsion would be something different according as his mind was conditioned. And after reading Kant I understood better the place of the will in the question of belief and disbelief. Just as belief could not be a matter of the intellect alone but must be, I was already persuaded, a matter of the heart as well; so the will I saw should play a part. There must be a decisive action. Only so would a personal response be possible. And only so could I perhaps reach a state which I now believed to be higher than that negative capability of Keats. This stage consisted in what T. S. Eliot has described as an ability to combine the deepest scepticism with the profoundest faith.[3]

[1] *The Friend*, p. 67. Bohn edition.   [2] *Ibid.*, p. 70.
[3] In a broadcast talk on Valéry.

A Subjective Approach in Religion

In belief there was an attitude of mind which still preserved those elements of uncertainty and mystery; it was in the presence of these that belief consisted as opposed to knowledge. And it seemed to me that every believer had something essentially agnostic with his *Credo*, whereas nearly every disbeliever I'd met seemed to have no doubts at all and implied *Scio* in his attitude of unquestioning rejection.

In Keats's injunction to let the mind be 'a thoroughfare for all thoughts, not a select party,'[1] I recognised the refusal ever to shut the door of the mind against any idea however uncongenial to one personally; the rejection of a Maginot line behind which a mind may be enclosed and safe from all attacks. And although I now believed in a benevolent Creator, and in the strong possibility of man's survival of death, I did not find it possible to turn a deaf ear to all the arguments that could be produced against these beliefs.

Emerson has said that the saint is a sceptic once in every twenty-four hours. I wondered if it could be said that the sceptic is a believer just as often. How frequently is he stabbed by the thought that perhaps after all the theists are right and that there may be a God? Just as the believer is continually pierced by the doubt whether God exists. It is difficult to know. Most discussion is dishonest and primarily eristic just because our minds are not 'a thoroughfare for all thoughts' but only 'a select party.' And criticism in aiming at a personal victory rather than discovery of the truth, breeds only anger, blindness and strife.

Jeremy Taylor has written:

' He (God) sees and deplores it, that many men study hard and understand little; that they dispute earnestly and understand not one another at all; that affections creep so certainly, and mingle with their arguing, that the argument is lost, and nothing remains but the conflict of two

[1] Keats's *Letters*, No. 158 to G. and G. Keats, 17 Sept., 1819. *Op. cit.*, p. 425.

adversaries' affections; that a man is so willing, so easy, so ready to believe what makes for his opinion, so hard to understand an argument against himself, that it is plain it is the principle within, not the argument without, that determines him. . . .'[1]

It is plain too that such arguers sought to resolve or to shelve uncertainties and doubts once and for all. But I was convinced that there could be no one decisive action in either belief or unbelief which blinds one for ever to the existence of a possible alternative.

Yet to many still, as it was to Locke, the existence of God is demonstrable by the cosmological and especially by the teleological arguments. [2] Voltaire, too, thought that 'all nature cries out to us that he does exist.' And although Kant in the *Critique of Pure Reason* refuses all force to the physico-theological argument for the existence of God, because the whole tendency of his system required this, yet we are told that

' In conversation he praised in the highest terms the teleological argument, and spoke freely of final causes and their utility in religion. One day he was heard suddenly to exclaim, *There is a God*, and then forcibly develop the evidence of this truth which nature everywhere presents.'[3]

(So it was not only poor mutts such as I who believed more than they could prove.)

'A short time before Kant's death, an intimate friend asked him what he promised himself with respect to a future life; he appeared absorbed, and after reflecting answered: " Nothing certain." Sometime before he was heard to reply to a similar question, " I have no conception

---

[1] *Dissuasive from Popery*, quoted by S. T. Coleridge, *The Friend*, p. 322.

[2] The cosmological argument is based on the existence of the universe; the teleological on purpose or design, on final causes.

[3] Stapfer, *The Life of Kant*, p. 43 (Thomas Clarke, Edinburgh, 1836).

of a future state." Upon another occasion he declared himself in favour of a kind of metempsychosis.'[1]

He is recorded as saying, 'I do not fear death; I know how to die. I assure you, before God, that if I knew this night was to be my last, I would raise my hands and say, God be praised. The case would be far different if I had ever caused the misery of any one of his creatures.'[2]

'How deliciously old fashioned,' the more tolerant of disbelievers patronisingly may cry. And I suppose that they would attribute to the then prevailing climate of opinion the fact that of the eight philosophers I had used as hunting grounds, all had believed in God, except McTaggart. But I did not think that this could be the whole story. True, their belief could prove nothing; and it was undoubtedly easier in their day to be convinced of God's existence when the universe appeared less immense and mysterious than it does in our time. Now scepticism is our natural climate, and belief demands a profounder faith. Yet nothing could destroy that 'most intimate essence' in the heart of man.

So, too, with the question of man's survival: as the universe expands, the natural—if superficial—assumption is that man's importance in the scheme of things tends to be diminished. Belief in immortality is no longer common. Yet I found it inextricably entangled with belief in God. And each of my eight philosophers was persuaded of its truth in one form or another. Aristotle may perhaps be queried in this respect; call him a 'draw.' That was seven to one for God and six to one for immortality, with one to play—Hegel.

[1] *Ibid.*, p. 43.   [2] *Ibid.*, p. 52.

5. Hegel shows me a philosophical meaning behind Christian doctrine

---

'It is the Philosophy of Religion which is the unfolding,
the apprehension of that which God is, and it is only by
means of it that our philosophical knowledge of his nature
is reached.'

Philosophy of Religion, Vol. I, p. 90

Heine is quoted as saying, 'I have seen Hegel seated with his doleful air of a hatching hen upon his unhappy eggs, and I have heard his dismal clucking.' Yet it was Professor Sterrett's opinion that no serious reader could be the same man intellectually after reading Hegel as he was before; and for my own part, I thought there might be an element of truth in this, at least as far as the *Philosophy of Religion* was concerned.[1] Tedious, prolix and redundant as it was, yet, through all the turbidness spirit spoke to spirit; and in spite of much weariness of flesh and faintness of heart, I was led on by poetic leaps and bounds from one shock to another as the various eggs hatched out.[2]

According to Hegel it is not until we view God as Subject or Spirit that we know him. He is 'the unity of infinite and finite, and our sole concern is to find out how the finite is incorporated

---

[1] J. M. Sterrett, *Studies in Hegel's Philosophy of Religion*, p. 11 (Swan Sonnenschein, 1891).

[2] A fuller account is given in Text X, p. 303 of those matters in the *Philosophy of Religion* which were relevant to my search.

with the infinite.'[1] Hegel argues that not only is finite spirit devoid of meaning apart from its vital relation to the infinite and only intelligible in that relation, but that the true infinite comprehends in its very nature a relation to the finite and cannot exist as the purely non-finite. The true finite is an essential phase of the infinite in God's nature—a finitising of himself in us. (This is akin to the conception of God as creating the world out of nothing but himself.) And it is only so far as it is taken back into God that the world of finite spirit has any reality and is known as at-one-with Absolute Spirit.

Of Spinoza's God, Hegel says:

' The Absolute Substance of Spinoza certainly requires something to make it Absolute Mind, and it is a right and proper requirement that God should be defined as Absolute Mind.'[2]

And Hegel claims for human thought the power to know reality, maintaining the ultimate identity of thought and being. Religion is the Divine Spirit's knowledge of itself through the mediation of finite spirit.[3] It is the Absolute Spirit himself relating himself to himself.

My joy at finding someone at last to whom God was Absolute Mind and yet not inaccessible to those who were neither philosophers nor men of learning, and someone to whom religion must be something for all men, was quickly damped. For my discovery that Hegel's view of Christian doctrine was fundamentally sympathetic, shook me so much that I wondered whether I should turn aside and by-pass it altogether; I thought the moment had still not arrived when I was ready to examine the claims of Christianity. But as I looked through the pages of the *Philosophy*

[1] *Philosophy of Religion*, Vol. II, p. 126 (Kegan Paul, Trench & Trubner, 1895). Translation by E. B. Speirs.
[2] Quoted by Sterrett, *op. cit.*, p. 17.   [3] *Op. cit.* Vol. I, p. 206.

of Religion I soon realised that here was the very work which might help me to understand much of what I found inexplicable and meaningless in the Christian religion, that it might bridge the gulf I saw yawning between it and reason.

Yet to Hegel God is no less than Absolute Person.[1] Man's personality is grounded in God and through it God reveals himself to man and man believes that he may rise to eternal, infinite life. Such communion would not be possible between man and some merely hylozoic, unanthropomorphic something for there would be no grounds for communion.

Stated baldly, the idea of God as Absolute Person came as a thunderbolt. Had I journeyed so far from what had repelled me in Christianity only to find that the road had been circular and brought me back to my starting post, to that very anthropomorphism whose rejection appeared to me as the first essential in a search for God?

But although I could formulate what I thought God was not, I was utterly unable to express what I felt the divine unanthropomorphic something, in which I believed, would be. It was impossible to imagine. And, believing as I did that man could enter into a relationship of some kind with the divine, I now had to admit the difficulties presented by a relationship where all grounds of communion were wanting. There would have to be something also in the divine which was present in the human if any relations at all between the divine and the human were to be possible. For Hegel, the Spirit whereby man knows God is 'the Spirit of God himself,'[2] that Essence which impels itself into phenomenal being.

This led me to another shock. I found that Hegel believed in the triune nature of God and saw in the Christian doctrine of the Trinity the only adequate statement of divine activity; the expression of God's self-revelation with its element of self-

[1] See *Logic*, pp. 89, 91 and 236. Quoted by Sterrett, *op. cit.*, p. 18.
[2] *Philosophy of Religion*, Vol. III, p. 304.

sacrifice—a truth so essential that without its light it would be impossible to know God or understand human history or the meaning of nature.[1]

But the ordinary conception of the triune nature is a compound of picture thought, of sensible and philosophical elements; this half conceals and half-reveals. Therefore philosophy is necessary to convert conceptual into organic thought. Representations of the universal and the infinite in forms of the contingent and finite cannot be adequate and no absolute representation of the Absolute is possible. All metaphors are anthropomorphic, and it is necessary that the soul should do battle ceaselessly with anything that shackles, that it should spiritualise where once it literalised.

In spite of my will I began to see a meaning behind the metaphors; to realise that it was against the literalisation that I had rebelled and not against the philosophical ideas themselves since the Church did not bother to give us the living ideas behind the bare dogmas. It was not surprising that dogma slept or was as dead as a skeleton. Why did the Church allow men to remain tied to their picture-thinking, which was tantamount to dragging a corpse around? It was small wonder that any self-reflecting mind cut itself loose from such a burden. But need there have been a corpse? If the Church had given men the inner meaning behind the mere outer expression of the dogma, that might have been no dead burden but a living truth which could have borne fruit in the human spirit. Not once during my so-called Christian days had I heard the Church warn against the abuse of metaphors; and such was my malevolence towards it in my agnostic period that I assumed that it had introduced doctrine in order to be esoteric and give itself importance as the sole interpreter of such cryptograms. But never had its interpretations been in language that I could understand. It was what Hegel would have termed 'religious knowledge filtered through finite images, and sieved

[1] See *ibid.*, Vol. III, pp. 11-13.

through a mesh of narrow and rationalising logic.' It was 'thought bound fast to a picture.'[1]

Hegel's acceptance of the doctrine of the Trinity naturally necessitated an even bigger blow for me: his belief in the Incarnation—that ultimate offence against reason, charged with the maximum of antecedent improbability. Now I began to see how it might be construed. I read on eagerly, fascinated and yet appalled by the horror that it might be true. I did not wish it to be the truth. I hated the very thought. I hated organised religion. I hated the Church (though I was not at all clear how I defined it). I hated dogma although I was persuaded of its necessity in religion. I almost hated the Founder of Christianity for what I thought were arrogant claims on his part. And I don't mean St Paul whom I used to consider its true founder.

But I could not stop reading. The doctrine of the creation and of the relation of man and nature to their Creator, Hegel finds to be inalienably bound up with the triune nature of God. It is the Divine nature to create, and creation is God's positing an 'other' which is not an 'other.' His creation, belonging to his essence, involves the finite as his own self-revelation and self-posited object. Hegel says that love is the expression of the eternally triune nature of God. It is necessary for love to create and love 'another'; albeit in loving this 'other' God does but love himself. This doctrine of the creation, as arising from the love inherent in his nature, implies a relation to humanity which can be termed an essential predisposition to incarnation. This propensity becomes actualised in Jesus Christ.[2]

The Incarnation, Hegel considers, is the unity of God and man as an external fact. This essential constituent of religion occurs in some form in every religion. In Christianity, the God-Man is the perfect revelation of living truth, for it is only as *Deus nos personat* that the truth can be known. Christ's coming is the

[1] See *ibid.*, Vol. I, p. 145 f. on metaphors and pictorial figures, etc.
[2] See *ibid.*, Vol. III, pp. 10-12, 25 and 111.

consummation of the Divine self-necessitated creation. It is in this immanent divine love—a conception made possible only by the Christian doctrine of the triune nature of God—that the source and cause of all creation is to be found. And this creation must continue on its course until love returns home, and God is all. For creation, as a free movement, is an act that is always being done, and not one that is performed once and for all. From the Godward side the entire process is an interchange of love, a movement of self-conscious life. From the human side, this movement in the finite sphere displays 'all the seriousness and pain and labour and patience of the difference' struggling back towards reunion with its source. Here are included the creation, the atonement and reconciliation of the universe to God.[1]

But the God-Man is to the Jews a stumbling-block; to the Greeks foolishness. To the mere understanding it is preposterous and ridiculous.

Yes, I was a Greek or a Jew all right. But I passed on (except that in Hegel one never really passes on; one turns the corner and there is everything all over again), from the Trinity and the Incarnation, to the Holy Spirit and the Spiritual Community, i.e., the Church.

Here was another knock. Hegel shows how the Church would be the natural flowering on earth of the Spirit in its Spiritual Community.[2] He insists also on the importance, the value, the necessity even of dogma.[3] Thus, the Trinity, with the Incarnation and the Holy Spirit, the Church, dogma, all are approved. I was amazed and horrified. But why should I have been so? I did not have to subscribe to any of Hegel's beliefs. The fact was that his arguments in their favour impressed me deeply in spite of my natural antipathy to his creed. The whole thing began to make sense, to be coherent. I certainly did not as yet believe, but my

[1] *Ibid.*, Vol. III, pp. 73-79, and Vol. I, pp. 70, 77 and 151.
[2] *Ibid.*, Vol. III, pp. 97, 100-108.   [3] *Ibid.*, Vol. III, pp. 125-127.

spirit quailed at the attack on the very bases of my disbelief when I saw how the whole Christian edifice might have securer and more solid foundations than I had hitherto suspected. If Hegel's interpretation of Christian theology were correct, he was undermining all my reasons for its rejection to which I clung with a passionate and almost pathological intensity. My quarrel had been with a conception of organised Christian dogma taken at its surface level and divorced from any inner meaning. And although I had always suspected that I had failed in some degree to understand it, I had never imagined Christian doctrines as pearls and myself in the role of the swine. Now that possibility had to be considered.

If the doctrine of the Trinity, instead of being rejected as a mathematical conundrum unworthy of consideration by the adult mind, could be viewed as 'an expression of God's self-revelation with its element of self-sacrifice,' then indeed love would be the expression of the eternally triune nature of God. Further, Creation itself could be seen as 'arising from the love inherent in the triune nature'—that triune nature which implies a relation to humanity which can be termed an essential disposition to incarnation. This would serve to reinforce the conviction that had so strangely and apparently inconsequentially arisen in me after reading Spinoza.

This was a very different view from that presented by the usual ' picture-thinking' to which the majority of unreflecting Christians were tied. I thought, on the one hand, of all the great minds that had been purely Christian: of St Augustine, St Anselm and Origen (in spite of his 'heresies'), of Aquinas, Descartes, and Pascal. Could they have believed in Christian theology if in fact it were at all as I had conceived it to be? But when I considered, on the other hand, all the ordinary Christians I knew, Christianity seemed to be not entirely respectable intellectually. There is no doubt that, like many others who were unduly influenced by the climate of opinion, I had evinced mediocrity of mind by being something of an intellectual snob.

Not only had I never ignored the climate but I had been all too ready to interpret Christian theology in terms of the lowest common denominator. Nothing could be true, I thought, which was held by most of the Church members I knew. Their views represented for me everything I deplored in the way of facile belief. I had no patience with an easy acceptance which appeared never to have come to grips with an honest appraisal of the difficulties involved. And I had a self-righteous dislike of men's preference for mental comfort to a desire for truth.

But now I began in honesty to wonder if my disbelief had sprung from as pure a source as I had always assumed. Possibly I had been too greatly influenced towards disbelief by the intellectual level of those 'believers' I had met in my youth. And I had probably rejected beliefs—just as McTaggart has warned us against doing—largely because I suspected that they were held for the wrong reasons. But if I refused to examine a dogma because it brought mental comfort to people who did not wish to think and wanted only to feel 'secure,' was not my rejection as ill-founded as their acceptance, and with more than a tinge of arrogance attached? Moreover, was it so certain that I would not reject even Hegel's interpretation of the doctrines of the Trinity, the Incarnation and so on, just because they offered me the very antithesis of mental comfort?

Hegel's philosophy was notoriously abstruse, and it is well-known that he himself said 'One man has understood me and even he has not.' It would be only too easy to misconstrue his statements. But I found no loophole here; for his interpretations of Christian doctrine appeared unambiguous enough. William Wallace sums up Hegel's doctrinal representations thus:

' For the Son of God, in the immediate aspect, is the finite world of nature and man which, far from being at one with its Father is originally in an attitude of estrangement. The history of Christ is the visible reconciliation between man and the eternal. With the death of Christ this union, ceasing to be a mere fact, becomes a vital idea—the spirit of God which dwells in the Christian community.'[1]

(Incidentally, I wondered whether this might not be taken as an explanation of why 'the Comforter' could not be sent until the union of man and the eternal through Christ's death had been accomplished. This union had to 'cease being a mere fact,' and become 'a vital idea.')[2]

There seemed to be no possibility of explaining away Hegel's attitude to Christianity (although his interpretations might sometimes be most unorthodox). He even states that positive pre-Christian religions are not true revealed religion, but only stages of the self-explicating idea. As moments in the process of the idea they are not false, but only so in their historical aspect as actual religions. Christianity, although it contains, and is the fulfilment of, all preceding religions, is neither the result nor the sum of them. Revealing the intrinsic unity of the Divine and human nature, it is the Absolute religion, and neither temporary nor finite like preceding religions.[3]

It seemed that the time was now ripe to learn something more of these other religions: of Hinduism and Buddhism, and to look into Judaism and Islam. Things were moving too fast in a direction in which I did not want to go. But escape was not to be so easy; and before I could alter my course I underwent a further—and surprise—attack from Christian forces

---

[1] *Hegel* in *Encyclopædia Britannica*, 11th edition.
[2] See Hegel, *Philosophy of Religion*, Vol. III, p. 110.
[3] Quoted by Sterrett, *op. cir.*, pp. 57-8 and 252-7.
(*Moment*, a constituent factor in a unity. E.g., the Three Persons are moments in the Godhead.)

6. *The impact of Kierkegaard's Christianity on my unbelief*

> ' Faith, the personal realisation of the reason by its union
> with the will.'
>
> S. T. COLERIDGE, The Friend

It was one thing intending to think no more of the claims of Christianity until I had examined eastern religions; but quite another to resist the burning curiosity I felt when chancing upon an old copy of *The Times Literary Supplement* whose front page invited me to 'Choose, Leap, and Be Free.' I had to know what I was asked to choose, where I was to leap, and how I could become free.

I had scarcely heard of Kierkegaard and I could not guess what I was to find in that fateful article. I read it. Then I reread it. Then I read it again. My heart was pounding and the blood singing in my ears. Although I had been profoundly disturbed by Hegel, the greater impact of Kierkegaard's thought concerning the Incarnation astounded me, reaching something deeper than the mere intellect. It struck a chill like that which awakens one when the bedclothes have slipped on to the floor in a night of bad dreams. I found myself in an alien land, defenceless, comfortless, where everything familiar had crumbled away. For it now appeared to me that Hegel must be right, the Incarnation no fable, and Christianity as a whole no mere theological fantasy. I suffered a sharp attack of unwilling suspension of disbelief.

I showed the article to various people to test reactions. But my friends remained unmoved, the bedclothes well up round their ears—and perhaps over their eyes too, I thought, since they saw nothing startling in Kierkegaard's approach to Christianity. They failed to be shaken out of what seemed to me their complacent habit of thought. Maybe, I wondered, there was something wrong with me. Or perhaps I was already 'conditioned' by my previous readings, in particular of Kant, towards a better understanding of the part the subjective must necessarily play in all thought; of Hegel towards a philosophic interpretation of Christianity. Or, again, perhaps it was that Kierkegaard placed his emphasis on the precise spot where the shoe of Christian theology most pinched me—the scandal of particularity. For my disbelief in the Incarnation stemmed fundamentally from the enormity of the idea that God should have entered into time and space—become a part of history on one small planet in the immensity of the universe, for thirty-three years out of the whole of time. And from the inability I experienced to reconcile such an event with my own idea of what a God in any way transscendent must be.

But Kierkegaard forestalled my every objection; and where most Christian apologists had discouraged my inquiring spirit by their unconvincing talk about the reasonableness of the Incarnation ('Surely, since God so loved the world, that is just what he might do—become incarnate.' Well, I had lacked the evidence to start with that he really loved the world; and how could God be predictable from a human point of view?)—where they had attempted to explain away my difficulties, Kierkegaard accentuated the unreasonableness, underlined the *skandalon* of the Incarnation, showing it to be impossible to believe in the God-Man through the understanding. It is the Absolute Paradox which lies beyond the confines of reason. To expect a man to affirm (as 'history') that God has endured human birth and allowed himself to be crucified seems like expecting a man to subscribe to the absurd.

But it *is* the Absurd, says Kierkegaard. This eternal truth which is the very core of Christianity, the belief in the God-Man, is to the Jews an offence, to the Greeks foolishness.

Yes, indeed, I saw again that I was a Jew or a Greek, or both. But now my nationality was beginning to sit less comfortably upon me. For that passage concerning the Absolute Paradox dogged me pretty well night and day for months. And with it went another disturbing idea. Kierkegaard says that it is not possible to argue about God, that it is probable that he exists, that it is very probable, that it is extremely probable—therefore God exists; and from that he goes on to show that in the same way it cannot be said of the God-Man that Jesus being a man of goodness, of great goodness, of such exceeding goodness that therefore he is God. No, God is something absolutely qualitatively different, and it is only by the leap of faith that he can be reached. And without risk no faith is possible. Therefore, the greater the risk the greater the faith.[1]

This conception of faith had for me an entirely new emphasis. It still appeared to be a wilful determination to believe a thing which the every-day, commonsense judgment rejected. But my attitude of derision was now arrested. I saw that faith might not only be justified in being wilful, but that its very essence lay in a personal, subjective response to the Christian challenge.

But this indeed was the thin end of the wedge. It was tantamount to infiltration by the enemy forces. Before long I should be believing in the Incarnation; and I most passionately did not want to do that.

Against that possibility I struggled for months, veering between faint belief, with an attendant sinking feeling in the stomach, and the old familiar doubt, accompanied by a better appetite. The question of the Incarnation pursued me remorselessly, bedevilling all my waking hours.

[1] *Concluding Unscientific Postscript*, p. 188, Oxford University Press, 1941.

I read the last four works of Kierkegaard: *Sickness unto Death*; *The Point of View*; *Training in Christianity*; *For Self-Examination*. Also Lowrie's *Short Life of Kierkegaard*,[1] and a small book, *Sören Kierkegaard, a Study* by Melville Chaning-Pearce—a *multum in parvo* of the greatest value and to which I am indebted for most of the matter contained in the Note on Kierkegaard's thought (Text XI).[2] Later I was to read much of the *Journals* and the *Concluding Unscientific Postscript*.

Throughout my life there have been a few books which at the time of reading, because they disturbed my peace of mind so much, I heartily wished I had never opened, and yet which I could not put down. Such was *Oliver Twist* when I was nine years old. Such, too, were the works of Kierkegaard now. The thought of the God-Man pursued me far more relentlessly than Bill Sykes had ever done.

The monstrousness of the Paradox appalled me. This coming of the eternal into time, the penetration of existence by essence, of becoming by being offended reason by its absurdity. Yet I could not dismiss it from my mind as I could have dismissed ordinary absurdities. This Absurd was absolutely *other*. It was the infinite qualitative difference between God and man which made this Paradox an offence.[3] It could not be removed, nor could it be grasped by negating the reason. All reason could do was to recognise that here, because it was utterly other, was something that was not contrary to, but higher than, itself.

And I saw that there was no way round this offence. For it is the prime declaration of Christianity that it must appear as an offence to anyone who has not died from the autonomous self of nature into a new life of the spirit. True Christianity Kierke-

[1] Princeton University Press, 1946.
[2] James Clarke & Co., Ltd., 1946.
[3] *Sickness unto Death*, pp. 199 and 209, Oxford University Press, 1941.

gaard pronounces to be a treason against humanity.[1] And Christ must be the sign of offence in order to be the object of faith. Whoever does away with faith or with the possibility of offence, does away at the same time with the God-Man. And whoever does that does away with Christianity.[2]

This made Christianity something which was to be believed rather than comprehended. And I remembered that St Augustine urged men to believe in order to understand. That of course presupposed faith in someone who spoke with authority and understood those things which, although beyond human reason to grasp, men were asked to believe. The God-Man, for Kierkegaard, spoke with such authority. But without faith to lay down the understanding, that was what I recognised as impossible.

Yet the whole emphasis of Kierkegaard's thought I found to be upon the personal apprehension and appropriation of truth. A man must choose whether he will believe in Christ or be offended by him. For here there can be no question of proofs; they are all equivocal and can be used *pro et contra* by the reasoning intellect to which they belong. Thus, for the Christian, sin lies in the will, not in the intellect. And the opposite to sin is faith.[3]

It was the need for this decisive choice that haunted me: offence or faith. The conflict was bitter—the conflict which Kierkegaard sees as the main tribulation through which men must pass in order to enter the Kingdom. (And let not the preachers, he says, lead their hearers to suppose that these tribulations are merely sickness, economic problems and worries about the future. No, tribulation comes, Christ said, 'because of the Word.'[4] For the object of faith is the Paradox, the 'Absurd,' which is the fact that God has come into being in time.) I had to

---

[1] *For Self-Examination*, pp. 154-5, Oxford University Press, 1941.
[2] *Training in Christianity*, p. 143, Oxford University Press, 1941.
[3] *Sickness unto Death*, p. 132.   [4] *Training in Christianity*, p. 115.

decide whether to make that 'leap' to appropriate this truth. For reason is unable to grasp what faith believes. Faith is against understanding.[1]

This choice I saw as an expression of the will where the whole of me would be involved, intellect included. I knew that Kierkegaard's fight was not against the natural reason but against the tyranny of rationalism encroaching by a speculative philosophy divorced from life, and a reason, cold and abstract, on the inherent right and superior capacity of the whole man to make existential decisions rooted in life—this whole man conscious of a dimension of reality which is beyond the reach of the intellect alone.[2] And this consciousness by the whole being was, I now saw, the way to that other kind of knowledge which, though not patient of proof, yet held firm, and of the existence of which I had had intimations before ever I set out upon my search.

Here with Kierkegaard, I was no longer concerned with a Cartesian kind of truth which is what is true in abstract thought, in the intellect alone. True apprehension and assent are to be grounded in total existence—what is true for life. That alone is true which can be 'proved upon the pulses.' For Kierkegaard belief is being.

Throughout my search I had tried to keep a just recognition of what I saw as arguments from reason, and what I felt upon my pulses when there was conflict between the results of the two approaches. Naturally diffident, I had at first been inclined to think that a greater reasoning power in others was more likely to arrive at truth than was the response of my own pulses which I sometimes feared might be influenced by the mere familiarity of an idea. But in the course of my journey of discovery I came to see that some ideas—even those diametrically opposed to anything I was disposed to believe—produced in me a response such as only a complete authenticity could elicit. Such were the inner meanings

[1] *Ibid.*, pp. 28 ff.   [2] See Chaning-Pearce, *op. cit.*, p. 38.

of the doctrines of the Trinity and the Incarnation. True, I had long been familiar with the dry bones of the dogmas. These I had found easy to dismiss. But now that Hegel and Kierkegaard had brought an unfamiliar life and content to them, I saw my attitude of disdain changed to one of acute mental discomfort. Although I could reject dead, meaningless conceptions with a clear conscience in spite of the recognition of my desire to do so, I now seemed unable to dismiss these same doctrines once they had been filled with a living but unfamiliar meaning, however much I wished to. There was here something in the nature of authenticity, however far beyond proofs of reason. Moreover, I saw that unless I had the courage to accept whatever my innermost self might believe to be the truth—in spite of any mental anguish involved in such acceptance—the whole of my search would become emptied of meaning, the purpose of my very being betrayed.

And not all my fears or distress of mind could stop my reading Kierkegaard. To desist would have made me a coward in my own eyes, when not even the terror of Bill Sykes had let me cast *Oliver Twist* away. And had I burned the works that so much disturbed me, the power of the God-Man to pursue me would not have been allayed—his power and the need for a decision.

But to make a decision of such tremendous import was beyond me as yet. I had to struggle again with the gospels, to read, to think—perhaps, God knows, even to pray. If I decided after all this to be offended, that would be the easiest way intellectually; for Christ was an offence. Yet such a decision might be the betrayal of everything in me except the common-sense part of my reason. For there was that about the Paradox that held the rest of me in a grip I could not loosen. What made me unable to reject such an absurdity and to question the rightness of such a rejection? The choice of being offended would bring me a certain mental comfort at a common-sense level, but—and this I saw was the rub—could it ever silence the suspicion that here, perhaps, I had been offered the pearl of great price, the one thing needful, and that in cowardice I had thrown it away?

Yet, on the other hand, could I ever pay this price? 'Blessed is he who is not offended in me.' Blessed?—when since all merely human faculties must fail to grasp the Paradox, and life must therefore be founded upon a bottomless chasm that can only be crossed by the leap of faith? And even then faith would continue to be a tension, for, Kierkegaard tells us, it can never be a thing attained and perfected once for all, (as Law reminds us it is not 'a thing done, but . . . a thing continually doing';[1] always in the making, dynamic not static.) Faith and doubt are interlinked in a dialect humanly indiscerptible. The believer is always veering between a state of faith and not-faith. And since it is faith alone which matters, all philosophy which seeks for certainty is vain and fatal to faith and can have nothing to do with Kierkegaard's conception of Christianity. Certainty is to be obtained only in the infinite, where man cannot remain but only repeatedly arrives.[2] There is to be no seeking of rational proof for the intellect, but only faith's authority for life. And it is the constant presence of the Paradox that engenders the pathos of the life of the intellect.

Clearly, such would be a very uncomfortable life. But throughout my search I had become increasingly aware that desire for the mental comfort which I so much loved, when it became an end in itself was always quite deadly in its effects upon the mind and the spirit. Kierkegaard's crucifixion of the understanding, however, might well mean a martyrdom of endurance;[3] and I was no good at enduring. The natural mind and will, conditioned as they are, react, I knew, against the Paradox, turning naturally to homocentric humanism and requiring continual

[1] William Law, Mystical Writings, p. 22.
[2] Concluding Unscientific Postcript, p. 75.   [3] Ibid., p. 496.

mortification and conversion.[1] How, even if I found it needful, could I embrace the tension of such a life?

It was certainly true that, as he claims, instead of using all his energy to make as many converts as possible without regard to the genuineness of the Christianity they were entering, Kierkegaard makes it abundantly clear what the requirements of Christianity really are although not one single person should be persuaded to enter it. This, rather than imply that there are such difficulties attached to Christianity that one must needs apologise for it if men are to be prevailed upon to enter it. It must be presented as something so great, as indeed it is, that it is from us that the apology should come that we presume to call ourselves Christians.[2]

I saw now how rare was the true representation of Christianity, and how common that those who sought to defend it merely betrayed it.[3] It was superhumanly difficult or it was nothing. And Kierkegaard was always striving to make it harder not easier. He speaks scornfully of battalion Christians—those who have been enticed into the Church merely to swell the ranks—and of man's dishonesty in making titular Christians by the million to put up a parade of zeal.[4] These tons of nuts without kernels, these empty shells are under the illusion that they are Christians. Just such a hollow nut had I been in my youth. And most of the Christians I had known led completely worldly lives, taking—as Kierkegaard suggests the majority do—everything pleasurable from life whilst indulging occasionally in a mood of enjoyable piety. This, he says, resembles Christianity about as closely as a little sickness and slight stomach-ache resemble cholera. I had never before experienced the collision with true Christianity.

Christianity, he tells us, did not come to win souls cheaply,

[1] Chaning-Pearce, *op. cit.*, p. 81.
[2] *The Point of View*, Supplement, pp. 156-160 (O.U.P., 1939).
[3] *Ibid.*, p. 77. Also *Training in Christianity*, p. 225.
[4] *That Individual* (published with *The Point of View*), pp. 139-40 (O.U.P., 1939).

and progress in numbers has only shown retrogression in truth. For if the price is lowered the unconditional is thrust out of the world.[1] He shows how 'imitation' of Christ is the only valid argument of Christianity, and how that, now this has been abandoned, there has been a steady reduction in the price demanded for being a Christian. As a result of this Christianity has become so low-priced and mawkish that many are revolted[2]— as indeed I had been. Now, thinking about Christianity has been substituted for 'imitation,' with the aim of advancing beyond faith. When people believed with true faith in Christianity they were willing to die for it. But when it is cheapened we get idleness and then doubt, and finally wonder at the need of Christianity at all. (This described pretty accurately the stages of my lapse from Christianity.) To suffer for the doctrine has quite gone out of fashion. But Christ does not want mere admirers, talkers of piffle. He wants real disciples.[3] And for a Christianity tainted with a false gentleness, the only remedy is severity.[4]

In these common-sense days, Kierkegaard finds that man has lost the conception of what is absolutely required of him. Now that no one any longer aims at it, the absolute is considered impracticable and ridiculous. So the situation becomes reversed, and men see the fault in the requirement and therefore require that it should be changed.[5] (How true this was in my own case.) It is crazy they say to will the impossible, and the only sensible aim is that which we are capable of fulfilling. Thus common-sense corrodes away the absolute until it falls apart bit by bit, and with it faith is undermined and all reverence for it. But it is Christ that men do away with when they seek to do away with the absolute requirement. Christianity demands that man must be

---

[1] *For Self-Examination*, pp. 215-16.
[2] *Ibid.*, pp. 197-8.   [3] *Ibid.*, p. 207.
[4] *Training in Christianity*, p. 222.
[5] *For Self-Examination*, p. 168.

changed to suit the requirement.[1] But men for the most part, as I well knew, do not wish to be changed.

Christianity must be transferred from the region of speculation, doubt and piffle (the objective) into the subjective where it rightly belongs.[2] Certainly according to Kierkegaard I had pursued speculation and piffle. I saw now that I had had an exaggerated fear of a subjective approach to ultimate questions. And although fairly early in my search—as an indirect result of reading Descartes —I had begun to distrust abstract reasoning as the sole method of attaining truth, it was not until I read Kant's *Critique of Practical Reason* that I had realised the inevitable and paramount importance of the experiencing subject. But that, I thought, had taken me out of the sphere of philosophy into that of religion. And with Hegel's *Philosophy of Religion* I seemed to have entered the realm of theology, for although he appeared to pursue a speculative philosophy, his language derived far more from mysticism than from the demands of logic.

With Kierkegaard I was undoubtedly in the realm of religion, but his Christianity was very different from that with which I had been familiar in childhood. He himself had experienced a sharp interior conflict between two forms of religiousness which he termed A and B. Therefore it was no purely abstract difference which he found between them. Religiousness A is 'natural' religion or religion in general; one of immanence and consisting mostly of vague pietistic emotions, largely unitarian in flavour, of the 'first immediacy' and not attached to anything in particular. (That certainly was the only religion I had ever known.) By religiousness B, he understands one of transcendence and divine grace; true, full Christianity.[3]

He saw that the speculative philosophy of his time found Religion A to be larger and therefore superior to Religion B, for the Hegelian influence inclined men to view Christianity as a

[1] *Ibid.*, p. 170.   [2] *Ibid.*, p. 217.
[3] *Concluding Unscientific Postscript*, p. 506 ff.

stage in the world's journey and encouraged the idea—even more rife nowadays it seemed to me—that 'progress' consists in not sticking at any one stage. (I remembered how much larger, and more profound and altogether superior I had found Pantheism to Christianity.) But why call this Religion A Christianity? he asks.

For Kierkegaard, Christianity is something completely other, something qualitatively different from all other religions. And Religion B is sharply differentiated from Religion A by the entry into it of the God-Man, Christ—the Incarnation as a historical fact. Eternity has entered time, being and essence have invaded becoming and existence at a particular spot and at a particular moment in history. It is therefore in virtue of this that true Christianity, Religion B is unique among religions and thus cannot form part of a ' Federation of Faiths.'

Religion A is a religion of time and within the temporal, and Kierkegaard tells us that the temporal is not and never can be the element of spirit.[1] Stripped of doctrine, it sets aside everything distinguishing it from other religions—man's contrite heart and need of grace, his redemption by Christ—and makes of its essential essence a mere burlesque. It is real religion and possibly excellent of its kind, says Kierkegaard, but it is not Christianity. It can therefore be included in a World Federation of Faiths.

The life of Christ on earth, he tells us, will never be a past event. It is with man, accompanying every generation, possessing eternal contemporaneity for believers.[2]

But it is useless, Kierkegaard tells us, to try and disperse the rabble of doubts by reasons; and extraordinarily stupid to attempt a defence of Christianity. The only force able to effect such a dispersal or defence is 'imitation.' Proof lies in the 'following.'[3] But if one does not wish to be a follower, then one had better shut up and go home.

[1] *The Point of View*, p. 82.
[2] *Training in Christianity*, p. 68.   [3] *For Self-Examination*, pp. 88 and 199.

' Full Christianity '

If the ideas of Hegel disturbed me, the reading of Kierkegaard only increased my inner conflict as the forces of the enemy penetrated deeper and their attacks became sharper.

I decided on an armistice, or perhaps it would be truer to say a retreat. To get away from this question of the Incarnation, or even perhaps to collect reinforcements, I turned to works on Hinduism, to the *Upanishads* and the *Bhagavadgîta*.

PART FIVE

Four great religions—
what I learned from them, and
what I rejected

' All truth, no matter by whom it
is spoken, comes from the Spirit.'
ST AMBROSE

1. *Hinduism*

I found the vastness and comprehensiveness of Hinduism bewildering, with its clusters of creeds and cults and innumerable sects where monotheism, pantheism, and apparent polytheism all have a place. There appeared to be no common creed and therefore little dogma; an insistence on a strict observance of practice whilst allowing the greatest freedom in belief. It was in this I thought that lies the great appeal it has for some modern westerners, those to whom, as to Professor Radhakrishnan, it is a curious obsession of Judaism and Christianity that belief in a particular doctrine is necessary to salvation.[1] Hinduism I found to be quite free from such pre-occupations, being admittedly less a form of thought than a way of life.

Gandhi is reported as saying that the only concrete belief common to the whole of Hinduism is the sacredness of the cow.[2] But *karma* seemed to be a fundamental doctrine generally: as a man sows so shall he reap. The past is an inescapable record which even death cannot wipe out, and according to one's actions rebirth will be in the body of a higher or lower being or animal—the doctrine of *metempsychosis* or the transmigration of souls, another general belief. Thus, through these two doctrines, it is understandable that for the Hindu not only is the future conditioned, but that free-will is not admitted by him as an unrelated, undeter-

---

[1] *The Hindu View of Life*, p. 37 (Allen & Unwin, 1927).
[2] L. S. S. O'Malley, *Popular Hinduism*, p. 14 (Cambridge University Press, 1935).

mined factor in human behaviour. It is said, moreover, that absolute prescience cannot be attributed to God for men are his fellow-workers.[1]

The transmigration of souls I had finally rejected in the course of reading Plato. For it did not seem to me reasonable to suppose that anything which could pass from the state of human to animal or *vice versa*, could be the same persisting entity. And with the belief of most Hindus that one Spirit, the *atman*, is common to all life and the separate existence of man's soul an illusion, it was not easy to understand what distinguishing entity it was that passed from one body to another other than a kind of balance sheet, *karma*.

But that man's will was free only relatively, being limited by its conditioning, seemed undeniable. And some aspects of the doctrine of *karma* were obviously true. There was a kind of automatic 'judgment' wrought into a man's nature as divine law. Every human could dwindle into a condition characteristic of a lower form of life through sheer non-use of intelligence or of mercy. It was easy to feel oneself shrinking after a peculiarly feline remark, and to see oneself a lesser creature after some paltry meanness, a mere vegetable during an attack of that despairing sloth, *accidie*. But shrinkage was one thing, a complete change of garment quite another.

As to God's prescience, could the question have any meaning, I wondered. For presumably he was outside time, and for the divine mind past, present and future could not exist.

To the Hindu, I was told, evil is nothing ultimate and should be conceived as the distance which the Good has to travel.[2] That seemed to be another aspect of the idea that evil might be only the distance between Creator and created.[3] Heaven and Hell, too, in Hinduism are nothing external to those experiencing them. They are higher and lower states in a continuous activity.

[1] S. Radhakrishnan, *op. cit.*, p. 76.
[2] *Ibid.*, p. 124.   [3] Simone Weil, *op. cit.*, Vol. II, p. 588.

Radhakrishnan speaks of the consubstantiality of Spirit, human and divine, as the basic conviction of spiritual wisdom. (This was similar to what I had found in Hegel.) And this leads to the statement that the difference between man and God is not qualitative but only quantitative.[1] ' The soul enchained is man; free from chains it is God.'[2] Men are God-men. But according to another Hindu writer, the question whether man's spirit is one with the Supreme Spirit (*advaitism*), or is an individual entity is one which has divided Hindu philosophers into two parties.[3] The *Madhva* sect, for instance, do not believe that human souls are identical with God. Neither did I, and not because 'l'accent du pays où l'on est né demeure dans l'esprit et dans le cœur.' I had tried and rejected the idea with the rest of Pantheism in my youth.

Vagueness in religious belief I found to be with the Hindu an intrinsic good. He reacts against anything in the intellect which divides, analyses and categorises—against what Jung terms the male principle in the human psyche. It is largely from this that springs the great tolerance of Hinduism and its bewilderment by the heated controversies amongst Christians.[4] It accounts too, for its capacity to embrace other creeds and adopt religious ideas of other nations, even at the same time those that appear to Westerners as being mutually exclusive.

One of the chief characteristics of Hinduism seemed to be that of all-absorbency, as a vast, limitless sponge, chiefly owing to an indiscriminate toleration. This I found to be its strength and yet its deficiency. (*Tolerance*, I thought, was one of the tiresome ' haloed' words like *religion*. Neither was inevitably good.) And although the gentle vagueness and natural lenity of Hinduism removed all desire for religious persecution, so too did it

[1] *An Idealist View of Life*, pp. 103-4 (Allen & Unwin, 1932).

[2] Ramanuja, *Sayings*.

[3] Gokul Chand Narang, *Real Hinduism*, p. 71 (New Book Society, Lahore, 1947).

[4] R. C. Zaehner, *At Sundry Times*, p. 57 (Faber, 1958).

prevent discrimination against the most debased forms of worship.

But this tolerance is undoubtedly to some one of the attractions of Hinduism, and this, together with its way of life emptied of all but a minimum of dogmatic content offers scope to many western intellectuals who wish for religious experience undisciplined by any doctrinal thought.

Western intellectuals who have embraced what they call ' Vedanta for the Western World,' hail it as a new religion which has come into history. One wonders what it has that Christianity, a truly historical religion, has not got. And I was reminded of Talleyrand's counsel to the man who sought advice on the invention of a new religion. He recommended that the revolutionary should first get himself crucified and then rise again on the third day.[1] But undoubtedly it is by what Modern Vedanta has *not* got that modern intellectuals are attracted—revelation, a personal God, Christian doctrines generally and those of the Incarnation and Resurrection in particular.

But I found it hardly surprising that those who had not troubled to dig down to the richer soil beneath the barren looking surface of Christian doctrine, which fails so signally to influence the western climate of thought, should prefer eastern religions into which they could read their own predilections. And undoubtedly to anyone interested primarily in religious experience the Indian climate of opinion would be far more congenial than any western one. For Indians themselves are as essentially religious, from all accounts, as Europeans are essentially secular. The average Hindu, I believed, had more religion in his little toe than the average westerner had in his whole body. Yet I was persuaded that no European could really make Hindu truth his own, however great was the latitude in belief. He would, I thought, be reading his own notions into it. As Jung has said of westerners

[1] Quoted by Algernon Cecil, *A House in Bryanston Square*, p. 339 (Eyre & Spottiswoode, 1945).

who try to practise Chinese Yoga, the points of departure are different. What is organically foreign is not to be imitated.[1]

Jung shows, further, how western man is all too apt to appropriate unreflectingly the spiritual treasures of the East, and to emulate blindly the eastern way.[2] This he sees as a positive danger against which it is impossible to warn a man sufficiently. He particularly mentions our infection by theosophy; whilst his translator, Cary Baynes, speaks of the 'occult thought' so rife amongst millions in Europe to-day as being entirely devoid of true comprehension of eastern ideas, and thus a real danger in our world through their complete distortion.[3]

In all honesty I had to cry 'touchée' here, for in my youth I had sampled many queer pseudo-eastern confections, none of them true Hinduism or true Buddhism, but rather a bogus syncretism. At first I had eaten with appetite merely because they were not Christianity with which I was in a huff because it offended me; but before long I felt that I was being enervated and nauseated with a diet of cheap sweets. Mentally and spiritually I was becoming pot-bellied through starvation; my teeth were rotting. I longed for good wholesome bread. Although it was to be a long time before I found that, at any rate I never nibbled synthetic confectionery any more.

It had given me, too, a great distaste for syncretism in religion. There was a good deal of talk from time to time of the desirability of forming a world religion which would unite men in one immense brotherhood, in the place of the five great religions which seemed only to sharpen human antagonisms. But although it was essential that all understanding of eternal truths should grow, the general idea behind syncretism appeared to assume that the eternal truths themselves could be altered or done away with according to men's requirements. As Kierkegaard said, men do not wish to change themselves to suit the absolute; seeing the

[1] *Secret of the Golden Flower*, p. 80 (Routledge & Kegan Paul, 1931).
[2] *Ibid.*, p. 79.   [3] *Ibid.*, p. vii.

fault in the absolute it is this which must be changed to suit them. And in syncretism this amounts to an admission that there are no eternal truths. Based on human predilections it seeks in the relative, the finite and the transitory that abiding place for the spirit of man which can only be found in the absolute, the infinite and the eternal.

But if, then, a religion of syncretism was rejected, what alternative remained but a religion of revelation? True, there was still the most irrefragable theory to be pursued unless what Simmias termed 'some safer raft,' a word of God, could be found.

I had yet to examine three religions which claimed to be revealed, to be this 'word of God': Judaism, Islam and Christianity. I decided that it was imperative to approach them in a less prejudiced way than that in which I had approached Christianity in my youth, when the very fact of the claim to revelation had roused all my antagonism like the quills of a defensive porcupine.

As a child, the picture I formed of revelation was of the usual old man with a long white beard and dressed in the customary shapeless white gown, lifting the lid from an immense black and steaming cauldron (slightly confused in my mind with 'tall Agrippa' and his inkwell into which he dipped the naughty boys, in *Struwel-Peter*). The children of men crowded round to peer in at the contents and when the lid was raised, somehow the Jews were always in the best places for viewing; or perhaps the old man raised the lid just at that angle so that only the Jews could see inside the cauldron. The lid was not lifted completely off— only gently raised, and visibility was impaired by the clouds of steam which arose from the pot.

Now I saw revelation in quite another manner. It was God lifting a lid from no cauldron but rather a layer of darkness from the human mind which man could not see to remove alone— God pulling back the curtains of night, man struggling out of his sleep to meet the eternal day.

And although I had fought against this 'revelation' as a mere stratagem of the Church, I began to wonder if I were as free from its effects as I supposed. For I found within me, quite early in my search, certain assumptions which refused to be dislodged, and which might well owe their presence to the fact that, during my school days at least, I had had a more or less Christian background. Thus I assumed that God was good, and that the world and we ourselves had been created for some purpose that he would enable us to know; and, moreover, that we could in some manner and in some small measure know something of God himself. And what I now realised was that if I believed that God would enable man to know not only the purpose of his creation but something of the divine nature itself, I should have to think again, and think hard, about the reasons for my rejection of revelation.

This I knew had been mainly due to my hatred of the Church. I could not believe that anything taught by that stuffy old Mrs. Grundy who delighted in narrowness and obscurantism, could possibly be true. And certainly until I read Kierkegaard and Hegel I found it easy to dismiss 'all that guff' as quite meaningless jargon. Now they had shown me that it might have a meaning vital and profound. Moreover, I saw that for anyone who could believe in the Incarnation, God could be known in his historical manifestation in time and on earth. But of that I did not now wish to think. I would stick to my investigation of Hinduism.

The Hindu castes I learned, are *Brahmans*, the priestly class; *Kshatriyas*, the warriors; *Vaisyas*, agriculturalists; *Sudras*, the sweepers. The enormous importance attributed to the caste-system derived, I saw, from the Hindu belief in *dhamma* (variously translated as law, duty, religion, or sometimes as virtue or even social custom). It means generally both the way things are and the way they should be. And because of this it was easy to see why caste has such a strong hold on the Hindu mind. In the *Bhagavadgita*, I read that the work of the members of these different castes 'is fixed by reason of the Qualities in each,' and Krishna announces that it is better for a man to do his own work badly than to do another man's work well.

Besides this belief in *dhamma*, another source of Hindu inspiration comes from the Vedas. In the early ones I found the idea of monotheism. God is sole deity, simple and alone; omnipresent and omniscient, beyond the range of human comprehension. By his grace sin can be destroyed and its deathly consequences averted.[1] But in both Vedas and Upanishads there are two aspects of God: the pure, absolute and incomprehensible, independent of matter and individual creation—the impersonal aspect; and the Creator and Lord of all—the personal aspect. Professor Radhakrishnan points out that there is no contradiction between the abstract and impersonal Absolute and the personal God who is the cause, director and goal of the world—the highest conception open to the logical mind. The difference between the Supreme as spirit and the Supreme as person is one of viewpoint and not of essence: God as he is in his pre-cosmic nature—unchanging reality; and God as we see him in relation to the universe.[2]

It had often surprised me that so many Christians assumed that man was God's sole preoccupation. Hegel was particularly at ease in Zion with his belief that God cannot exist as the purely non-finite and that 'God is movement towards the finite.' That God was this movement was intrinsic to his triune nature and its manifestation in his Incarnation—if true. But I doubted that this could be the whole story. A God whose *raison d'être* was man would necessarily be something less than God, and man so singularly favoured something more than human. And I understood the agnostic's derision of the idea of a God existing primarily for man.

And yet, if man was made in God's image, if he contained a divine spark—as I believed he was and did—God must necessarily

[1] See particularly the *Rig Vedas*, I, III and X.
[2] *An Idealist View of Life*, pp. 107-8.

find in his creation a major preoccupation. For the divine essence, I was persuaded, was a concern that nothing it had made should be lost. I revolted only against the idealist theory of Hegel that 'without the world God is not God.' Although the Absolute could not be known as God if there were no men to worship him, the divine existence was eternal whatever one called it, and quite independent of the existence of man. (And I now saw how easily an atheistic neo-Hegelianism had arisen.)

Here were matters obviously too high for me. But that could never stop my brooding upon them. Hinduism, however, offered no light on the purpose behind creation. For even in the Gîta, the apex of Indian theism, there appears to be no purpose in creation; it is an illusion useless except as a plaything.[1] Moreover, to a westerner, revelation in the Upanishads—lovely as they are— seems to be inconsistent with itself.[2]

So, in spite of all that I respected in Hinduism and those things that I thought I might learn from it, I knew that I could never believe in a purposeless creation, in *advaitism* or in *metempsychosis*. And I doubted whether any westerner could ever really understand any sect of Hinduism sufficiently to make the religion his own. (I saw, conversely, in the many misrepresentations of Christian belief by Hindu writers, how hard it was for the Indian mind to grasp Judaic-hellenistic thought.)

It has been said only fifty years ago that from a study of history it is clear that the west has always sought to influence the east without ever trying to understand it. Never emerging from our own houses, and reading only our own literature, we view problems solely from our own standpoint. And then we wonder how these stubborn men can reject the offers made to them by Rome with such profusion of compliments and benevolence.[3]

[1] Zaehner, *op. cit.*, p. 129.
[2] For extracts from the Upanishads and the Bhagavadgîta, see Text XII, pp. 322. ff.
[3] Prince Max of Saxony. Quoted by Gerald Vann, O.P., *St Thomas Aquinas*, p. 72 (Hague & Gill, 1940).

I deplored the unthinking arrogance of the average westerner. Moreover, I questioned the wisdom and rightness of 'foreign missions.' If what is organically foreign is not to be imitated, is the eastern mind to be persuaded to adopt alien western thought? How is the Hindu to be reconciled, for instance, to an idea so repugnant to him as the resurrection of the body? It seemed that growth towards new ideas could come only from the inside as they had done in the amazing *Brahma-Samaj* movement through the efforts of Rāmmohun Roy, Debendra-nāth Tagore, and Keshab Chandar Sen.

The beliefs of this sect have been stated by Pratap Chandar Mozoomdar, one of the four teachers ordained by Keshab the reformer of Hinduism, in a conversation with Sir Monier Monier Williams in 1884:[1]

'Our most common name for God is Hari which means "The Taker away of sin and all evil."

We hold that God did not create the world all at once, but by gradual evolution.

We do accept Christ in our own way. We regard him as our supreme Exemplar. He was the Spirit of God incarnate—the ideal of the life of God in man. We do not believe this of anyone else. Paul conforms most nearly to the Christ-like pattern—Christ is the concentration and combination of all.

We accept Christ's death as an atonement spiritually. But there is no mere mechanical and material application of Christ's merits. If we are to profit by Christ's death we must go through the same processes. Christ's death was the victory of pain and suffering over pleasure and carnality. It was also a self-sacrifice. It was God living and dying for the good of the world. It effected a reconciliation between sinful man and God. In this sense we recognise the Atonement. Any one who adopts the same principle of self-sacrifice helps to effect reconciliation between man and God. Christ has taught us to die.

[1] Monier Williams, *Brahmanism & Hinduism*, pp. 522-3 (Murray, 1887).

We believe in his spiritual, but not in his bodily, resurrection.

Our Heaven is an eternal condition. We do not believe in the transmigration of souls. Our Hell is a temporary condition, like the Purgatory of the Roman Catholics.

We do not believe in a personal Devil. Evil is negative, and sin is a positive act proceeding from weakness or disease of the will.

We have Birth, Marriage and Funeral Ceremonies. We also have Baptism and a rite called *Homa* (using fire as a symbol). Moreover, we have a ceremony corresponding to the Christian Communion, performed with rice and milk which are supposed to have the same symbolic significance as bread and wine—that is they typify union and assimilation as food is assimilated.'

Why, I wondered, was I so deeply interested in this movement in the direction of Christianity—the religion that I had rejected? Was it merely that I was like the average Englishman who grumbles at everything whilst he is at home and yet finds no better way of life in all his travels? If so, what had militated against my youthful preference for the exotic and the unfamiliar?

It was the historicity of Christianity I realised that had begun to have an influence on my mind. And curiously enough it was a note preceding the translation by Christopher Isherwood and Swami Prabhavananda of the *Bhagavadgita* that made me realise this. It is here stated that to the true seeker after spiritual reality in reading the Sermon on the Mount and the *Bhagavadgita*, it is a matter of but little moment whether a historical Jesus or a historical Krishna actually lived.[1]

A parallel view I was to find expressed by Professor Braithwaite when he implies that it is not necessary to believe in the truth of the Christian story as long as thinking about this story retains its causal efficacy.[2] But who, I wondered, could suppose

[1] Phœnix edition, p. 29 (1947).
[2] R. B. Braithwaite, *An Empiricist's View of the Nature of Religious Belief*, Cambridge University Press, 1955 (The *Ninth Eddington Memorial Lecture*).

that such efficacy would long survive the establishment of this story as a work of imaginative fiction? Could the bare conception of a perfect life of selflessness ever be the same source of inspiration as the actual living of such a life? Moreover, this view assumes that religion is only ethics. Stripped of all that compels a personal devotion to one who has actualised the highest potential idea, 'causal efficacy' and such a 'spiritual reality' can have little to do with religion and cannot rise above an ethical philosophy.

How was it possible to believe it of no importance whether a historical Jesus actually lived? To me, it was a matter of life and death.

It was clear, I saw, that I had not escaped even now from the pursuit by the God-Man.

2. Buddhism

Gautama is said to have declared 'I am the all-subduer, the all-wise; I have no stains; through myself I possess knowledge; I have no rival; I am the chief Arhat—the highest teacher; I alone am the absolute wise; I am the Conqueror; all the fires of desire are quenched in me; I have Nirvana.'[1]

I found this a staggering pronouncement by one who 'never claimed to be other than a man; he had taken the idea from Brahmanism which held that its saints could surpass all gods, Brahma only excepted.'[2]

However difficult it might be—owing to the enormous gap in time between his death and the recording of his teachings—to have certain knowledge of his sayings, it appeared beyond doubt that Gautama placed himself above all other beings; and that his claims for himself were even more comprehensive than those of Christ. Where Christ stated that he could do nothing 'but for the Father,' Gautama refused to affirm or deny the existence of an Absolute; it was something in which he was not primarily interested. For him man is potentially the Absolute. And being a thorough-going empiricist he found only one thing verifiable; the state of flux in the universe generally and in men in particular. There is therefore no entity which can be called 'man.'

[1] *Maha-vagga*, I, 6, 8. Quoted by M. Monier Williams, *Buddhism*, pp. 134-5. (Murray, 2nd ed., 1890.)
[2] Monier Williams. *ibid.*, p. 135.

Not only, then, would I find in Buddhism nothing about God or about the soul as I understood it, but I would have to abandon all hope of finding here any views of the meaning of life, for, since there is no God either as a person or as a principle, and no human soul in the Platonic sense, there can be no idea of a divine plan underlying history. To Gautama, as to all Hindus, there is no history. And religion means purely personal salvation. It concerns itself with eternity, the achievement of *Nirvana*, alone and unaided by grace.

This salvation and the release from suffering are to be attained by knowledge and practice of the Four Noble Truths, and the treading of the Noble Eightfold Path.[1] Personality is the cause of everything evil, and desire for personal existence and personal possession must be eradicated before *Nirvana* can be achieved. Impermanence is the fundamental truth of life, therefore only pain and sorrow are to be found here. Thus, the purpose of life is to escape from its misery. But it is only the monk who can achieve salvation.

I felt as if torn in two by primitive Buddhism. On the one hand I could scarcely bear the idea that only pain and sorrow were to be found in this life, in this world the wonders of which were inexhaustible, and with its beauties of which one could never tire. And where, too, love was given and received, where there was family life, friendship, such joys as enriched man's heart and mind. It seemed to be a choice of death, a wicked denial of life, a wanton waste and stark ingratitude to whatever Powers were responsible for Creation. At times it even appeared to me ignoble to seek cessation of suffering and a snug invulnerability by embracing the Noble Truths and treading the Noble Path.

Yet, on the other hand, I understood that the negative way could not be so facilely judged. To some it was the only way to salvation—salvation from the self; the only means of realising that the ego is nothing, to escape from being mere natural man

[1] See Text XIII, p. 339.

Buddhism

by seeking to merge the self in something greater. But still I wondered need the discipline have been quite so violent? Only broken morsels given in alms for the monk's one meal (and even then he had to fast sometimes as well), rags from a dust heap for clothes, roots of trees for an abode; and no sexual act of any kind, no stealing of even a blade of grass, no killing even of a flea or a plant, owning no possessions beyond his three cloths, a girdle, bowl, razor and water-strainer (to avoid swallowing animalculae); remaining in one spot for three or four months during the rains when itineration would mean trampling on vegetable and insect life, the refraining from a recumbent position, and the visiting of cremation grounds for meditation on the corruption of the body.

If all had become monks, there would soon have been no more children and eventually no more people to be saved. Gautama himself must have foreseen this difficulty, for it is said that he put the existence of Arhatship—the higher practices for which the Order was founded—at one hundred years. And we are also told that his anti-matrimonial doctrines did give rise to murmurings; 'He is come to bring childlessness among us, and widowhood and destruction of family life.'[1] The fact that primitive Buddhism lasted such a comparatively short while and never gained any real stability in India was due, I thought, to the intensity of its demands and the conflict between its main tenets and human nature.[2]

Although the achievement of *Nirvana* constituted salvation, it was difficult, I thought, for a westerner to understand what it was, since there was no entity, which experienced this bliss. But Professor Zaehner holds that belief in the non-existence of the self can only be attributed to Gautama if by 'self' the empirical ego alone is understood.[3] To speak of an unchanging state of peace and deathlessness implies something which is conscious of

[1] Monier Williams, *ibid.*, p. 88.
[2] Ninety-six sects were observed in the fourth century in India. See Monier Williams *ibid.*, p. 158.   [3] Zaehner, *op. cit.*, p. 96.

such a state. For it to be an object of experience there must be some person or thing which experiences. And the Buddha does sometimes refer to a 'self' which, seemingly unconnected with our general idea of what constitutes a man is, like *dhamma* or *brahman*, a permanent something. Definition of this, Gautama deliberately avoids.[1]

His conception of *dhamma*, according to Irving Babbitt, is one of human law which is not unlike Arnold's 'great power not ourselves that makes for righteousness'; to this alone does the Buddha bow.[2] Moreover, in the desire for *Nirvana*, Babbitt sees no craving for annihilation which he finds explicitly censured in Buddhist scriptures, but rather the longing for the matchless security of a state free from change and corruption. And this escape from the flux and the relativity of life is man's highest good because it is an escape into the eternal.[3] If, therefore, as Zaehner observes, Christians dismiss either Hindu or Buddhist religion as inferior because it finds no purpose in human life, it might well be pointed out that to him who knows the eternal everything else will be added.[4]

But although the quest is fundamentally for the eternal, what lies beyond the flux cannot be defined in the only terms we have —those of this flux. And for Gautama 'mind' was part of this; therefore an intellectual formulation of the state of *Nirvana* is not to be hoped for. He would not speculate upon its nature (any more than Plato, I remembered, would define the Form of the Good), but he implied that it was of the nature of immortality. And that it was the release of the immortal *Atman* which constituted an experience of this immortality. (This appeared to be similar to the thought expressed by Ramanuja: 'The soul enchained is man; free from chains it is God'). This release, we are told, is the prime function of Indian religion. All questions

---

[1] *Ibid.*, p. 169.
[2] *The Buddha and the Occident*, p. 80 (O.U.P., New York, 1936).
[3] *Ibid.*, pp. 96-7.   [4] Zaehner, *op. cit.*, p. 19.

as to the existence, nature and laws of God are of secondary importance.[1]

Without denial of the ego or personality, there is no salvation possible. Indeed, denying the self is the fundamental basis of Indian ethics. The *Atman* is common to all forms of life, one with the spirit of the universe. No man owns his own. Thus the ego is an illusion; it lacks permanence and is therefore, according to Gautama, unreal.

It was in this idea of dying to the ego that I found one link with Christianity—the dying in order that we may live; the seed that abiding alone must perish but which falling into the ground brings forth much fruit. 'Ye are members one of another.' It was quite plain, however, that with the average Christian the idea is purely notional (as Newman uses the term) and that few attempt seriously to make it real. The whole conception is alien to the general mentality of the westerner. It has even been said that our present inability to think of ourselves as other than individuals is the most powerful argument for man's fallen state.[2] That could well be true; and, if indeed the Fall had ever taken place, how much better than the westerner has his eastern brother, in this respect, readjusted himself since then.

But although Buddhism has in common with Judaism and Christianity, belief in an Eternal, the Buddhist believes that spirit must be separated out from matter if it is ever to be free. The ideas both of incarnation and re-incarnation are repugnant to the Buddhist. It is therefore easy to understand that any suggestion of a resurrection of the body would be to him the last straw.[3]

So, too, the Christian belief that God is love is utterly illogical to him, since detachment is considered in itself a virtue.[4] And the compassion of Gautama is as detached as the love of Christ is attached and passionate. Christ overcomes suffering by accepting

[1] *Ibid.*, p. 43.
[2] Gerald Heard, *Is God in History?* pp. 54 and 59 (Faber, 1951).
[3] Zaehner, *op. cit.*, p. 23.   [4] *Ibid.*, p. 21.

it; the Buddha conquers it by repudiation. Here, I saw, with Simone Weil, the overwhelming greatness of Christianity in seeking a supernatural use of suffering rather than a supernatural remedy against it.[1]

Undoubtedly, it is on the ground of ethics that Christianity and Buddhism come closest together. In the *Dhammapada* I found many resemblances to the Sermon on the Mount.

Babbitt sees a similarity, too, between the Christian and the Buddhist attitude to belief. He finds in the Buddhist will to act upon the Four Noble Truths, the one means of their becoming known to him. Knowledge proceeds directly upon this use of the will. This order is similar to the Christian injunction that we must not seek to know in order to believe but rather believe in order that we may know. Knowledge in matters religious waits upon the will, and is the result of doing certain things.[2] This might be compared, I thought, with Wycliffe's saying that good life is necessary to right belief.

And although by the use of a will to refrain a man may gradually find himself exchanging what is transitory for what is eternal, and thus effecting a final escape from impermanence altogether, without the practice of meditation or spiritual recollection there can be no subsistence for the religious life at all. Gautama teaches that this meditation is the prime essential in a man's life. The illusion of the separate or lower ego (*manas*) is to be eliminated by constant meditation. The importance of this is paramount.

That was what I revered in primitive Buddhism—the persistent effort in thought. To Gautama, it is said, the radical diseases of human nature are conceit and laziness, and these must be eradicated by continual struggle and recollection. Spiritual indolence is the chief of all offences, and the putting forth of spiritual strenuousness the prime virtue.[3]

But this recollection and spiritual effort came hard, I knew, to

[1] *Op. cit.*, Vol. II, p. 387.   [2] *Op. cit.*, p. 86.   [3] *Ibid.*, p. 91.

western man. Perhaps that was why he was so secular-minded. Or perhaps he could not meditate because he was not naturally religious. I didn't know which was cart and which was horse, and whether it was with him a lost faculty or an intrinsically alien one.

One of the most interesting things for me about primitive Buddhism was the fact that it suffered a complete transformation from its original atheism. I was reminded of Sidgwick's saying that mankind neither will nor can believe in a Godless universe. And although I had often heard 'man's need to worship' spoken of pityingly at the best, and contemptuously at the worst, I had never, even in my most agnostic days, been quite convinced by the Freudian attempts to explain this trait. It was, I thought, due to men's fundamental need to worship that from the primitive Buddhism which in India 'gradually and quietly lost itself in *Vaishnavism* and *Saivism*,' arose *Mahayana* Buddhism. Although this started its theistic movement by a simple veneration for the extinct Gautama as a perfect saint, it soon grew into actual worship of the Buddha. And this was followed by canonisation of the most celebrated *Arhats* who were his immediate disciples; by the doctrine of *Parivarta*—the turning over of merit to the benefit of others, similar to the theological basis of the Catholic 'indulgences,' by the doctrine of vicarious salvation; and even belief in a goddess, *Kwan Yin*, as a sort of Madonna figure. None of these doctrines, however, belongs to true Buddhism.

In my youth, just as I had felt Pantheism to be so much broader and more profound than Christianity, so, too, I had preferred Buddhism—without understanding much about it—to the Christian religion. I had loved what I thought was its absence of dogma. But now I found many doctrines: *karma, metempsychosis, anatta,* the *skandhas, dhamma, Nirvana,* the *Atman;* and that it would hardly be possible to be a Buddhist without embracing the Four Noble Truths and treading the Noble Eightfold Path. I had admired Buddhism too as containing no proselytising element. But now I saw that, like every religion which claimed to possess good tidings for mankind, and a love (or compassion) for humanity, it did contain this and that it could hardly be consistent without such an activity. The whole purpose of the itineration of the monks was to preach the misery of this life and the means of escape from it through the higher practices of Buddhism.[1]

So I found that what most uninformed people admired about primitive Buddhism—lack of doctrine and a proselytising element —were just those things which were not its true characteristics. Its supreme virtue of overcoming the self by a life of almost superhuman self-denial, and of eliminating the idea of the separateness of the lower ego, *manas*, through constant meditation, was one which was barely recognised. Many esteemed Buddhism without understanding it, and certainly without any feeling of self-commitment. It was easy and comfortable to revere Gautama as 'the most undogmatic of men,' to praise his wisdom and his tolerance because these fitted in with one's own agnosticism and disillusionment. But Gautama, like Christ I thought, would not have wanted admirers and 'talkers of piffle.' He would have wanted disciples—men that would wish to be changed—rather than an admiration which costs one nothing.

I saw, too, that much of the esteem for primitive Buddhism was founded, as mine had been, on a revulsion against Christianity. But for myself I now knew that I could never embrace a religion where the existence of God and the human soul were so problematic, and with its resultant self-sufficiency and complete faith in the self, unaided by grace. And not only that; there was also the Buddhistic approach to this world that I could never accept. The vanity of life? I believed in its infinite value. I loved life and the way of affirmation on this very odd but strangely fascinating

[1] Jung tells us that now that the Christian myth has become so enfeebled in Europe, the Buddhists consider the moment ripe for a European mission. See *The Secret of the Golden Flower*, p. 145.

planet. And, above all, I thought that love was in itself of supreme worth; that love which cost one everything was the highest human faculty and also the essence of the Divine; that compassion, detached and undisturbing, was but a shadow of a greater substance. The negative way I knew was not for me.

3. Islam

It was not surprising that I found nothing original in the essence of the religion of Islam, for Mohammed (567 or 569-632 A.D.) never claimed anything for it but a revival of an old faith, a return to the primitive creed of Abraham.[1]

Renan, I read, has said that if monotheism, pure and simple, is to be a life as well as a creed, it almost demands the prophetic office. The Creator is too far removed from his creatures to allow of a sufficiently direct communication with them. His power, his knowledge, his infinity overshadow his providence and his love.[2] The Arabs themselves, I learned, looked up to Adam, Noah, Abraham and Moses as prophets. Mohammed does likewise, and adds Christ to their number, holding that each successive revelation had been higher than the preceeding one, though each was complete in itself as being adequate to the circumstances of the time. But was there, Mohammed asked himself, any reason to suppose that Christ had been the last of the prophets, and that his revelation was absolutely as well as relatively final? And were there not evils enough in Arabia and in the world generally to call for a further communication from heaven? For some hundred years before Mohammed the advent of another prophet had been expected. Now the

[1] Although chronologically Judaism should precede Islam, it suits the purpose of this work that Judaism and Christianity should be contiguous.

[2] Quoted by R. Bosworth Smith, *Mohammed and Mohammedanism*, p. 132 (Smith, Elder and Co., 1876).

time had come. Why should he not be Mohammed himself?[1]

The essence of Islam I found to be not merely the belief in the unity of God. Mohammed started indeed with the dogmatic assertion that the one God and Creator of all things is omnipotent, omniscient and omnipresent. But God not only lives; he is righteous and a merciful ruler; and it is the duty of all men to worship him.

It appears that at one period, that of the *Fatrah* (the interval when no *Suras* were given),[2] Mohammed considered whether first Judaism, and secondly Christianity, as he knew it, contained the message he had to give. Amongst several reasons for his not accepting Christianity, one is to be found in the picture presented to him of Christ. This was the Christ, not of the Canonical, but of the Apocryphal Gospels, and even these only from general tradition. Some of these I had read, and I marvelled that, Mohammed's information being limited to such miraculous imbecilities, he should have revered Christ so much.[3] From the Koran it is clear that there are only two or three passages which suggest any acquaintance with the synoptic Gospels.

The mystery of the Trinity, we are told, was another stumbling-block. For this conveyed only the idea of Tritheism, and Mohammed was also led to believe that the Virgin Mary was one of the Persons of the Trinity. But it has been suggested that in his denial of God as the Father of Jesus Christ, Mohammed, not being a theologian, is rejecting only the crude picture of a Deity in human form co-habiting with the Virgin Mary.[4]

The Incarnation and the Crucifixion he denied as being

[1] *Ibid.*, p. 133.

[2] *Suras*, chapters of the Koran. For extracts from the Koran, see Text XIV, p. 340.

[3] See Montague R. James, *The Apocryphal New Testament* (Clarendon Press, Oxford, 1953).

[4] R. C. Zaehner, *op. cit.*, p. 203.

altogether too degrading. He cannot believe that God would ever have allowed Christ to be crucified (much as the old Cumberland woman felt when she said, 'It is so long ago, let us hope it isn't true'). He preferred to think that someone else was substituted for Christ. (This Gnostic doctrine it is said may have been adopted by Mohammed as likely to reconcile the Jews to Islam as a religion embracing both Judaism and Christianity, if they might thus find the doctrine of the atonement removed. Jesus could then have been believed to be another prophet like Elijah who had been miraculously taken from the earth.)[1]

But perhaps the most important reason of all for Mohammed's rejection of Christianity was the fact that Christianity as he knew it had been tried and had failed. It had been known for three hundred years in Arabia, and had not been able to overthrow, or even weaken, the idolatry of the inhabitants. Also such Christians as Mohammed had ever met occupied themselves with every question about Christ except those concerned with a true discipleship.[2]

I found little new in the religion.[3] Allah is One, and the Merciful. The spirits he had created resented his subsequent creation of man. One spirit Iblis (Diabolos) refused to bow and so became Shaitan (Satan) and brought about Adam's fall through spite. It is curious that Iblis should have been expected to worship a mere man. And in this Zaehner sees Mohammed as regarding Adam as divine, otherwise God would not have commanded the angels to worship him, and Iblis would not have been damned for refusing to do this. The likeness between Christ and Adam is referred to in *Sura* III (XCVII) where it is said that Jesus is as Adam in the sight of God. This consists in the fact that neither of them had a human father. Both, according to Zaehner, are

---

[1] See J. M. Rodwell, *The Koran*, p. xvii (Williams & Norgate, 1861).
[2] Bosworth Smith, *op. cit.*, p. 277.
[3] But over one hundred sects of Islam are listed in the *Encyclopædia Britannica* under *Mohammedan Religion*.

believed by Mohammed to be special creations into which God
has breathed his spirit.[1]

According to a tradition of Mohammed every new-born child
is touched by Satan with the exception of Mary and her Son
between whom and Satan God interposed a veil. Thus the passage
in *Sura* III (XCVII) ' I take refuge with thee for her and for her
offspring, from Satan. . . . So with goodly acceptance did her
Lord accept her, and with goodly growth did he make her grow,'
has been thought to imply the Immaculate Conception of the
Virgin Mary, a doctrine in Christianity supposed by Gibbon to
have been ' borrowed from the Koran.'[2]

In Islam God creates the world *ex nihilo*. Man appears to have
free-will. No redemption is necessary. Allah forgives those that
believe. But Hell awaits nonbelievers, and a sort of purgatory
exists for the Jews and Christians who do not accept Mohammed.

Muslims accept all that is miraculous in the Christian religion;
the Virgin birth, miracles, the Ascension and the Second Coming.
They believe Christ to be the Messiah.

In spite of many imputations against Islam, I did not find it
possible to believe that a religion with such frequent fasts, prayer
five times daily, and its programme of almsgiving and pilgrimages,
could be an easy and sensual religion. Nor did I understand how
the charge of being a fatalist could be maintained against anyone
with as strong a belief in prayer as Mohammed possessed.

It might be asked, as F. D. Maurice has done, why Mohammed
had considered a new Bible necessary five hundred years after the
Jews had declared it complete.[3] For there was little new in the
Koran; even the denial of the Incarnation had been anticipated
by the Jews. Undoubtedly Mohammed found the evils of the
world in general and of Arabia in particular sufficient to call for
a new prophet and further pronouncements from heaven. For his

[1] Zaehner, *op. cit.*, p. 206.   [2] Rodwell, *op. cit.*, p. 499.
[3] F. D. Maurice, *The Religions of the World*, Boyle Lectures, 1846 (John
W. Parker, 1847).

countrymen his acceptance of the role of prophet and their conversion thereby from idolatry to worship of the Unity of the Godhead are enough justification for the birth of Islam—if justification be needed.

But although it seemed that the westerner might learn much from Islam: the habit of frequent prayer at regular intervals throughout the day, together with the attitude of mind which gave its name to the religion—the resigning or submitting oneself to God—it can but be asked what has the theology of Islam to offer the west that cannot be found either in Judaism or in Christianity?

4. Judaism

It was clear in the poetic myth of Genesis that God made man in his image, giving him dominion over all the rest of creation. And that man succumbing to the temptation of a lesser creature, disobeyed God and denied this law of creation. Each of his descendants manifests the same proclivity to serve that which he was meant to rule, and to disbelieve in the God he was created to obey. But however 'natural' this propensity becomes, there remains always a sense of anomaly and contradiction in the heart of man.

Throughout the Bible I found God portrayed as seeking to awaken in the creature he had made a consciousness of his true condition. A direct relationship to the Creator is assumed, however the creature might be denying it. And after 'the Fall,' man is still intended to have dominion over the earth. The whole history of the chosen people is a history of men brought out of darkness into the light and consciousness of their state as children of God made in his image and intended for this dominion.[1]

Although I recognised the proclamation ' There is one God ' to be the leading characteristic of the Old Testament, I saw that it was not its monotheism alone which set it apart from other sacred writings. For in the early Vedas too, I had found a sole deity. It was in their attitude to this Being that the difference between the Hindu and Judaic sacred writings was total and

[1] F. D. Maurice, *ibid.*, pp. 198-9, to which work I am indebted for much of this short account of Judaism.

fundamental. In the Old Testament I found a record; all is announced as coming from him; it is an account of a vividly personal God dealing with his people—a people chosen above all nations. He reveals himself as ruler of his creation, demanding unquestioning obedience; a God of justice, punishing only where punishment is due, but hating iniquity and chastising it deservedly. His revelation is progressive; his presence terrifyingly real. There are no speculations about him, no reflections concerning absorption into his essence. Nothing is set forth as a thought or a dream about God.[1]

And in the personal relationship between God and his chosen people—something absolutely fundamental in Judaism—and in the living experience by the prophets of a transcendent God, I saw again the utter difference between the Hindu and Jewish approach to the Deity. For the Indian generally *advaitism*[2] is accepted as true, whereas to the Jew the Lord remains the Lord of heaven and earth, and man remains his servant. In Hinduism and Buddhism there is no creatureliness. But with Yahweh no union is possible; a gulf yawns between his transcendent holiness and the nothingness of man. Eternal Being is not immanent in the world; he stands apart and the creature is not required to share this life.

It had always surprised me that once one separated the religion of the Hebrews from that of the prophetic movement, the cultus they practised was clearly not much superior to that of the surrounding nations. It was obvious that the Mosaic religion was neither spiritual nor other-worldly, and that the idea of the spiritual nature of God could have been but little understood. Moreover, it was not at all clear why the Hebrews were the chosen people unless it was due to the conception of Yahweh peculiar to them: of God as wholly 'other' and admitting no confusion between the human and the divine. And I was reminded that the prophets themselves point out that 'chosen' denotes no favouritism

[1] *Ibid*, pp. 136-8.   [2] See page 163.

which deals out privileges, but rather does it mean a conferring of responsibility. His people are to be immediately open to his Word. Their religion was thus revealed through the mouth of his prophets: 'Thus saith the Lord'—the Lord who spoke to their spiritual sense when their minds were immediately exposed to his Word.[1]

It has been said that the early Christians made the major blunder of saddling themselves with the Old Testament in which is found, together with some fine poetry and wise morality, the history of the barbarities and treacheries of a Bronze-Age nation, battling for their rights under the patronage of its anthropomorphic tribal god. Christian theologians, we are told, attempting to justify to men the ways of this tribal deity, sanctified this ancient darkness as revelation.[2] But as Edward Caird has observed, it was just that transmutation in Hebrew thought effected by the prophets which was the impressive fact about the story of the Jews. (And what appeared to me to argue most strongly for this revelation.) They changed a fear of something greater than nature into a profound reverence for something which is spiritual.[3]

This change is to be seen throughout the Old Testament from Abraham's learning to reject the idea of human immolation to its culmination in the declaration that God prefers mercy to sacrifice. And from Israel's worship of God as a national deity, it could be seen how Hebraism came gradually to take its stand on the spirituality of God.[4]

In reading the prophetic books of the Old Testament, I found an absoluteness in their statements about God that did not pretend to be conclusions from the prophets' own reflections about him but are proclaimed as the very word of God; a word that they are compelled to utter because it is his own utterance. Sometimes these messages, far from being in agreement with the prophet's

[1] C. H. Dodd, *op. cit.*, p.107. [2] Aldous Huxley, *Ends and Means*, p. 283.
[3] See E. Caird, *op. cit.*, Vol. I, pp. 387 ff.
[4] For extracts from the Old Testament, see Text XV, p. 349.

own customary reasonings, appear as the result of wrestlings with God, culminating in an almost reluctant acceptance of the office of mouthpiece for the divine proclamations.

It was curious, I thought, that this people, small in number and of little importance culturally should not only have embraced monotheism and worshipped one God, but that they should have had this deeply-rooted conviction that he was something wholly 'other.' And since it seemed that this race was continually sinning and falling away from God in unfaithfulness, it looked as if its enlightenment might be due to no merits of its own. The extraordinary persistence with which it continued to produce prophets had something of the appearance of a divine intervention, almost as if there were a determination on God's part not to let this people go; as if there were a purpose they had to fulfil, however many prophets they wore out in the process.

That God revealed himself through the prophets has been believed through subsequent generations; their testimony accepted as true and acted upon. And as Bishop Gore has observed, that which so greatly adds to human powers and raises mankind lastingly to a height which it had before been unable to attain, must necessarily be grounded in reality.[1]

If I could not be convinced like Pascal that the prophecies were the strongest proof of Jesus Christ, I did at any rate find it impossible to explain them away completely and satisfactorily. There was always an element of doubt which remained, and as Pascal has said:

' Quand un seul homme aurait fait un livre de prédications de Jésus-Christ, pour le temps et pour la manière, et que Jésus-Christ serait venu conformément a ces prophéties, ce serait une force infinie. Mais il y a bien plus ici. C'est une suite d'hommes, durant quatre mille ans, qui, constamment et sans variation, viennent, l'un ensuite de l'autre, prédire

[1] *Philosophy of the Good Life*, p. 264 (Everyman, 1935).

ce même avénement. C'est un peuple tout entier qui l'annonce, et qui subsiste pendant quatre mille années, pour rendre en corps témoignage des assurances qu'ils en ont, et dont ils ne peuvent être détournés par quelques menaces et persécutions qu'on leur fasse; ceci est tout autrement considérable.'[1]

It certainly did appear possible to argue that a special providence had preserved Jewish nationality not only from extinction but from being largely absorbed by its more powerful enemies. And from that I found it no far cry to entertain the idea that the preservation of Israel might well have been for the sake of its faith, then only a religion for a particular nation—that it might broaden out from a narrow nationalism into a religion for all mankind.

It seemed as if the character of Judaism was not to be understood apart from some consummation. Its explanation did not appear to lie within itself. And it has been said that the prophets point to a completion of history which shall be a completion in a Person. They see a King who shall be the manifestation of God, *the* Man, the Deliverer and Ruler who should establish righteousness and unite heaven and earth. For him David and his line are the preparation.[2] ' Except such a manifestation were really presented to them in a Man—except it were really shown to be true that Man was made in the image of God, and had dominion over the creatures, and that Death and Evil were not his masters, the visions of the Jewish seers were delusions.'[3]

The question for me then remained: ' What do Old Testament records mean if they have their completion in themselves, or if they have *not* their completion somewhere else? '[4]

For a short summary of present-day Jewish belief, see Text XV, pp. 360-361

---

[1] *Pensées*, Article X, *Preuves de Jésus-Christ par les Prophéties.*
[2] F. D. Maurice, *op. cit.*, p. 151.   [3] *Ibid.*, p. 201.   [4] *Ibid.*, p. 155.

PART SIX

Christianity

1. *The Incarnation*

'In the beginning was the Word, and the
Word was with God, and the Word was
God.'
'And the Word was made flesh, and dwelt
among us, (and we beheld his glory, the
glory as of the only begotten of the
Father,) full of grace and truth.'

ST JOHN I, I and 14

At last the moment had come when I was obliged to face the
question of Christianity. Always before, I had been able to justify
procrastination by deciding that the time was not yet ripe. Now
I could do so no longer, for of the great religions of the world,
only Christianity remained to be considered.

I had by now read many Christian works and reread the New
Testament and commentaries on it. Before, I had formed my
own opinion of Christ independently of much that I found in the
Gospels and commentaries. Anything in them that didn't fit in
with that, I assumed to be wicked interpolations by an infamous
body—the Church. That this was a method a shade too facile for
the attainment of a balanced view never occurred to me in my
youthful temerity. Now, having lost both youth and audacity,
I was conscious of the uselessness, the barrenness of the results of
reading the New Testament in a spirit which was fundamentally
distrusting, lightly discarding the testimony of those who had
lived the nearest to Christ.

That there would have been accretions still seemed to be
inevitable. But what now puzzled me was that if there had been

the large-scale tampering with the texts which I had hitherto suspected, how was it that this had been effected to so little purpose. Why had so many inconsistencies, so much stressing of Christ's humanity been allowed to remain? However that might be, I had tried to approach the gospels in a new spirit, not as before searching for 'pretexts for unbelief' as Coleridge suggests many do—and I certainly had done—not any more seeking for texts with which I might castigate the Church and demolish all its doctrines.

I thought I could bring to this re-examination of Christianity a *tabula rasa*. But I soon found how impossible this was and how utterly unable I was to wipe the slate of my mind clean from all that had been written on it by Hegel and Kierkegaard. And the difficulty I now encountered in rereading the New Testament was that I simply no longer believed Christ to be just a great teacher, another prophet. I had come to see that this theory created more problems than it solved.

That brought me up sharp once more against the only other possible solution—that of the God-Man. But was it a possible solution? I could shirk the issue no longer. Before, when I had found what I feared to be the truth, I had been unable to stay still and face it. I had tried to run away. But nowhere I ran could I find an abiding place. Cleave the wood and lift the stone as I would, everywhere lurked the same fear—that the Incarnation might be true.

Although the difficulties I had to face in Christianity were still the same as before, the shock I had experienced on reading Kierkegaard had disturbed my confidence in some of my rejections. His words had battered against my unbelief, and disbelief was shaken from its positiveness. Moreover, I was now no longer able comfortably to shelter behind the scandal of particularity as an insurmountable obstacle to belief. In reading Christian works recently, I had seen particularity as inseparable from historical revelation, although I did not profess to understand

196

why God's revelation should come to one race and not to another. It has been said that this particularity should be no more surprising than the possibility that it is only on this planet that life has appeared, or than the fact that of all the species of earthly life only one has developed powers of reason, and but few have attained to civilisation, and of those few to civilisation which is scientific and progressive.[1]

Mindful now of what I had learned from Descartes, I thought the Incarnation was not to be disbelieved primarily because it could not be imagined. If God were to enter human life he would necessarily become subject to those conditions which limit human life—those of time and space. He must appear at an exact spot in one country, at one moment in history. Of course it still seemed absurd that God should limit himself by time and space and should enter history. But as Kierkegaard incessantly repeats, the Incarnation *is* the Absurd, the Paradox. It is 'natural' to be unable to believe in it. It cannot be understood. The late Archbishop Temple said that no one had a right to believe in the Incarnation who had not first found it incredible.[2] I certainly had the right to believe it, then, but I needed more than a right in order to be able to accept what must surely be the most fantastic story in all the world and for all time.

I remembered Hegel's doctrine that the creation arising from the love inherent in God's triune nature implies a relation to humanity which can be termed an essential predisposition to incarnation. The propensity becomes actualised in Jesus Christ. Further Hegel says:

' The need felt by Spirit to know God as spiritual in a universal form . . . was created by the gradual advance of the World-Spirit. This immediate impulse, this longing

[1] Dr. Clement Webb, quoted by C. H. Dodd, *The Bible Today*, p. 107.
[2] Quoted by the late Bishop of Lichfield, University Sermon, Cambridge, October 10, 1948.

which . . . craves for something definite, the instinct, as it were, of Spirit which is impelled to seek for this, demanded such an appearance in time, the manifestation of God as the infinite Spirit in the form of a real man.'[1]

This I considered in conjunction with the idea expressed by Georges Berguer that Jesus, in his death and resurrection, had incarnated actually an inner experience that was potential in the human soul for centuries. He brought into life and actualised the dream—potential and secular—of the people.[2] And Fr. Victor White has pointed out that the myth which has been lived out and fulfilled in fact and history, voluntarily and consciously, is not thereby destroyed. But it has ceased to be mere myth.[3]

Jung, speaking about the anticipation of the Christian mystery of redemption in the Orphic, Dionysian and Heraclean myth cycles, states that the Christian projection differs from all these manifestations on account of the historic and personal figure of Jesus. Through him the mythical happening was incarnated and thus entered history as a mystic and unique happening.[4]

I had often been told by Christians that it was not possible to pick and choose from Christian theology; that one must take it all or nothing. The whole corpus of theology was indivisible. I thought then, what a pity. But now I began to understand the possible truth of this. For I saw how God's essence as love might necessitate his triune nature, which, again, involved Incarnation. And how the Fall and the Atonement were inextricably bound up, in their turn, with the Incarnation. Moreover, it was not just a well-integrated story that I began to discern; it was a possibility of truth conveyed through myth.

---

[1] *Philosophy of Religion*, Vol. III, pp. 75-78. See also Sterrett, *op. cit.*, p. 206.
[2] Quoted by Gerald Vann, *The Water and The Fire*, p. 57 (Collins, 1953).
[3] *God and the Unconscious*, pp. 227-8 (Harvill Press, 1952).
[4] *Integration of Personality*, pp. 223-4 (Routledge & Kegan Paul, 1952 ed.).

But the God-Man 'is the extraordinary combination which directly contradicts the understanding.' No ' likely story ' this. It was not surprising that I found it well-nigh impossible of belief.

And yet the question would not let me be. Many of my friends—theists with a Christian tincture at that—thought it completely unimportant whether God had incarnated in Christ or not. And it was obvious that the question was generally ignored as having not the slightest significance for modern men. And I supposed that it was because they had never bothered to get at the ideas behind Christian doctrine that they did not see that the Incarnation—bound up with the Trinity—if true, was the only evidence we have of the love of God for man. If that wasn't a matter of life and death, I wondered what was. I saw with increasing force the meaning of that extraordinary statement of Christ's ' He that believeth on me hath eternal life.' And I had to decide whether to believe in him or be offended.

I could not forget my conception of the Incarnation as a crude, human superstition which sought to limit by time and space and 'personality,' the infinite, eternal God who is Spirit; and how æsthetically repugnant I had found the whole idea. But now I was no longer a convinced Arian. My attitude was ambivalent.

For if I could not accept Christ's divinity what was I to make of those high claims of his, his self-assertion? The old argument cropped up again that either he was God or he was not good. I could not explain away his claims, for they were too subtle and all pervasive. He said ' I am,' not merely ' I know.' He was the culmination of prophecy. And how was I to interpret the way in which, undoubtedly, he distinguished in the relationship between God and himself ('my Father'), and that between God and the apostles ('your Father') ? It is clear that he assumed a special relationship with God, and with the Spirit. Moreover, there is no record of his praying with his disciples. We read frequently that he went apart to pray.[1] There was also Peter's confession which I had to consider, and the fact that Jesus did not deny that he was the Christ, the Son of God. Also his own confession to the high priest.[2] And again his identification of himself with the One who is offended by transgression: 'Ye did it unto me.'[3]

Yet nowhere did he state explicitly 'I am God.' I began to understand that it might be no part of Christ's approach to the heart of man to impose direct recognisability. Was not this, I wondered, one of the temptations that Christ overcame when he resisted the suggestion that he should display his divine powers in such a fashion as to win an easy recognition from mankind? There must be no compulsion to belief. We are not to believe by a scientific or logical necessity independent of ourselves. We are to be free to choose. And I remembered that Whitehead had observed that it was Plato who first assured us that the divine principle in the universe is a persuasive agent and not one of compulsion. And how the power of Christianity lies in its revelation in act of that which Plato's outstanding intellectual vision saw only in theory.[4]

Belief, I saw, was not to be equated with invincible knowledge, since a thing known and proved certain cannot be an object of faith. And faith, which Christ asked of man before all things (for indeed love was part of faith) could only exist where there was an element of risk. I saw now that it might be part of the divine plan of giving man free-will that he should exercise his free choice even—or perhaps above all—in the acceptance or the rejection of the God-Man. Direct recognisability according to Kierkegaard would be paganism. For it would destroy the need for faith, and

[1] See Jean Guitton, *The Problem of Jesus*, pp. 76-7, on this subject (Burns, Oates, 1955).
[2] See *ibid.*, p. 85.
[3] See *ibid.*, p. 82. For some of Christ's sayings, see Text XVI, p. 362
[4] *Adventures of Ideas*, pp. 161-2.

thus, I thought, might deny man the one response which made his salvation possible.

Yet I thought still of how bitterly I had revolted against the seemingly arrogant claim of Christianity to be unique and how this had deterred many interested in religion from joining its ranks. But I knew now that if Christianity was not unique then it was sheer nonsense.

Professor Arnold Toynbee in his *Christianity among the Religions of the World,* asks that Christians should deny the uniqueness of their religion. He pleads that the doctrines of the Atonement and of the Resurrection are found in the nature religions also. But as one reviewer has observed, it is not pretended that in any of these there was an historical redeemer who was slain and rose from the dead. They may be beautiful and edifying stories; but in Christianity we have a birth and life and death which are historical happenings. Whether we accept or reject the claims of Christianity, the reviewer concludes, it is completely absurd to profess that such a religion can be anything but unique.[1] It remained true, however, as Professor Gabriel Marcel has observed that it is very nearly inevitable that a historical religion should appear as a scandal to anyone outside that religion.[2]

But there were many who could not bear the tension which that uniqueness imposed upon the Christian. Would I be able to bear it? Or alternatively was I prepared to deny Christ's own claims for himself; and also the whole meaning perhaps of God's revelation to the Jews?

And yet I still hoped for some means of escape. Was I then one of those to whom Etienne Gilson refers as being most anxious to find truth but not eager to accept it? I was perhaps like Annanias and Sapphira who tried to keep back something for the self. And that something in my case was intellectual comfort. I looked for something that would lessen that

[1] *Times Literary Supplement.*   [2] *The Mystery of Being,* Vol. II, p. 133.

tension which the uniqueness of Christianity imposes upon the Christian.

But nowhere could I find a satisfactory compromise. Modernism offered no refuge since it had made a travesty of Christian theology. As Santayana has observed, modernism is suicide; the final concession to worldliness which the double-minded make in their half-belief. It is a mortal step which concedes everything. The modernist has left off being a Christian in favour of becoming an amateur of Christianity. Believing in no part of it in the way in which it demands to be believed, he wishes to reconcile the world with the Church, ignoring that the message of Christianity was the overcoming of the world.[1] No, it wouldn't do. I saw that the modernist wants what he considers to be the best of both worlds, and deaf to the warning that we are to suffer ' because of the Word,' he, too, seeks a fatal compromise in the pursuit of intellectual comfort. He must change the requirement since he does not wish to change himself. But debasing truth in order that it may be acceptable to men—that, says Maritain, is the great sin. And Kierkegaard shows how whittling away doctrine—especially that of the Incarnation—gradually diminishes the absolute until it falls apart bit by bit. With the unconditional thrust out of man's life all his efforts are like attempts to sew without first making a knot at the end of the thread. Moreover, he declares that everyone who has not in some way or another suffered for the doctrine is guilty of setting his shrewdness to spare himself.[2]

Christians, I saw, have to suffer for the Word just because it is unique. They have to endure the obloquy of the world because they cannot deny this uniqueness of Christianity; they must accept the scorn of non-Christians who see in their loyalty to this religion without parallel nothing but bigotry and an inferiority

[1] *Winds of Doctrine*, pp. 49, 51, 56-7 (Dent & Sons, 1926 ed.).
[2] *For Self-Examination*, p. 215.

to followers of other creeds who claim no such uniqueness for their religions.

So be it. Perhaps to one who really believed, it would be a small price to pay. He might count the world well lost.

But for myself, I had not faith. I had only a cessation of disbelief.

2. Faith

'The Sea of Faith
Was once, too, at the full, and round earth's shore
Lay like the folds of a bright girdle furl'd.
But now I only hear
Its melancholy, long, withdrawing roar,
Retreating, to the breath
Of the night-wind, down the vast edges drear
And naked shingles of the world.
                    MATTHEW ARNOLD, *Dover Beach.* 1.21

Humanity clearly was now bereft of faith. It had seeped away from us, as Jacob Wasserman has said, like water from a cracked cup. Any that remained was abnormal, and to an age accepting experimental evidence as alone able to verify truth it seemed like madness. Those to whom, like Pascal, faith was god-sensible to the heart although not to the reason, lived now as the lunatic fringe in an alien land.

It did not surprise me then that by men like Newman and Kierkegaard, the intellectual climate of the age was felt as an agonising tension. Like Pascal they knew the might and value of reason as well as most; but they knew too its limitations, and considered it inadequate to treat of things beyond the natural law. Newman, we are told, drew no comfort from Paley's argument from design, finding it ' beautiful and interesting to the believer in a God; but, when men have not already recognised God's voice within them, ineffective, and this moreover possibly from some unsoundness in the intellectual basis of the argument.'[1]

[1] *University Sermons*, p. 70 (Rivingtons, 1872).

He substitutes the argument from conscience as his foundation of belief. It might be said, however, that the reactions of our conscience depend upon our belief in God rather than prove his existence, and that conscience itself is but a habit of thought in which we are taught by our parents and our teachers in youth, or which we have absorbed from the tradition of that society in which we live. Yet I had never been able to dissever man's recognition of goodness as the positive norm and evil as contradiction, from the existence of God as the Form of the Good. And although the argument from conscience might have no rational justification, Newman believes that something like Pascal's *esprit de finesse*, a certain disposition of mind, a pectoral logic, could establish the authority of conscience. ' The safeguard of Faith is a right state of heart. This it is that gives it birth; it also disciplines it.'

It is not only faith that he finds going a long way beyond what is demonstrable. Scepticism goes equally far. Both believer and unbeliever view evidence in the light of their antecedent presumptions, as I well knew. Hume's rejection of miracles was the outcome not of an examination of the evidence, but the result of antecedent belief which obliged him to reject all evidence for them in advance. Antecedent improbability is considered—as indeed I had seen in the attitude of some scientists to the work of the Society for Psychical Research— to justify refutation of the evidence unexamined.

Again, I felt Newman was right in recognising that in questions that lie near our hearts it is almost impossible to rule out all prejudices. I had found within myself an ineradicable conviction that God, if he existed, was good, and that he was not indifferent to his creation and that there was a meaning and purpose in the life of man. Perhaps this was because only so could life make any sense for me. And I would not care to deny that the emotional factor must contribute something to our judgments. For both believer and unbeliever judge by the effect produced on their minds. The same evidence convinces some whilst it fails to impinge on the mentality of others. Newman considers it right that conclusions should be reached 'not . . . by a scientific necessity independent of ourselves, but by the action of our own minds, by our own individual perception of the truth in question.'[1] Obviously, therefore, conclusions will vary. Evidence itself is incapable of being conclusive.

This was again very like what I had found in Kierkegaard. So, too, Newman's statement that belief is essentially free and dependent upon an act of the will. Evidence is never of such overwhelming nature that we are forced to believe. No human testimony can render a man *quite certain* that he is hearing a message from God. The merit of faith derives from the fact that it is an act of free-will done with the help of grace, and not a mere consenting to conclusions whose logical necessity forbids the intellect to dissent.[2] Faith for Newman, was not a result which must be arrived at through premises, but the outcome of an act of the *will* born of a *conviction* that to believe is a duty.[3]

But he shows, too, that faith is not solely a matter of the will.

' Faith is a gift of God, and not a mere act of our own, which we are free to exert when we will. It is quite distinct from an exercise of reason, though it follows upon it. I may feel the force of the argument . . . I may see that I ought to believe; and yet I may be unable to believe. This is no imaginary case; there is many a man who has ground enough to believe, who wishes to believe, but who cannot believe. It is always indeed his own fault, for God

[1] *Grammar of Assent*, p. 242 (Longmans, 1947).
[2] *Thèses de Fide*, thesis 12; Gregorianum, XVIII, p. 237. Quoted by Philip Flanagan, *Newman, Faith & Belief*, p. 126 (Sands, 1946).
[3] From a letter to Mrs. William Froude, from Ward's *Life of Cardinal Newman*, I, p. 242. Quoted P. Flanagan, *op. cit.*, p. 125.

gives grace to all who ask for it, and use it, but still such is the fact, that conviction is not faith.'[1]

How much, I wondered, did this apply to me? I had exercised a certain amount of reason, and had felt the force of the arguments for much of the metaphysical significance behind the Christian doctrines. Moreover, Kierkegaard's presentation of the God-Man had persuaded me that I ought to believe. But could I do this against my inclination? Perhaps a growing conviction might increase like a smouldering fire until it burst into the flame of faith, burning up every resistance to it like so much dead wood. That was what I should have liked—to be freed from that awful need to decide, that personal responsibility. But I saw that Newman was right, and that conviction was not faith.

Had I those good dispositions then which Newman finds necessary to faith—the readiness to co-operate with grace? He sees the principles inducing a man to search as affecting the results of such search; without a feeling of personal responsibility there can be no understanding of religion. ' Men consider that they have as full a right to discuss religious subjects, as if they were themselves religious.'[2] And, further, one can either go out to meet the truth, or consider that the truth ought to come to one. ' To be easy in believing is nothing more or less than to have been ready to inquire; to be hard of belief is nothing else but to have been loth and reluctant to inquire.' Examination of the evidence in an impersonal manner as if it had no concern for him and he were favouring Almighty God, shows that such a man is 'a critic and a judge, not an inquirer, and he negotiates and bargains, when he ought to be praying for light.'[3]

This was exactly how I had approached the Bible in my youth

[1] *Discourses to Mixed Congregations*, p. 224 (Longmans 1909).
[2] *University Sermons*, p. 198.
[3] *Sermons on Various Occasions*, p. 70 (Burns, Oates, 1870).

—but now I thought I was not entirely devoid of good dispositions.

In the *Early Journals* I found him admitting that Faith was the most difficult of all graces; for it is the believing of something which is beyond the grasp of reason and contrary to the imaginings of our fallen nature.[1] And faith further requires humility to submit. Speaking of those who are persuaded of the truth, but yet await assurances of more than the familiar moral certitude before submitting, Newman says ' They do not reflect that their present difficulties are moral ones, not intellectual.'[2] (As Kierkegaard said, sin is in the will and not in the intellect.) Newman says, ' You must make a venture; faith is a venture';[3] an exhortation similar to those of Kierkegaard.

I saw that I had been trying to get the best of every world. I had still wanted the 'most irrefragable theory.' I had looked for arguments for and against Christianity, seeking to prove or disprove by means of apologetics. I was waiting for 'evidence' so overwhelming that it would compel belief, thus hoping to make of faith something painlessly and effortlessly inevitable, something that might happen of itself without my having to 'make a venture'; cheap grace as Pastor Bonhoeffer would have called it. I did seem to be expecting 'assurances of more than the familiar moral certitude'; perhaps a sort of *coup-de-foudre* in the manner of the conversion of St Paul.

In fact, I was unwilling to take any risks—to throw myself overboard. I remembered, however, that Kierkegaard had said that the man who never let go of probability could never commit himself to God. And that all religious adventure must be on the farther side of this probability. And in the *Nature of Metaphysical Thinking*, Professor Dorothy Emmet has shown Faith to be a

[1] *Early Journals*, Book 1, p. 161. (From *Autobiographical Writings of J. H. Newman*, Sheed and Ward, 1956.)

[2] *Discourses to Mixed Congregations*, p. 188.

[3] *Loss & Gain*, p. 385. Quoted by P. Flanagan, *op. cit.*, p. 136.

positive response of the whole man, volitional, emotional and cognitive, a self-commitment, an affirmative response to a challenge to his decision. For a man to believe on a mere balance of probabilities, accepting what is most likely to be true, has nothing to do with faith. She finds it no part of the working of faith to turn probability into certainty. But it lifts a man right out of the theoretic domain.[1]

And Kierkegaard defined a believer as one who dared, through his own choice to make a leap to appropriate truth. This cannot be done by testing knowledge and 'proving' theories, for eternal truth lies always beyond the territories of scientific knowledge. I knew that before Kierkegaard I stood convicted of paltry sagacity, effeminate common-sense and a shoddy servitude to probability. I was a coward certainly; for I felt I could not bear that tension inherent in the acceptance of Christianity—if it were to be anything more than Religion A to me.

Yet I knew, too, under all the struggle that there would be only one direction in which I could go if I were not to betray everything I revered. I would have to submit to what in my innermost thinking I now believed to be the truth however great the demands it made upon me intellectually, psychologically and ethically. The responsibility was mine to cease troubling myself with faith in my doubts and with doubts in whatever particle of faith I had.

But having decided this, I can give no further account as to the precise moment when conviction took on another quality. I only know that one day I found I was 'there.' I had arrived on that other side. And if the trumpets sounded for the sinner that repenteth, I did not hear them. I had no pious feelings, no exaltation; nothing but a sense of surprise at there having been accomplished in me something that had to be done. As far as I remember, I did not even say Thank you.

[1] P. 139 (Macmillan, 1945).

3. *Dogma and religion*

'Quamdiu vivimus, necesse habemus semper quaerere.'

When I first heard of dogma in my early schooldays, I formed a picture of an old and ugly bulldog who somehow was a dog and yet a mother. And I disliked him a good deal with his puppies bearing the strange names, Incarnation, Atonement and Resurrection. Whereas the term 'free-thinkers' evoked a picture of beautiful young men and maidens free-wheeling down a steep hill when everyone else was in Church on Sunday. Sitting on my hard pew, irritated by my clean and prickly combinations and the hateful hat which were my Sunday lot, how much I envied these creatures of my imagination! And the steep hill had no connection in my mind with the Gadarene swine; for I loved the free-wheelers as much as I hated cross old Dogma.

Throughout my childhood, the name 'free-thinker' was synonymous with 'unbeliever,' for except in religious circles no believer was considered free to think; and I grew accustomed to the thought that acceptance of dogma necessitated a sacrifice of intellectual freedom. In the binding authority of doctrine I saw the petrifying of truth, and in submission to this authority the paralysis of reason.

For human knowledge based on evidence was necessarily by its very nature a matter of change and increase. It was obvious that there could be no such thing as scientific dogma, since all scientific conclusions must be provisional, awaiting the results of further observations. And my failure to believe in revelation made me see in religious dogma an absurd attempt to place outside its proper category a purely human statement which, I thought, should be subject to change and decay like any other theory. Perhaps if I had read earlier of Plato's changeless Forms, or of Leibniz's 'eternal truths,' I might have understood at least the possibility of the existence of truths which were unalterable and subject to neither time nor fashion. I might, too, have been a shade less confident in my uninformed attacks on Christianity for its 'outworn creeds' and 'dead dogmas': in my denouncements of its very essence—its changelessness.

But I, like the non-Christian world, assumed that anything that could not change must be dead. And certainly dogma was dead as far as the majority of human beings was concerned. I could not but think that the Church itself was largely responsible for that. Though rightly aware, I now saw, of its primary function of safeguarding revelation, it appeared too often content that belief itself should be static and remain at a superficial level, as if all that mattered was that sheep should safely subsist on the bare bones of the Christian dogmas. Some found the marrow for themselves. Other hungry sheep looked up and were not fed; whilst many, as I myself, wandered from the fold in search of better nourishment.

Even now I still had great sympathy with those who rejected revelation, since I could not forget my own youthful dislike and misunderstanding of it. I had seen it as an ingenious invention of the Church whereby anything it wished to promulgate it could announce as 'revealed.' This implied a private telephone line from the Church authorities straight to a heavenly propaganda department. Moreover, all their conversations were secret and privileged. No one could 'tap' the wires and so be enabled to check on the reports of the conversations issued from time to time.

I had profoundly mistrusted such a procedure and believed that the Church had introduced doctrine to supply 'jobs for the boys,' to keep its theologians occupied; and to give itself a position as sole interpreter of these esoteric and obscurantist theories which it alone could understand. The doctrine of the Incarnation particularly enraged me. I thought that if the Church wanted recruits how foolish it was to keep potential ones away by its zeal for such a doctrine as well as those of the Trinity and the Atonement. Dogmas of religion were to me so antiquated as to be little more than medieval superstitions unworthy of consideration. They were dead; why wouldn't they lie down and make an end of the farce? Or else be flexible, fluid, adaptable to modern requirements—in fact, cease to be dogmas?

But now I had come to believe in revelation through believing in those things that had been revealed; in the very doctrines that I had so scornfully rejected—the Incarnation, the Trinity, the Atonement. And in reading the Old Testament I had seen what appeared to be the hand of God in the history of the Jews. Again, in the succession of the prophets I found it not easy to deny that God had revealed his will to men, his commandments and his truth.

At the very outset of my search I had found McTaggart's idea that without dogma it was impossible to have religion. It was one that I disliked very much. For not only had I considered it broadminded to despise dogma but I had also known a stage when I thought religion ought to be something warm and woolly and comforting, just an amorphous mass of uplifting thoughts with vague yearnings after the Infinite, and an ethical content that could be summed up in the words, ' Be nice.' What more could possibly be wanted?

But McTaggart scorns the notion that it is liberal and tolerant to use dogma as a word of abuse, and asks on what, if we reject it, can we hope to base religion? He adds that Christ himself held various dogmas which he believed to be of the utmost importance, such as personal immortality, the existence of a personal God with the Fatherhood as a metaphor. To which might be added, I thought, his belief in Judgment, heaven and hell, and the necessity for repentance, faith and love in the achievement of salvation. It might be possible perhaps to be vaguely religious without dogma, but for a religion, I now realised dogma was as essential as a skeletal frame was to the human body.

Newman saw that 'granted the fact of revelation, Religion cannot but be dogmatic.' 'From the age of fifteen, dogma has been the fundamental principle of my religion. I know no other religion. Religion as a mere sentiment is to me a dream and a mockery.' He believed that the so-called religion of the heart when it was without orthodoxy, could have but the 'warmth of a corpse, real for a time, but sure to fail.'

But Newman saw also that 'it is not at all easy (humanly speaking) to wind up an Englishman to a dogmatic level.' And this reminded me of the remark of a shrewd foreigner that the only dogma to which the British cling with passion, is that nothing can be demanded of a Christian which is distasteful to an Englishman.[1] And certainly the general opinion appeared to be that it couldn't possibly matter what one believed as long as one tried to be averagely decent.

For a long time I had heard talk about yielding to the intellectual pressure of the age and preserving only the more valuable characteristics of the Christian religion—its ethics—whilst 'moving with the times.' Doctrine has no longer any value. And that, surely, was not surprising when it was understood only at a surface level. Of what possible worth could it be to men to believe that the nature of God is triune without their seeing how such a nature is necessitated and expressed by love? Of what value to them to assent to the doctrine of the Incarnation without recognising in it the supreme—perhaps the only—evidence we

[1] The Rev. M. B. Dewey in a University Sermon, Cambridge.

213

have of God's love for man (and what superlative apathy to find the question of the Incarnation of no moment one way or the other). For severed from that inexorable divine concern that no man shall be lost, the dogmatic definitions are cut off at the roots and die of inanition. Nothing which is emptied of meaning for him can impinge on man's belief. And I thought that the letter of doctrine had died because it had been severed from the spirit which alone gave it life and significance.

That left ethics as the be-all and the end-all of religion. But even if an ethical philosophy couched in pious terminology could satisfy the majority of men, the preservation of ethics apart from doctrine might not be as simple as some thought. This, it is said, is clearly shown in John Morley's essay, *On Compromise*—not so much in the intention of the author as in the light of the event —where it is apparent that Christian moral standards survive Christian dogma by no more than one generation. Once the creed is dropped, the standard falls.[1] But although the Church was the main object of his attack, Morley did not fail to recognise the importance of distinguishing between truth and error, and he himself, we are told, approved of Pope Paul III's telling the Council of Trent that 'belief is the foundation of Life and that good conduct only grows out of a right creed, and that errors of opinion may be more dangerous even than Sin.'[2]

It has been suggested that, as in ethics, perfect freedom is to be experienced only in the service of God, so thought within the bounds of theology may be the freest.[3] But speaking of the theologians of his day, Hegel has said that the importance which was once attributed to the doctrines themselves is now assigned to their history. Zeal and erudition are expended on externalities and controversies about them. They are regarded as convictions

[1] A. Cecil, *op. cit.*, p. 208.
[2] B. Willey, *More Nineteenth Century Studies*, p. 280.
[3] B. Willey, *Christianity Past and Present*, p. 50 (C.U.P., 1952).

which belong to *others*. 'With the true content, with the knowledge of God, such theologians have no concern. The truth which they have for our spirits is shoved on one side by this historical treatment.'[1]

It seemed undeniable that—as has been remarked—men are now more concerned to trace the history of an idea than to decide upon its merits; and that it is a fact that a belief for which a historical explanation has been found, its origin and development discovered, ceases to exercise authority over the mind. For once we know how it came into being and why it was credited, we no longer feel obliged to believe it ourselves.[2] And now that it has ceased to be vital to our lives, doctrine has been replaced by secular dogmas—for man cannot live without faith in something—belief in man, in progress, in liberty, in human rights, together with the agnostic's dogmas that nothing can be known and that all truth is relative and subjective. The truth or falsity of Christian doctrine matters nothing to the world at large.

We are therefore indifferent to the only 'evidence' we have of God's love. For I could not deny that the universe alone offers not a shred of evidence for this love of man; rather the contrary, or at best—in view of universal suffering and wretchedness—a complete indifference. It was not surprising that the agnostic who judges alone on direct evidence, should be bewildered by any talk of God's love.

The Christian finds this evidence in the Incarnation. And, too, he argues that man is called upon to bear no suffering—mental or physical—no dereliction, that has not been borne by the God-Man. Moreover, the Christian does not believe that this temporal scene is in itself a rational whole. It begins to promise intelligibility only when viewed as the first act in a drama of which the true significance will not be completely understood until the last

[1] *Op. cit.*, Vol. I, p. 38.
[2] B. Willey, *More Nineteenth Century Studies*, p. 279.

scene of all.[1] Above all, he has a conception of the love which emanates from the Divine Nature—implicit in all doctrine—as differing from and far outdistancing human love.

Kierkegaard has warned against the false gentleness, that sickly sentimental gentleness of Victorian divine love, and George MacDonald saw in God's love something terrible in its inexorability—the one thing from which escape was impossible.[2] But it seemed that many would prefer this love to be the lesser, purely human kind which we associate with a weakly indulgent and foolishly compliant parent who seeks to intervene between cause and effect. And it is no comfort to these to be told that God will burn away from us all that separates us from him. For most of us do not mind being separated and all of us very much dislike being burned. The tendency nowadays is for the removal from the Christian picture of every idea that might be unwelcome to us. Thus Reinhold Niebuhr shows how for the present day it must be a wrathless God who brought sinless men through a Christ without a cross to a Kingdom where there is no judgment. God's wrath and the sense of our sin are utterly alien to modern thought. But Pascal tells us that ' la plus cruelle guerre que Dieu puisse faire aux hommes, dans cette vie, est de les laisser sans cette guerre qu'il est venu apporter.'[3]

It is perhaps not surprising that some of the arguments for another sphere of being should be unworldly. And I did not think that it was to be expected that the believer should get the better of any argument with the unbeliever. For it is the agnostic's world; one where there are no evidences which he would accept as such for what the believer believes. And it is the agnostic's language that the world uses; it does not understand the language of the believer who fails to establish for his beliefs a case founded solely upon evidence and reason. It is useless for the Christian

---

[1] F. A. Iremonger, *William Temple*, pp. 235-6 (Cúmberlege, O.U.P., 1948).
[2] See *Anthology of George MacDonald*, ed. C. S. Lewis, p. 25 (Bles, 1946).
[3] *Op. cit., Pensées Diverses sur la Religion.*

to attempt to speak of faith and of truths that are beyond reason. The agnostic is interested only in what can be known, and for him there can be no truths ' beyond reason ' to which men could attain by other means. He is invulnerable to the cuts by the sword of the spirit, whereas the believer is only partly so to the thrusts of the rapier of reason, since he lives in two worlds, that of the spirit and of reason. He feels the wounds although he knows them not to be mortal. To him belief is being, an integral part of life; whereas to the agnostic it is only a more or less negative thing, detached and peripheral in character; a sort of 'your guess is as good as mine' without importance or value.

But it was just this believing in an idea with all one's strength that took one, I saw, out of the self and enabled one to live in that idea. And if the idea were eternal then whatever lived in it would be eternal too. Just as Spinoza has said that if the soul should be united with some other thing which is and remains immutable, the soul must also remain permanent and immutable.[1] Thus, where before I had seen only a source of bewilderment and unbelief in Christ's pronouncement that ' he who believeth in me hath eternal life,' now I perceived an immortal truth to which Plato and Spinoza in their different ways had subscribed. And I was more than ever convinced that it was only in losing his own life that a man could save it. And further that love was the cause, the means, the doctrine, the goal of all eternal life.

But nowadays the problems of civilisation are so acute that it is generally thought that these should be man's primary concern, and that even to consider belief in eternal life is a mere fiddling whilst Rome is burning. Emil Brunner, however, has pointed out the utter fallacy of this view, showing that our present difficulties have attained their incomparable complication just because there is no longer a general belief in such a life. We are gripped in a sort of time-panic.

[1] *The Short Treatise*, Part II. Quoted by W. Hale White, *op. cit.*, p. xci.

To Dostoevsky, a believer in eternity, this world was primarily a testing place where we are to choose between good and evil. To him, we are reminded, it was neither possible nor even desirable to rid the world of suffering, since our sojourn here was designed so that we might achieve the greatest good—humility, and avoid the greatest evil—pride; and he saw it as against our fallen nature that unvarying good fortune should incline us towards this humility.[1] Constant favours at the hands of 'the bitch-goddess Success' only increased idolatry, inflamed pride and encouraged the illusion of self-sufficiency. It was the sorrows and afflictions of life that had the power to awaken consciousness and to redeem evil, to teach us humility and the acceptance of our appointed place in the scheme of things, to remind us that salvation lay in our being bound up with our fellow-beings, not only in the communion of sinners but also in the communion of Saints.

Because it was a separation from the supernatural, humanitarianism appeared to Dostoevsky as the most powerful anti-religious factor in Europe, and therefore the kind of atheism most to be feared. Obviously, with a disbelief in the transcendent, man was forced to seek perfection within the time process; without reference to the supernatural, human values were the only significant ones. But all evil, according to St Augustine, was a mistaking of means for ends. And earthly life instead of being a means of attainment to a more abundant life, has become an end in itself. To most of us it now seems fantastic that Hegel should have approved, only a hundred and fifty years ago, of the attitude of the Middle-Ages to life when

' the world of the living was a mere forecourt or anteroom to the greater world of the dead, and the worth of all human things, both in the knowledge and the use of them

See article on *Dostoevsky* in *Times Literary Supplement*, Sept. 20, 1947.

was estimated entirely by their reference to that other world.'[1]

' Medieval ' is now generally a term of abuse whether applied to ideas or sanitation. But Emile Cammaerts has told us that from the first to the fifteenth century civilisation in the west waxed stronger on the Christian belief, ' God made man'; but that from the sixteenth century to the present day it has waned rapidly on the principle that 'man made God.' The worship of man is the basic cause of failure. It is the most grievous error ever made.[2] And it has been observed that since the Renaissance, belief in man's subjection to superhuman powers is considered a sign of ignorance, timidity, or of his slave mentality, and of a lack of appreciation of human reason's creative power. Anthropocracy is enthroned in the place of theocracy in which man was conscious of his own smallness and frailty, and his subjection to powers stronger than himself—the creature dependent on the Creator.[3] Now the second commandment has annulled the first.

Yet in the present climate of secularism, it seemed that man was becoming increasingly depersonalised. It was not the whole man that was the object of devotion. And in spite of a constant improvement of his economic and social conditions, there was a deep sense of frustration. And it was clear that, whilst such betterment was inalienably part of man's responsibility for his neighbour, alone it was not enough. It might bring freedom from want and a reduction of physical suffering, but what of any true satisfaction and contentment of mind? Love of money now seemed to have usurped joy of craftsmanship, acquisitiveness to have become the purpose of life. But they did not satisfy. And the suicide rate remained high.[4] Thoreau even found that most

[1] E. Caird, *Evolution of Religion*, Vol. II, p. 286.
[2] *Flower of Grass*, p. 83 (Cresset Press, 1944).
[3] Semyon Frank, *God with Us*, pp. 150-51 (Cape, 1946).
[4] See e.g. the figures for Sweden where economic and social conditions are excellent.

men lived a life of quiet desperation. Be that as it may, there certainly appeared to be little meaning in the lives of the majority. For man's hunger was not only an affair of the stomach. His chief unhappiness arose from ignorance of his purpose; his chief need was to find a meaning in life. And enlightenment on either was something that could not be afforded by a humanism—however benevolent—which limited both to the striving for a Paradise within earthly confines.

St Augustine knew what he was talking about when he said of man's relation to his Creator:

' Thou hast made us for thyself, and our hearts are restless till they rest in thee.'

And I could not believe in an automatic transportation of the soul at death, however pious and ' blameless,' from an earthly to a heavenly state regardless of the soul's capacity to love God— which was eternal life. If the chief end of man is to glorify God and enjoy him for ever, a 'good' man will be, according to Plato's meaning of 'good,' one who loves God with all his heart and soul and strength, thus fulfilling the function for which he was created. It was only that kind of goodness which qualified, I thought, for eternal life. But if a man rejected God through vincible ignorance, what then?

Hell had already been out of fashion for some time when I was a child. So the idea instead of engendering fear provoked only derisive laughter. And I heard people who scarcely believed in God say comfortably that he was a God of love and so of course there could be no hell. But as I grew older I was amazed by their inconsistency. If God existed, then subconsciously they blamed him for all the misery in the world he had created. They rebelled furiously—and perhaps understandably—against the idea that he could (or would) interfere with the laws of nature in performing miracles. Yet it seemed that, at the same time, they did expect him to interfere between cause and effect, and they demanded that at death a human heart should be changed against a man's will and that he should have thrust upon him a heaven to which he neither aspired nor was in any way susceptible. And it was often those who most loudly decried any 'personality' in the divine nature who were most ready to expect that every law of cause and effect should be set aside as if by an indulgent parent. (Out and out atheists and agnostics were at least more logical than these half-believers.) I did not believe that God punished or rewarded like a human potentate. Or that there could be any morality without freedom. Therefore the whole totality of divine love could not force salvation on a man whose will was set against it. And that was why I had often thought something like Purgatory might exist, although I had been brought up to consider that papistry was the only sound argument for the existence of the devil.

Since I had come to believe that man was made in God's image, the idea had constantly recurred to me that it was just this divine spark in him which could make hell possible. But for that, could he have been made for God? And but for that it was clear that he could perish utterly and comfortably. It seemed to be that awful burden of the divine in him that made hell possible—his separation from God. For hell could be nothing else but that—man's persistence in the error of original sin: 'I am my own.'

At one time I believed that the soul could perish from inanition; that the divine spark unfed by the desire for God might flicker fitfully and then die out, allowing those without love of God to perish completely and painlessly. (And how impossible to feel the desirability of what must appear in the form of retribution at the hands of however impersonal and just a law of cause and effect, except it be a means to a greater good and not an end in itself.) But later I saw that this was where the terrible inexorability of God's love came in. It was part of the divine essence that it could not let go of any soul as long as this still had the will to choose, the potentiality to cast itself at the ever-pursuing feet with a cry, ' My God, you win.' I only hoped that, as has been said, God always wins the last trick.

We are told that everyone is free deliberately to choose this separation, to make his own hell consciously and with his eyes wide open. Hell is not God's punishment of man but man's rejection of God. Man's will was free to the end of life to choose good or evil, God or self. And if, as we are also taught, the tree must then lie as it falls, I thought that the moment of death, that moment of complete nakedness, might teach something that we had refused to learn through any other means: the meaning perhaps of the choice on the one hand of the poverty, the barren-ness, the cold, dark prison of the ego, and nothing but the ego to all eternity; and on the other, more than we ever can have 'willed or hoped or dreamed of good.'

Perhaps it would be only in that moment that one might wholeheartedly cast off the desire so often felt for a death of annihilation.

> ' How gladly would I meet
> Mortality my sentence, and be earth
> Insensible! how glad would lay me down
> As in my mother's lap! There I should rest
> and sleep secure; . . .'

There was too much I feared in the thought of survival. ' In the evening they shall examine thee on love.' I should come poorly out of that supreme test; far, far worse than some humanists who spent their time denying God and succouring his children. And then, too, there was that divine and agonising blow-lamp, the thought of which filled me with dismay; what the mystics describe as a flame burning up the baser metals, and Newman saw as the divine effulgence consuming yet quickening the soul.

But with all doctrine, how can men see other than in a glass darkly? I believed with Plato that 'a man of sense ought not to say, nor will I be too confident' that any suggestions relating to another world can be exactly true. But 'I do venture to think that something of the kind is true.' Revelation mediated through the human and the finite cannot escape the limitations inherent in a treasure which must necessarily be in earthen vessels.

Yet religion itself, as Whitehead remarks, was by no means necessarily a good.[1] And I thought William Law's declaration incontrovertible: 'When religion is in the hands of the mere natural man, he is always the worse for it; it adds a bad heat to his own dark fires and helps to inflame his four elements of selfishness, envy, pride and wrath.'[2]

This Pascal recognises in his terrible saying, 'Jamais on ne fait le mal si pleinement et si gaiement que quand on le fait par conscience.'[3]

So religion, because it has been brought into disrepute by mere 'natural man' is often dismissed as a bad thing generally. I thought it would be equally irrational to condemn science altogether because of the uses to which it has been put. But Lord Russell states that religion does no good whatever and that it is a disease resulting from fear, and a cause of inestimable misery to the human race.[4] Ideas of good, however, vary; and naturally his opinion must be largely influenced by the fact that he finds all creeds to be false or meaningless. Jung, on the contrary, maintains that organised religion has been the greatest psycho-therapeutic system the world has ever known. Moreover, he finds the source of many people's neuroses in the stifling of their religious promptings through an adolescent determination to be only

---

[1] *Religion in the Making*, p. 17 (C.U.P., 1926).
[2] *Christian Regeneration.*
[3] *Op. cit., Pensées Diverses sur la Religion.*
[4] *Why I am not a Christian*, pp. xi, 18 and 37 (Allen & Unwin, 1957).

rationally enlightened. And he has also stated that amongst all his patients of over thirty-five, the problem of each has been that of discovering a religious view of life. Every one of those patients became ill as the result of losing that which living religion gives to its followers. And none of them was completely cured who did not recapture his religious view.[1] It must, however, be added that although Jung shows a passionate concern to defend the psychological value of religion, and although he does not now believe this to lie in sublimation, all religious belief for him is only 'psychologically' true.[2]

It is still frequently said by the followers of Marx and Freud that religion is an opiate or a neurosis, but it has been observed that had Marx warned people against *using* their religion as an opiate, and had Freud shown them that what they *called* religion was actually their neurosis, both thinkers would have uttered profound though common truths. And although their original statements that religion is the opiate of the people, and that it is a neurosis may blind the superficial thinker to the real problem, the attempt at debunking religion may effect some good in shaking the 'religious' amongst us out of our complacency.[3]

Thomas Hobbes remarked that 'It is with the mysteries of our Religion as with wholesome pills for the sick, which swallowed whole have the virtue to cure; but chewed are for the most part cast up again without effect.'

I found the exact opposite to be true in my own case. Unchewed, I had been unable to swallow one single 'mystery of religion.' Whereas the constant chewing of each, both severally and together, gave me no desire to cast them up again.

The fact that the doctrines of the God-Man, the Trinity, the

---

[1] *Modern Man in Search of a Soul*, p. 264 (Routledge & Kegan Paul, 1933).
[2] See Raymond Hostie, S. J., *Religion and the Psychology of Jung*, pp. 112, 114, 116, especially, also pp. 133 ff. (Sheed & Ward, 1957).
[3] Karl Stern, *The Third Revolution*, p. 151 (Michael Joseph, 1955).

Virgin birth, and so on are not peculiar to Christianity alone, I had often advanced as an argument in its disproof. Whereas the commonness of those beliefs I now saw only serves to illustrate the essentiality of the thought behind them. They are archetypes according to Jung who tells us that such ideas were never the result of invention. In the infancy of thought, such ideas came to people before they knew how to produce thoughts. The dogma of the suffering God-Man is thought to be at least 5,000 years old and the doctrine of the Trinity, he thinks, may be even older.[1]

The picture that the doctrine of the Trinity and that of the Atonement had evoked in my mind was not unlike the one that Matthew Arnold describes:

'. . . a sort of infinitely magnified and improved Lord Shaftesbury, with a race of vile offenders to deal with, whom his natural goodness would incline him to let off, only his sense of Justice will not allow it; then a younger Lord Shaftesbury, on the scale of his father and very dear to him, who might live in grandeur and splendour if he liked, but who prefers to leave his home, to go and live among the race of offenders, and to be put to an igno-minious death, on condition that his merits shall be counted against their demerits, and that his father's goodness shall be restrained no longer from taking effect, but any offender shall be admitted to the benefit of it on simply pleading the satisfaction made by the son;—and then, finally, a third Lord Shaftesbury still on the same high scale, who keeps very much in the background, and works in a very occult manner, but very efficaciously nevertheless, and who is busy in applying everywhere the benefits of the son's satisfaction and the father's goodness.'[2]

[1] Jung, *Psychology and Religion*, pp. 56-7.
[2] *Literature and Dogma* (1873) pp. 18-19.

It was almost impossible not to be influenced by 'picture-thinking.' The doctrine of the Trinity was incomprehensible to the human reason. And why should I be surprised that the nature of God should be a mystery to my finite mind? It was perhaps a measure of my arrogance that I had tended actively to disbelieve any revelation that I could not understand. I was personally affronted that the Church should have put forth anything so absurd and unacceptable to human reason. Three persons with one nature, distinct but not separate? 'A likely story.' Each possessing the whole Godhead? 'Impossible.' And so on. But now I no longer expected to understand.

It has been said that on a unitarian conception of God it is impossible that brotherhood should be a reflection of God's nature. But that if it was a triune God who created us in his own image, man might, according to his limited capacity, imitate in his relationship with other men, that divine fellowship of the Blessed Trinity.[1]

Hegel has said:

' The Trinity has been reduced to a relation of Father, Son and Spirit and this is a childlike relation, a childlike natural form. The Understanding has no category, no relation which in point of suitability for expressing the truth can be compared with this. At the same time it must be understood that it is merely pictorial, and that Spirit does not actually enter into a relation of this kind'.[2]

For Hegel, as we saw, the divine self-activity is adequately stated only in the doctrine of the Blessed Trinity. He finds Love to be the expression of the eternally triune nature of God with its necessity to create. And in God's relation to humanity Hegel sees an essential predisposition to Incarnation, a propensity which becomes actualised in Jesus Christ.

[1] The Rev. H. A. Williams, in a University Sermon, Cambridge.
[2] *Op. cit.*, Vol. III, p. 25.

Just as the God of Aristotle could have only himself as object of thought, since nothing else could be adequate; so the God who lives a life of infinite love loves himself infinitely. But here is no egoism. In the triune God there is infinite love between three who are infinite. Love infinitely given and infinitely returned cannot be grasped by man.

4. *At-one-ment*

> 'That they all may be one; as thou, Father,
> art in me, and I in thee, that they also may
> be one in us:'
>
> ST JOHN XVII, 21

> 'So we, being many, are one body in
> Christ, and every one members one of
> another.'
>
> *Epistle to the Romans*, XII, 5

The doctrine of the Atonement was declared by St Anselm to be ultimately unfathomable. I could therefore only hope to understand something of the part in it which man was called upon to play.

C. S. Lewis has said that the 'Substitution' of the Anselmian doctrine of the Atonement cannot be regarded as a mere legal figure of speech—a fiction that we cannot fit into what we believe to be the universal process—but that it is indeed the supreme example of such process. 'He saved others, himself he cannot save' is the perfect definition of the condition which prevails in the Kingdom. All salvation is, of necessity, always and everywhere, vicarious.[1]

The vicariousness of Christ's atonement, I now saw, lay in his complete innocence of sin. Only one who was not already involved in sin could voluntarily take upon himself its consequences. It was the difference between freedom and necessity. We were all in it anyway, necessarily; up to the neck in sin and

[1] *Arthurian Torso*, p. 123 (Cumberlege, O.U.P., 1948).

debt. And we remained in it I was convinced, in the sense that neither responsibility nor need for co-operation was removed. Christ made our sharing in the atonement not only possible but our very means of life. Salvation is not thrust upon men apathetic and idle and unwilling to be changed.

The theory of mystical substitution, of co-inherence, about which C. S. Lewis and Charles Williams have written so eloquently I found to be integral to the doctrines of the Incarnation and of the Atonement.

According to Charles Williams the bearing of one another's burdens can and should be far more literally true than is generally believed possible. 'Under God' any two souls can make such a pact; the one offering to take on the burden of grief or anxiety, the other agreeing to the transferring of the burden. Such exchanges, he held, could be made even without mutual consent; we can benefit without our knowledge much as when our god-parents undertake for us at our baptism. And substitution knows no limits by Time in the web of co-inherence.

This co-inherence is shown forth first in the Blessed Trinity. Thence it descends into man created in the divine image. Lost by him at the Fall it was the substitution of Christ which restored it to man.

'At the hand of every man's brother will I require the life of man,' proclaims a law of responsibility, and creates the web of co-inherence. It is in acts of substitution that we are to love one another. To take over the burdens of another is to fulfil the commandment of Christ: 'Deny the self, take up the Cross, follow me.' And yet 'My yoke is easy and my burden is light.' It is in the lifting of the cross that it is no longer a burden. Burdens become light when they are exchanged. But no such exchange is possible where there exist any hatred, grudge, jealousy, greed or pride; forgiveness of sins by those involved must be complete.[1]

[1] See Charles Williams, *He Came Down from Heaven*, pp. 114-133 where the subject is discussed (Heineman, 1938).

During recent years I had become increasingly convinced of the truth that we are in fact members one of another. And this truth I found confirmed by much that is recounted in *The Sixth Sense*. The research work, for instance, of the radio-engineer G. N. M. Tyrrell (as that of Whately Carington) led him to infer that at a subconscious level there is some sort of immediate linkage between men. This is borne out by Jung's discovery in the human subconscious of like symbols, throughout the ages and all over the world.[1] (This linkage fits in too with all I had read of Hindu philosophy.) And in Professor Gardner Murphy's view, instances of ESP even suggest that there is at some deep plane a lasting capacity in men to be *en rapport* with the whole of time and space as Bergson has postulated. And it is the relationship between persons which Professor Murphy suggests is the most active agent in the piercing through to our consciousness of ESP. The reason he gives for these break-throughs remaining so rare is that we are—especially in modern times and in the western world—so insulated psychologically from one another. The frequency and ease with which an individual appears to get flashes of ESP have been noticed to be in proportion as he feels himself not to be sharply divided from his fellow-beings. And he suggests that this apparent division may be merely a matter of biological organisation.[2]

Another growing conviction of mine was of the immensity of the power of thought. According to Bergson the purpose of the threshold of consciousness is to act like a lid in keeping out all mental images which are not required by the thinker's immediate concerns at any particular moment. But Professor Habberley Price thinks that it is not by our own little lids alone that the multitudinous ferment of ideas struggling for admission into consciousness, is held at bay. It is by their opposites that most

[1] Rosalind Heywood, *op. cit.*, p. 187.
[2] *Ibid.*, pp. 196-7.

ideas are neutralised. And this explains how telepathy can be discouraged by mutual inhibitions, and even prevented by scepticism.

Price suggests that thought may be a very dangerous matter. For he finds that anything thought of has some inclination to come about in fact. And if it does not, that this is due to opposing thoughts which cancel it out.[1]

All this may seem to have been a digression from the subject of mystical substitution. But actually I found it to have the strongest bearing on inter-subjectivity. And the belief both that we are not isolated individuals however much we may appear to be, and that thought is the most powerful force in the world psychologically, were the two factors which gave me some clue as to the meaning and value of prayer.

I knew that some people had no need to puzzle themselves over this. For them the nature of prayer demanded no clarification. But it was only for a short period of my life that I had been able to pray spontaneously and unreflectingly as if God were no more than a kindly Santa Claus whose main occupation was dealing with requests as to how the various stockings were to be filled.

My idea of prayer had not been entirely separable from the involuntary conception of God as a stingy and stubborn deity surrounded by bags of good things with which he was loth to part. But now I saw it not as the persuading of a hard-hearted potentate to relinquish his grasp on all those spiritual riches he was so inexplicably withholding from the men he was reputed to love, but as a means of unblocking all those interstices which men had closed up and through which alone grace could reach them—a sort of removal of obstructions in the plumbing systems of men's spiritual natures in order that grace might freely flow. In a less prosaic metaphor, St Augustine has told us the same thing; that God is everlastingly wanting to give us everything

[1] *Ibid.*, pp. 218-19.

231

that is good, but that our hands are always so full that there is nowhere to put anything.

Simone Weil has said that grace enters only where there is a void. She has warned us of the dangers of filling up in our being the cracks and interstices through which grace might come.[1] As we become aware of a void within ourselves, we try to fill it with anything which disguises for us its existence. By our escape-systems we render ourselves safe from God, hermetically-sealed against the infiltration of divine grace.

But this waiting empty handed, a patient standing in the void, I knew to be one of the most difficult attitudes in the world.

Yet now I knew, too, that there was an immediate linkage between men at some subconscious level and that thought had the power to effect a change for good—or evil—I believed that prayer was of paramount importance; it was the strongest force against evil that was accessible to men. I no longer thought of the Contemplative Orders as wasting their time. They were a strength for good, their monasteries power-houses of prayer. And Charles Williams seemed to be right in saying that all prayer for individuals must be filled with the intention of substituted love. It might be easy to dismiss the theory as a sentimental fancy —indeed, that is the stock dismissal for every poetic insight not to our taste—but not so easy perhaps to shuffle out of our responsibilities on the Day of Judgment, whatever that might mean. 'And in the evening they will examine thee on love.' And, 'At the hand of everyman's brother will I require the life of man.'

The taking on vicariously of the mental anguish, grief and sufferings, and even of the physical pains of others, and to suffer in their place has been practised, I read, by several of the Saints. But Charles Williams, who I believe spoke from experience, has warned that burdens are not to be undertaken recklessly.

[1] *Gravity and Grace*, pp. 10-11 (Routledge & Kegan Paul, 1952). See also E. W. F. Tomlin, *Simone Weil*, p. 46 (Bowes & Bowes, 1954) and Simone Weil, *Notebooks*, Vol. I, pp. 145, 147, 149, 198-9, 227, etc.

Bernanos has said that everything is grace, but that this can be uttered with perfect integrity only by a saint.[1] It cannot be understood on a monadist conception, but only on the plane of intersubjectivity. And Gabriel Marcel tells us that the greater the assertion by the ego of its own centricity in the organisation of consciousness, the greater the attenuation of the closeness of substance of being. And, conversely, the greater the realisation by the ego that its position is essentially relative, the greater the sense of this density. Our concern with being depends upon the degree of distinctness of consciousness we have of that unity which attaches us to our fellow creatures. He stresses intersubjectivity in his desire to accentuate the reality of what is already sensed: a community which has its roots in ontology. Human relations would otherwise be incomprehensible or would necessarily have to be regarded as purely mythical.[2]

Mystical substitution, co-inherence, intersubjectivity are subsumed in the doctrine of the Communion of Saints. We are told in 1 Corinthians XII, 26, that if one member suffer, all members suffer; if one member glory, all members glory. It was St Paul's teaching that the Saints, besides having individual functions, are bound together in a community of life whose purpose is charity in the truest sense; living and active in the service of all members through intercession and vicarious expiation.

And bound up with this doctrine is the much-abused and hence much-misunderstood doctrine of Indulgences, similar to the idea of *Parivarta* in *Mahayana* Buddhism, fundamentally only an extension of the theories of substitution and co-inherence to include conditions that are said to operate beyond this world.[3]

[1] *Le Journal d'un Curé de Campagne.*
[2] Gabriel Marcel, *The Mystery of Being*, Vol. II, pp. 16-17.
[3] That this is one of the dogmas that Swift, in the *Tale of a Tub* called 'Points tagged with silver'—those doctrines that promote the greatness and the wealth of the Church,' is not to be denied. But no amount of abuse can effect the truth of a doctrine, and as Edwyn Bevan declared, use is not to be condemned because of such abuse. (*Christianity*, p. 164, Home University Library, Thornton Butterworth, 1932.)

The chief difficulty in believing in the Communion of Saints arose naturally, I thought, from a lack of belief both in our inter-subjectivity and in immortality. The Saints seemed so far away and so long ago. The mind boggles at the thought that they are far more alive than anyone on earth. But if we believe in immortality as inevitable for the true lover of God, what reason remains for disbelieving St Paul? And it was the value of vicariousness in prayer, I thought, which gave force to the invocation of the Saints. We are told by the early Fathers that grace flows more readily into a soul through the prayers of others than through that soul's own attempts. It is yet another instance of ' He saved others; himself he cannot save.'

It was clear, however, that whatever form at-one-ment took it was a responsibility the shirking of which would be a complete rejection of salvation. But how hard and contrary to my fallen nature I found it to live actively as 'members one of another,' in the realisation that 'at the hand of everyman's brother will I require the life of man.' How heavy the burden of prayer for others (never quite free from my childhood's association with the effort of cleaning my teeth in the daily routine). Harder still to practise that absorption of evil demonstrated by Christ: the refusal to let evil bring out answering evil, absorbing it by the spirit within instead of hurling abroad retaliatory evil; that evil which can never die until it is so absorbed and prevented from breeding. That was a form of at-one-ment: to stop the rot of sin by turning every evil into an occasion for love. Hence one of the values of humility. Pride justifies the man of spirit (as opposed to spiritual man) in 'just' retribution.

At-one-ment demanded too, it seemed, the sharing of the guilt and sin of the world, accepting it, admitting ' There but for the grace of God go I.' And repentance, I had learned, was a passionate endeavour to know all things after the manner of the Kingdom,[1] to see them *sub specie aeternitatis*. But oh! this pen

[1] Charles Williams, *op. cit.*, p. 60.

and paper piety; how easy to write, yet how impossibly hard to 'subdue the least sin in myself.'[1] (Pascal has a word for it: 'Diseur de bons mots, mauvais caractère.') And as Professor Dodd reminds us, it needs no great imagination to see oneself in the role of Pilate, Caiaphas, the Pharisees, the mob, the cowardly disciples, the traitor Judas.[2]

But he adds that the recognition of evil becomes the occasion for some new good. The forgiveness of sins he sees as the renewing power of God, not only a device for easement of conscience but a creative act which transforms and uses every failure in a new growth.[3]

---

[1] Thomas Fuller, *Good Thoughts in Bad Times.*   [2] *Op. cit.*, p. 137.
[3] *Ibid.*, p. 138.

5. The Resurrection

'Why seek ye the living among the dead?'
                    ST LUKE XXIV, 5

'O fools, and slow of heart to believe . . .'
                    ST LUKE XXIV, 25

'. . . they have taken away my Lord, and
I know not where they have laid him.
And . . . she turned . . . and saw Jesus
standing, and knew not that it was Jesus.
. . . She, supposing him to be the gardener . . .
Jesus saith unto her, Mary. She turned
herself, and saith unto him, Rabboni;'
                    ST JOHN XXI, 13-16

It has been said that the certainty which the apostles experienced concerning Christ's Resurrection is a verifiable fact historically; but that he did rise from the dead cannot be in the same way historically verifiable.[1] And that although evidence and history are of the greatest importance, alone they could not as St John insists, reveal God or be intelligible of themselves. We need the enabling power of the Spirit in order to penetrate to the meaning of both.[2] I was reminded of Christ's saying, 'Flesh and blood have not revealed it unto thee, but my Father which is in heaven.'

Further, concerning the Resurrection, I had read that

'Without a corresponding power of spiritual discernment

[1] From a Sermon by the Rev. J. Sanders, Peterhouse, Cambridge, 1952.
[2] A. M. Ramsey, *The Resurrection of Christ*, p. 15 (Bles, 1945).

236

there could be no testimony to its truth. The world could
not see Christ, and Christ could not (there is a divine impossibility) show himself to the world. To have proved by
incontestable evidence that Christ rose again as Lazarus
rose again would have been not to confirm our faith but to
destroy it irretrievably.'[1]

I knew, too, that for the Christian there could be no escape
from that tension which exists between history and that which is
beyond history. (The strength of Christianity, it was said, lies
within that very tension.)[2] No decisive proof of the Resurrection
could ever be advanced by which man would be obliged to
believe by a scientific necessity outside himself. He is left perfectly
free to believe or to disbelieve in it on other grounds, chiefly the
nature of Christ's person. Yet certain facts of historical nature
must remain unexplained unless the Resurrection is accepted;
whilst various historical testimonies, it has been shown, all build
up its overwhelming probability.[3] And that was as far as one
could go in the way of 'evidence' I was persuaded.

But we are reminded that in the Gospel, we have a synthesis
of what is historical and supernatural, temporal and eternal, at the
heart of which is a Person.[4] Christ, being the God-Man, the
synthesis was possible only in him. I recognised, too, that the
risen Christ was seen only by believers, and I thought that, as has
been suggested, the Resurrection appearances were a matter of
revelation.[5]

I remembered my original view of revelation as a useful
stratagem of the Church to impose unlikely truths upon the
credulous minds of human beings too lazy and apathetic to think

[1] F. Westcott, *The Revelation of the Risen Lord*, pp. 11-12 (Macmillan, 1881).
[2] A. M. Ramsey, *op. cit.*, p. 16.   [3] *Ibid.*, p. 36.
[4] E. G. Selwyn, *The Resurrection*, in *Essays Catholic and Critical*, p. 281
(S.P.C.K., 1950).
[5] See Donald M. Mackinnon, *The Resurrection*, in *The Listener*, April 16,
1953.

for themselves. But I had trudged many weary miles since then on my own aching feet, to a point where I now saw it as the unblocking of a void that man had filled with any old junk that would keep out the draught. It was only when the void was open that light could penetrate. The light, I thought, shone always, so that it was not possible to blame God for not switching it on more often.

So with the Resurrection, it was the mind made susceptible by grace and faith that alone could see. As Hegel had said

'The Resurrection is something which thus essentially belongs to faith. After his resurrection Christ appeared only to his friends. This is not outward history for unbelief, but on the contrary, this appearing of Christ is for faith only.'[1]

Even in my unbelieving days I had found it impossible to be entirely convinced that the Resurrection appearances could be accounted for as being merely hallucinatory and, in the case of the five hundred witnesses, due to mass hysteria. I did not think somehow that a world-wide religion which had survived for 2000 years could be founded on a series of delusions. For I saw that it was the Resurrection which constituted the turning point in the life of Christianity. Men who could not only break faith with and desert their Master at the time of his greatest human need, but who were utterly deflated by the apparent failure of his mission—these men, only a few weeks later went out into the world fearless and convinced that Christ yet lived. In that belief these one-time cowards were prepared to die.

And much as I would have liked then to be able to account for the empty tomb by trusting the argument that Christ's body had rolled away into some cleft in the rock, I could not overlook the fact that it was in the interest of the Jews to produce the body and scotch the legend of a risen Christ. They would hardly have

[1] *Op. cit.*, Vol. III, pp. 91-2

neglected to search every fissure in the rock tomb to that end. And it seemed to me even weaker to suggest that the Apostles had removed the body and invented a legend. Feeble and often of a monumental stupidity they appeared to be but hardly capable of guile.

And many disbelievers must share these doubts since they find it necessary now to question also the empty tomb, in spite of the fact that even Strauss saw in the finding of this those facts about the Resurrection which are the least contestable.[1] But if such doubters think that the whole story was a legend invented by the Apostles, there is one other thing they will have to explain away. As Guitton has shown, to anyone meditating such an invention, it would be immediately obvious that the one event that must be recounted would be the coming forth of Christ from the tomb. Yet in the official stories of the Resurrection such an account is nowhere to be found.[2]

For Guitton, the Resurrection demands of faith a belief not in Christ's overcoming of the laws of biology, so much as in the triumph of a new supernatural life and its expansion. He says that the Resurrection can be viewed either as a return to normal life (which he finds unacceptable) or as a participation in the divine life. This raises the question of the difference between a terrestrial and a glorious body.[3]

St Paul conceived of Christ's risen body as a spiritual one which was not subject to the limitations of a material one. He says ' flesh and blood cannot inherit the Kingdom of God.' And Dean Selwyn thinks that there is reasonable ground for considering that this body was not physical in the ordinary sense of possessing metrical properties and therefore being perceptible to everyone. A glorified or spiritualised body would belong to a different order from what we call 'natural.' The supernatural or extra-cosmic body could not be subject to natural conditions of space and time. What is involved in such a transmutation

[1] See J. Guitton, *op. cit.*, p. 197.   [2] *Ibid.*, pp. 197-8.   [3] *Ibid.*, p. 127.

removing it from the category of things ruled by laws of natural science, place it in a relation to experience which has no parallel. We are ignorant of the potentialities of matter ingested by the Spirit of God, though it is not hard to believe that such would place it beyond the powers of corruption.[1] That for me was the only satisfactory attitude to the Resurrection.

And in the bearing it has upon the nature of men's immortality, Guitton reminds us of St Paul's urging his readers that, rather than seeking to be rid of the body, we should seek to clothe ourselves anew in order that the mortal within us may be ingested by life. Guitton sees the question as one of being what we are in a higher manner, with nothing annihilated but rather with all things 'super-being' and in a manner recreated through sublimation.[2] For this sublimation, he suggests, is a mutation without ablation: *vita mutatur non tollitur*. Indeed, he adds, the permanence of a self is demanded if there are to be any servants' wages; for without a memory how can a man be judged? And Guitton finds it difficult to see what, apart from Bergson's theory of 'pure memory,' memory could be without a sublimation of the body.[3]

According to St Thomas Aquinas the soul is not perfect without the body; thus resurrection is no mere superfluous extra. Could a soul divorced from its means of expression enjoy any life at all? Guitton remarks that death appears to rob us not of the soul and the mind which we believe are imperishable, but of their language and their sustaining power.[4]

How much of the self survived, or even what was this self— the 'soul' in Plato, the 'divine reason' in Aristotle, the 'mind' in Spinoza, the 'higher self' in Jung—it seemed useless to speculate. But it appeared reasonable to suppose that it could hardly exist unchanged in such a completely different environment; and it

[1] *Op. cit.*, p. 319. And it appears that ' Thou shalt not suffer thy Holy One to see corruption ' may be true at another level if one can believe the well-attested evidence for the incorrupt state in which many bodies of Saints have been found.
[2] *Op. cit.*, p. 134.   [3] *Ibid.*, p. 139.   [4] *Ibid.*, p. 140.

might well be those who had lived most closely and actively with the idea that we are members one of another whose sublimation might be the least hard to accomplish. For, as Charles Williams tells us, we shall be clothed with grace by one and all: never by the self. There will be no success of our own.[1]

> ' The glory which thou gavest me I have given them;
>   that they may be one, even as we are one: I in them,
>   and thou in me, that they may be made perfect in one.'

---

[1] *Op. cit.*, p. 132.

6. *The Church*

' The Church stands in darkness, in this time
of her pilgrimage and must lament under
many miseries.'

ST AUGUSTINE

Aldous Huxley has compared Church membership with travelling
on a vast luxury liner bound either for the wrong harbour or,
worse, for perdition. The implication 'within the Church no
salvation' is a nice *quid pro quo*. And although I knew that this
told me a good deal more about Mr. Huxley than it did about
the Church, my antipathy to the latter was so great that when I
saw the way things were going with me, I debated whether I
could try to become a Christian in isolation, dissociating myself
from any ecclesiastical body.

In my simple ignorance I had always thought that the Bible
had preceded this community, and that one sad day some villain
had said, 'Let's invent a Church.' This hideous invention by
St Paul and his accomplices I had seen as a distorting veil over the
simple beauty of primitive Christianity. And what, anyway, was
the point of a community when religion, I thought, was a purely
private and individual affair between a man and his Maker?

But Newman, I read, has said of this early Christian community:

' In assembling for religious purposes, Christians were
breaking a solemn law. This was a very strong act on the
part of disciples of the great Apostle who had enjoined

242

obedience to powers that be. Time after time they resisted the authority of the magistrate. Justification of such disobedience lies simply in the necessity of obeying the higher authority of some divine law; but if Christianity were in its essence only private and personal . . . there was no necessity of their meeting together at all . . . Gibbon says "it was impossible for Christians to omit the example of public worship." [1]

It seemed that it was not through isolated individualism that grace was primarily to flow, that sanctification was not directed primarily to a numberless multitude of souls in isolation, but rather through this *Ecclesia* (that which is summoned or called).

Could this, I wondered, be the meaning underlying the incredible statement 'Outside the Church no grace,' so palpably untrue without reference to such intersubjectivity? Where once I had seen only another example of the Church's narrow bigotry, I now saw that the paramount importance of the belief that we are members one of another did argue that salvation should not be through isolated individualism. We are to be saved only through this co-inherence in Christ's body. And in spite of its papal condemnation[2] there was a sense, I thought, in which Christian mutual dependence gave the proposition cogency. That meant for me the reluctant admission that an attempt to live a life of Christian worship in isolation from my fellow-Christians would be a betrayal of my most fundamental convictions. Since our very salvation depended on the love of our neighbour (under God) and on the overcoming of the confining bonds of the ego, I ought not to have been so surprised and horrified that a com-

[1] *Essay on the Development of Christian Doctrine*, pp. 235-6 (Pickering, 1878).
[2] We are told that the Jansenists in the seventeenth century followed St Augustine in holding that ' Outside the Church there is no grace'; but that against this was Rome. Clement XI expressly condemned this proposition in 1713. See Karl Adam, *The Spirit of Catholicism*, p. 191 (Sheed & Ward, 1934).

munity life should have been ordained as a means of grace. But I was utterly dismayed by the price I should have to pay for consistency. And because I felt no need for the Church, I longed to believe I had none; that I was immune from either need or duty.

I thought it was largely due to original sin that most people like myself disliked the idea of Church membership so much. At the Fall, Origen has said, the one nature was shattered into innumerable particles. It brought separation, contradiction into that nature. And the whole purpose of our redemption was one of restoration: of the unity of man with God and of the unity amongst men themselves. At long last I had come to see such a recovery as the whole purpose and meaning of life. But I had grown to prize and love my separateness; to be an autonomous part as an end in itself seemed infinitely more pleasant than being a member subject to a greater whole; and any suggestion that I should surpass my individuality by acting as one of a body, in living as one of a community, produced in me a strong feeling of antagonism and nausea. Although I could see Church membership as the obvious means of seeking to repair the damage done at the Fall—and in this sense I did believe that salvation from the self could be effected through the Church—I still longed to be the cat that walked alone. But even if I could refuse to take my part as a member of the *Ecclesia*, rejecting responsibility to other members in a corporate life of worship and prayer, was I willing to forgo the grace not only flowing through the sacraments but also arising from this unity as a body? For St Augustine says, 'If you have unity, whatever in it is another's is at the same time yours.'[1] And St Francis of Sales speaks of God having ordained that any worship or prayer undertaken in common is to be preferred to every kind of individual action.[2] ('When two or

[1] See Henri de Lubac, S. J., *Catholicism*, pp. 120 and 122 (Burns, Oates, 1950).
[2] *Introduction to the Devout Life*, p. 97 (Burns, Oates, 1948).

three are gathered together in my Name, there am I in the midst of them.')

And yet Pope Pius XI declared that men were not made for the Church, but the Church made for men.[1] We have been told, too, that we must neither exaggerate nor minimise the importance of our outward loyalty to the visible Church. It is to be no end in itself with any value apart from union with Christ in fellowship with other Christians. But equally there can be no complete interior union with the Head which does not result in exterior loyalty to, and participation in, the life of the Body.[2] For we are called to *become* a *Church*.[3] And I now saw it as mere exclusiveness that I should wish for special treatment, a private line by which grace might reach me in snug isolation.

Outward loyalty to such a body, however, was for me a duty to be performed against the very grain of my fallen nature. But my dislike of the Church, I found, was not due to all its iniquities: the medieval Inquisition, witch trials, persecutions and other abominations. Nor was it for any of the corruptions from which arose its responsibility in the great schism at the time of the Reformation and for which it had already been severely punished by the loss of most valuable elements. I did not expect the Church militant to be without sin since it was made up of ordinary mortals and was not a community that had already achieved salvation. Neither did I find it surprising that, as was constantly declared, it had failed. How could the Church militant ever be anything but a failure? Moreover, it was not possible, I thought, to dissociate oneself entirely from its iniquities and failures any more than from the common frailties of mankind in general. Nor did I find it possible to hate anyone or any body for crimes that were admitted and repented of, and, moreover, being atoned for

[1] *Allocution to the Lenten Preachers of Rome*, 1927. Quoted by H. de Lubac *op. cit.*, p. 26.

[2] Victor White, O.P., *God the Unknown*, pp. 181-2 (Harvill Press, 1956).

[3] *Ibid.*, p. 181. Quoted as J. Middleton Murry's idea from his *Price of Leadership*.

perhaps in some degree. The example of Cardinal Pole at the Council of Trent in 1545 when he confessed ' It is our ambition, our avarice, our cupidity, which have brought these evils upon the Kingdom of God,' is followed by the Catholic theologian, Karl Adam, in his admission of the justification for the Protestant motives. And also by Abbé Couturier in his appeal to priests in France to remember especially on St Bartholomew's Day, not only the massacre but the injustice that followed the revocation of the Edict of Nantes.

But much more significant than these isolated examples of attempts to accept responsibility and to atone for past crimes, is the fact to which Professor Dodd has called attention. He shows how the Church in our time is making history by being in many countries the only voice to uphold certain ultimate principles, by being the sole efficacious guardian of values. Anyone minimising this claim would but advertise his ignorance, he says, adding that to whatever depths it may sink, the Church yet carries the indelible signs of its origin.[1]

Not as a one-time sink of iniquity, then, did I dislike the Church. Nor was I alarmed by its narrow intolerance in matters of doctrine. For, as the late Archbishop Temple pointed out, the chief commission of the Church is to preserve and transmit true doctrine in order to elicit saving faith.[2] And now that I believed in the paramount importance of the truths behind the bare dogmas I wondered how saving faith was to be elicited without this evidence of God's love for man. Liberalism in matters of doctrine could arise from apathy and indifference, and a worship of broadmindedness was often the one requisite in matters of religion of those who had themselves no depth of conviction. Why should heresy be tolerated when it necessarily threw away

[1] *Op. cit.*, p. 141. By *Church* he understands 'the whole congregation of Christian people dispersed throughout the world.' (In this light it is easy to see our own responsibility in, and for, the Church.)

[2] *Readings in St John*, pp. 37-8 (Macmillan, 1939).

the baby with the bath water?—water, it must be admitted, that men's dirty hands had rendered so turbid that the baby was practically invisible. It was only fresh water and cleaner hands that were needed. But these, I believed with Santayana, could not be provided by modernism and the secularisation of the Church. For with them everything would be swept down the drain—the Incarnation first of all—until nothing remained and the unconditional itself, as Kierkegaard said, would be thrust out of the world; the truth debased to make it palatable to man.

What grudge, then, had I against the Church? Chiefly, I found this to be for her unenlightened popular propaganda, for her uninspiring teaching of doctrine, for her failure to emphasise the paramount importance of the truths behind these dogmas. I think that the intensity of my feeling about this derived from the thought that as I might so easily have missed these truths altogether had I not embarked on a voyage of discovery, others were probably being deprived of them quite unconsciously. And to me these truths were of such a nature as to reorientate men's minds; they were the light of life. It was not that I denied the truth of most of what was preached at its surface level; but, convinced that there was an almost infinite number of layers to every religious truth, I resented concentration on the most superficial and least fruitful plane. Moreover, I knew that unintelligent propaganda deterred many from accepting Christianity, often gifted and serious people who would have been, as Christians, no nuts without kernels. How true that those who expound Christianity so often betray it!—destroy it for others.

And to accord a central position to the peripheral as in the development of Mariology into Mariolatry was to detract from the pre-eminence of the cardinal doctrines (and how could anyone dare to say that the later accretions to Catholic dogma were of equal importance with the doctrines of the Incarnation, the Atonement, the Resurrection?) True, Mariology in some pure and simple form was necessary as a second line of defence for the doctrine of the Incarnation—the essence of divine love. But Mariolatry appeared to me as impure and complex and fundamentally an emotional self-indulgence. And it has been said that for over six hundred years theology has been steadily losing its battle with the Catholic folk-mind which by gradual steps is influencing the Church to admit the divinity of the Virgin Mary.[1] Indeed, Jung welcomed the proclamation of the Dogma of the Assumption as being the most momentous religious event since the Reformation,[2] and he criticises severely not only those who see in it nothing more than papal arbitrariness, but those who are content to accept a purely 'man's religion' devoid of metaphysical representation of woman.[3] But I believed the whole significance of the doctrine lay in its being a sign of the redemption of the flesh. The body that had known nothing but obedience to the divine Will was incorruptible. The flesh that through Eve's disobedience had fallen into a state of mere nature, was restored to its preternatural state in the perfect obedience of Mary. Her glorification might well be the result of an emergence of an archetype into consciousness,[4] but when importance is attached to either apart from the inner meaning of the doctrine, it seemed only too possible that the Catholic folk-mind might get alarmingly out of hand. And it has already been noted that many invocations of the Virgin imply the shattering suggestion that she alone is the essence of mercy whilst Christ is the severe Judge, less merciful.[5]

But it was not only Mariolatry that I disliked. There were also the Princes of the Church. Although I knew that they were by no means as rich as their silken raiment proclaimed, I hated their

---

[1] Alan Watts, *Myth and Ritual in Christianity*, p. 110 (Thames & Hudson, 1953).

[2] *Answer to Job*, p. 169 (Routledge & Kegan Paul, 1954).   [3] *Ibid.*, p. 174.

[4] See Raymond Hostie, S. J., *Religion and the Psychology of Jung*, pp. 198-210, for a discussion of Jung's idea of Quaternity (Sheed & Ward, 1957).

[5] Yves Congar, O.P., *Christ, Marie et L'Eglise*, p. 84 (Desclée de Brouwer, 1952).

pomps and vanities when the Son of Man had not where to lay his head.

I disliked, too, the Church's general attitude to the question of belief and doubt. It seemed to prefer the attitude of mind which was lazy and incurious and to which belief was nothing more vital than a habit, to one which insisted on asking every conceivable question and feeling every pronouncement of authority upon the pulses before the mind could make a truth its own. Of course there were notable exceptions: Pope Gregory the Great who observed that he derived less benefit from the faith of Mary Magdalen than he did from the doubt of St Thomas Didymus; and St Augustine who also found that these doubts did better service to future believers than did the firm confidence of the other Apostles. And I had even heard of an enlightened parish priest who had actually hoped for some small doubt amongst his flock as evidence that it ever reflected at all. (But No! everything was so safe, so smug—and so *dead*.) The truth was no good, I thought, unless it gave us life, and, as Christ intended, that more abundantly. And if questionings could further stir an awakening consciousness, then the more there were the better. It seemed that it was often in these minds which had achieved it by way of doubt that belief shone most brightly; for instance, in the case of Dostoevsky who said that it was in no childlike simplicity that he believed in Christ, but that his cry of adoration had come from the crucible of doubt.

Simone Weil has spoken of a purifying kind of atheism, saying that where we are confronted with a choice between faith streaked with scepticism, and scepticism streaked with faith, there may be more integrity in accepting the latter with all its anguish, than in seizing on the former and feigning that the scepticism is a deviation. We have to acknowledge our native scepticism which is our intellectual affliction, as we accept other afflictions in life, as a kind of necessity. It is through this scepticism that belief must percolate. And it is quite wrong to think that scepticism can be permanently annulled by an uprush of emotion.[1] The void must not be filled prematurely with belief. There must be an *attente*, a standing in the void, in order that grace may find us.

I had heard it shrewdly remarked by a Catholic that since the Reformation the Church has no longer trusted God—the God of Truth. Its policy became dictated by fear. What else could have given birth to such a monstrosity as *the Index*? Everything was to be made safe for the flock. But it is a law of this life that nothing can be made safe, whether it is man's happiness or his faith, and that all attempts to achieve safety by dodging everything that might threaten it only results in an impoverishment of whatever it is he is seeking to safeguard. Of what value would a faith be that could be preserved solely by a perpetual wearing of blinkers? The Church fed its members with a spoon and delighted in those who developed intellectual rickets. And its attempt to keep these childishly foolish brought the Church into deserved disrepute, and made its members children of darkness when they might have become children of light.

As to Roman legalism in the Church, it was better I thought to laugh at it than to be annoyed; for it certainly was laughable that it should seem necessary to specify the exact bargain that was being offered to anyone anxious to share in the expiation of sins of those in Purgatory. I believed that such intersubjectivity operated between this world and the next just as it did in this earthly sphere. But that particularisation should be introduced into so sublime a truth was to give to the belief an appearance of having feet of clay. Why did the Church have to spoil everything?

And in its worship I found there was too much opportunity for pious formalism, too much dragooning that made the yoke difficult and the burden heavy; too much insistence on piddling detail, too much talk of mortal sin connected with rules and regulations rather than with lack of charity. It seemed that the

[1] See E. W. F. Tomlin, *Simone Weil*, p. 60.

Church had complicated religious life for the Christian much as the Scribes and Pharisees had for the Jew; that it was repeating those very mistakes that Christ had spoken against.

Yet who appointed me judge in Israel? I was not unmindful of that question though quite unabashed by it. That there were blemishes in the Church was part of the difficulty of containing treasure in earthen vessels. But to blind oneself to the earth adhering to the truth was to love the Church more than the treasure. I believed with Coleridge that 'he who begins by loving Christianity better than truth, will proceed by loving his own sect or Church better than Christianity, and end in loving himself better than all '—especially his mental repose, I thought. To believe otherwise was to give force to Huxley's suggestion that the luxury liner can land one at the wrong harbour, or even in perdition.

Truly, there was a good deal on the Church's table that I could not stomach. Some I was bound to swallow—like the set-up of the Church. But in other things I saw that—as Fr. Tyrrell had pointed out—the catering was designed so that there should be something to suit all tastes and that one was not obliged to eat everything on the table. Von Hügel, however, warns us that we should not hug our fastidiousness, making it a matter of self-congratulation. (That might be my danger.) And it has been observed that men who are sufficiently humble to endure the pains and paradoxes of the earthly Church visible truly know the heavenly Church invisible.[1]

Maybe I was not humble enough to endure the paradoxes inevitable to the expression of the infinite by means of the finite. But in spite of that I did realise the necessity of some authority if the Church were to fulfil her obligations. The Bible, for instance, has been called the book where everyone finds what he wishes to find. And I thought Jung right in deploring the Protestant intensification of its authority as a substitute for Church authority,

---

[1] A. M. Ramsey, *op. cit.*, p. 98.

for as he observes some biblical texts are capable of many different interpretations.[1] (I thought of the Eunuch's reply to Philip, 'How can I [understand] except some man guide me?') And Professor Dodd tells us that at the Reformation things went further than was intended, and an absolute authority was claimed for the whole Bible exposed to the vagaries of private interpretation, in place of the absolute authority of the Church.[2]

The work of the Councils which resulted in this absolute authority, appeared to consist rather in defining what was already generally believed by the Church than in demanding belief in any article of faith because it had been defined.[3] And in that sense every member of the Church has some influence on its theology.

But alone, the recognition for the necessity of some authority would not have been sufficient to urge me on to the luxury liner whose every blemish was as clear as her fundamental seaworthiness. Impulsion was more radical. For very early in my search I had awakened to those two basic truths which I have repeated *ad nauseam* throughout this work: one, that we are in actual fact members one of another; the other that it is only by struggling ceaselessly to overcome the ego that we can attain to something of the divine. These two thoughts gathered force and intensity throughout the years. But I remained the old Adam on the old way. And even when the truth of Christianity broke upon me in all its force, I was still the old man though on a new way. There are the three stages, Charles Williams tells us, and what I needed was to be the new man on the new way.[4] For that grace was required.[5] And all salvation, I believed, was vicarious. This was an exchange of responsibility, not a shirking of it as so many western converts to eastern religions prefer to believe in

---

[1] *Psychology and Religion*, p. 23.
[2] *Op. cit.*, p. 21.   [3] See Charles Williams, *op. cit.*, p. 118.
[4] *Ibid.*, p. 119.
[5] Intentionally, I do not speak here of the sacraments of the Church—the outward and visible signs of this inward and spiritual grace—as being beyond the scope of this work.

their failure to wish to understand the nature of Christian at-one-ment.

Embarking on the luxury liner was the first step I took in humility, acknowledging in act what I knew in thought—my unity with all men in Christ, and especially my fellow-Christians —abandoning my snug and dearly-prized individualism.

So the end of one journey has been but the beginning of another, far longer and more arduous. And if at long last it brings me to the denial of the self through grace to be the new man on the new way, the harbour will be the right one for me.

Traherne has said:

'When you love men, the world quickly becometh yours.
The whole world ministers to you as the theatre of your
love . . . without which it were better to have no being.
Never was anything in this world loved too much but
other things too little; many things have been loved in a
false way: and all in too short a measure.'[1]

That the love of individuals for one another was of infinite value and of the utmost significance metaphysically had been for McTaggart one of the two most fundamental truths. And recently Sir Charles Sherrington has paid tribute to the paramount importance and worth of altruism.[2] Lord Russell, even more bravely, revives the word 'love,' saying that 'Christian love' or compassion is the greatest need of our age.[3]

It was only this love of individuals for one another that counted. A vague love of humanity in general was but a poor substitute; in fact, as McTaggart found, it was about as possible to love mankind in the abstract as to love a post office directory.[4]

[1] *The Divine Lover.*   [2] *Op. cit.*, p. 298.
[3] *Impact of Science on Society*, p. 114 (Allen & Unwin, 1952). Quoted by
C. A. Coulson, *op. cit.*, p. 111.
[4] *Some Dogmas of Religion*, p. 269.

And it seemed that the cost to anyone of the love of his neighbour was a measure of the value of such concern.

It was, I believed, because love was the essence of the divine that man as a child of God had this need of love, inalienable from his very nature. But although it might be more blessed to give than to receive, in the case of love it was infinitely harder. And I could not blink the fact that some 'good' people with a humanistic philosophy were far more proficient in this giving of love than were many of the so-called children of light, and in that respect— if anyone may dare to conjecture on such a matter—a great deal 'nearer to the Kingdom.' But although the source of such concern might be hidden from a man, I could not believe that it was anything but divine. *Ubi caritas et amor, Deus ibi est.* And recently an eminent agnostic has spoken of the sense of 'givenness' in the experience of devotion to his neighbour.[1] It is something that he cannot command, something that comes to him; and he is driven to conclude that this which is outside himself is good, or at any rate neither evil nor indifferent.

That was a tremendous admission for an agnostic, for in the recognition of a good existing outside and independent of the self there was much of the authentic flavour of religious experience. So, too, in the case of Lord Russell, his unswerving loyalty to truth and his passionate devotion to its cause seemed to argue belief in an absolute outside himself—a God of Truth. For if there is no such Absolute, why should man who is fallible and the victim of his own 'conditioning' be so dedicated to what must be mere opinion?

Although Voltaire's remark, ' S'il n'y avait pas de Dieu il aurait fallu l'inventer' might tell one more about man than about God, that did not mean that religious belief was therefore necessarily subjective. For, as Fechner argues, it is difficult to explain man's need to believe in those things which religion

[1] J. P. Corbett in a broadcast discussion with R. Gregor Smith. See *The Listener*, Jan. 21, 1960.

affirms if, in fact, these had no objective existence. If he merely invented them in order to fulfil a need, at least he did not create the circumstances necessitating such an invention. And why should the human demand for religious faith not be founded on the same objective reality which produced those men themselves who make this demand? Is it credible that nature should have constituted them in such a manner that their true satisfaction can only be found in an illusion—a belief in something which does not exist? Certainly, I had long ceased to find it so.

For without God and eternal life, man is nothing but what Sartre called 'une passion inutile,' a being whose existence Heidegger saw as a tragedy and a mockery. It seemed that human life had to be lived on two planes, and that failure to do so resulted in incompleteness of being and a sense of frustration. Man could either try to rid himself of that sense by living more intensely a purely horizontal life, by blocking up the interstices through which grace might enter into his being, thus making himself *securus adversus Deum*; or he could accept the concept of life as cruciform, with the horizontal beam dependent upon the vertical.

But his difficulty is that he is no longer content to believe; faith is not enough; he has to *know*, know for himself, know like God. (Perhaps that was the essence of the meaning of the Fall.) Yet Jung shows that there are things which it is impossible for man to understand metaphysically, where it can only be done psychologically. And many of these are the things most vital to man's being. D. H. Lawrence saw that it is not wickedness that kills men but their unbelief. Further, he has said:[1]

' The old Church knew that life is here our portion,
to be lived . . . in fulfilment. . . . The rhythm of life itself
was preserved by the Church, hour by hour, day by day,
season by season, year by year, epoch by epoch down

[1] *Apropos of Lady Chatterley's Lover.*

among the people. . . . We feel it in the south, in the country, when we hear the jangle of bells at dawn, at noon, at sunset, marking the hours with the sound of Mass or prayers. It is the rhythm of the daily sun. We feel it in the festivals, the processions, the three Kings, Easter, Pentecost, St John's Day, All Saints, All Souls. This is the wheeling of the year, the movement of the sun through solstice and equinox, the coming of the seasons, the going of the seasons. And it is the inward rhythm of man and woman too; the sadness of Lent, the delight of Easter, the wonder of Pentecost, the fires of St John, the candles on the graves of All Souls, the lit-up tree of Christmas, all representing kindled rhythmic emotions in the souls of men and women. . . . Oh, what a catastrophe for man when he cut himself off from the rhythm of the year, from his union with the sun and the earth. Oh, what a catastrophe, what a maiming of love when it was made a personal, merely personal feeling, taken away from the rising and setting of the sun, and cut off from the magic connection of the solstice and the equinox! This is what is the matter with us. We are bleeding at the roots, because we are cut off from the earth and sun and stars, and love is a grinning mockery because, poor blossom, we plucked it from its stem on the tree of Life, and expected it to keep on blooming in our civilised vase on the table.'

Hadn't Traherne, too, known the importance of not cutting oneself off from life when he said:

'You never enjoy the world aright, till the sea itself floweth in your veins, till you are clothed with the heavens and crowned with the stars.'[1]

But perhaps the trouble with most of us is that we do not

[1] *Precepts of Felicity.*

want life—certainly not too abundantly; it is not that we want too much but that we do not want enough, that we are too easily satisfied with the cheaper consolation prizes which are all that a horizontal life can offer. And cut off from the divine spring of grace most of our hearts are no more than cisterns likely at any moment to run dry. Maybe it is not their coldness that is at fault so much as their shallowness—a shallowness that allows pre-occupation with the mere toys of this world to silence that constant crying after Elysium, and to incline us to forget what we many of us feel in our deepest being—that we are too willing exiles from our home.

For ' God did infinitely for us, when he made us to want like gods, that like gods we might be satisfied.' And 'our enjoyment of the world is never right, till every morning we awake in Heaven.'[1]

---

[1] *Ibid.*

THE TEXTS

Texts

                                                        page

TEXT 1   SOCRATES' argument for the divinity of the soul, from the *Phaedo* 263

Note on Socrates' argument against materialism in the *Phaedo*

TEXT 2   Extracts from MCTAGGART's *Some Dogmas of Religion* 267

TEXT 3   Extracts from C. D. BROAD's *Mind and its Place in Nature* 270

Note on Bergson's view of the brain 273

Joad's theory concerning ESP, from *The Recovery of Belief* 275

TEXT 4   Note on PLATO's Forms, and on God in Plato's *Dialogues* 278

Extracts from Plato's *Laws*, with note 279

TEXT 5   ARISTOTLE's argument for God's existence 282

Extracts from Aristotle's *Nicomachean Ethics*, and *De Anima*, with notes 282

Note on the medieval Church and Aristotle's philosophy 284

TEXT 6   Extracts from DESCARTES's *Discourse on Method*, and the *Meditations* 285

TEXT 7   Ueberweg's short summary of the philosophy of SPINOZA 288

Extracts from Spinoza's *Ethics*, with notes 290

TEXT 8   Extracts from LEIBNIZ's *Monadology*, with notes 292

The Texts

TEXT 9   Note on KANT's three postulates   299

Kant on the arguments for God's existence   300

TEXT 10   Extracts from HEGEL's *Philosophy of Religion* together with notes from J. M. Sterrett's *Studies* in the same   303

TEXT 11   Extracts from KIERKEGAARD's *Journals, For Self-Examination, The Point of View, Training in Christianity, Concluding Unscientific Postscript*, etc.   316

Note on Kierkegaard's thought   319

TEXT 12   Extracts from the *Upanishads*, and from the *Bhagavadgîta*, with notes   322

TEXT 13   Extracts from the *Dhammapada*, and from *The Book of the Great Decease*   334

The Buddhist Creed, the Four Noble Truths and the Noble Eightfold Path   339

TEXT 14   Extracts from the KORAN, with notes   340

TEXT 15   Extracts from the OLD TESTAMENT   349

Note on modern Jewish beliefs   360

TEXT 16   VERBA CHRISTI: 362

On what the Christian must strive to be and do   362

On what the Christian can expect in this world   366

On the assurances granted to the Christian believer   366

What Christ said of himself   367

An Argument of Socrates for the soul's divinity, from Plato's ' Phaedo' (with Note). Note on Socrates' argument against epiphenomenalism in the ' Phaedo'

(PLATO 427-347 B.C.)

FROM THE PHAEDO:

Socrates: ' That which is uncompounded, and that only, must be, if anything is, indissoluble.

And the uncompounded may be assumed to be the same and unchanging, whereas the compound is always changing and never the same. (78c.)

Are these (ideas or) essences each of them always what they are, having the same, self-existent and unchanging forms?'

Cebes: ' They must always be the same.' (78d.)

Socrates: ' And what would you say of the many beautiful— whether men or horses? May they not be described as almost always changing and hardly ever the same?'

Cebes: ' They are always in a state of change.' (78e.)

Socrates: ' And these you can touch and see and perceive with the senses but the unchanging things you can only perceive with the mind—they are invisible and are not seen.' (79.)

' Well then . . . let us suppose there are two sorts of existence—one seen, the other unseen. The seen is the changing, and the unseen is the unchanging. And to which class may we say that the body is more alike and akin?' (79b.)

Cebes: ' Clearly to the seen.'

Socrates: ' And is the soul seen or not seen?'

Cebes: ' Not by man.'

Socrates: ' Then the soul is more like to the unseen, and the body to the seen?'

Cebes: ' That is most certain.' (79e.)

Socrates: ' And to which class is the soul more clearly alike and akin, as far as may be inferred from this argument?'

Cebes: ' I think ... that ... the soul will be infinitely more like the unchangeable—even the most stupid person will not deny that.'

Socrates: ' Yet once more consider the matter in another light: When the soul and the body are united, then nature orders the soul to rule and govern, and the body to obey and serve. Now which of these two functions is akin to the divine? and which to the mortal? does not the divine appear to you to be that which naturally orders and rules, and the mortal to be that which is subject and servant.'

Cebes: ' True. The Soul resembles the divine and the body the mortal—there can be no doubt of that.' (80.)

Socrates: ' Then reflect: of all that has been said is not this the conclusion? that the soul is in the very likeness of the divine, and immortal, and intellectual, and uniform, and indissoluble and unchangeable; and that the body is in the very likeness of the human, and mortal, and un-intellectual, and multiform, and dissoluble, and change-able.'

' But if this is true ... is not the soul almost or altogether indissoluble?' (80b.)

Cebes: ' Certainly.'

Socrates: ' And are we to suppose that the soul, which is invisible, in passing to the true Hades, which like her is invisible, and pure, and noble, and on her way to the good and wise God, whither if God will, my soul is also soon to go—that the soul, I repeat, if this be her nature and origin, is blown away and perishes immediately on quitting the body, as the many say? That can never be, my dear Simmias and Cebes.' (80D and E.)

We have been told that the purpose of the *Phaedo* is to show the divinity of the soul, and to justify the care of it and the 'imitation of God' as the right and logical rule of conduct. The immortality of the soul is but a consequence of this divinity. And we are warned not to view the arguments for the soul's immunity from death as so many 'proofs' possessing equal intrinsic value. Rather are they to be considered as a series of attacks on the problem.

Plato's own attitude towards the two main difficulties in the defence of the soul's immortality is to be found in the refutation of the unbeliever in the Laws, Book X, where it is asserted that mental life is not the effect of a physical cause and that physical reality itself cannot be explained by purely mechanical concepts. In the *Phaedo* the position of Socrates on these two questions of ephiphenomenalism and the mechanical theory of nature is stated and found to agree with that of Plato in the *Laws*.[1]

SOCRATES' ARGUMENT AGAINST EPIPHENOMENALISM, FROM THE PHAEDO

Epiphenomenalism cannot be reconciled with the appreciation of differences in moral worth (93-95). Socrates argues that ethical first principles are certainly true; a theory which seeks to con-

[1] A. E. Taylor, *Plato, The Man and His Work*, p. 177 (Methuen, 5th ed., 1948).

tradict them must be false. Ethics suppose a two-sphere struggle between the good and the bad, the higher and the lower, whereas the epiphenomenalist is limited to a one-sphere interpretation of human behaviour. No profound moralist could therefore accept epiphenomenalism.

The mechanical theory of nature might be translated into modern terms thus: the presupposition of ethics concerning the action of mind on body can only be reconciled with natural science by assuming that the mind when directing the body expends energy. Now if this expenditure continues without compensation, it is obvious that a time must come when the energy is exhausted. The issue now at stake is therefore: either Mind must follow the natural law of the Conservation of Energy, or it must be admitted that a mechanical theory of nature is not of universal application.[1]

The upshot of the discussion of this difficulty is that Socrates entirely persuades his listeners that the mechanical interpretation cannot adequately explain a single process in Nature (95a–102a).

[1] A. E. Taylor, *ibid.*, pp. 195-9.

'It is clear that if I am a mere effect of my body I shall cease when the body ceases. And it is also clear that, if I could not exist without this particular body, then the destruction of the body will be a sign that I have ceased to exist.

'But, besides death, there is another characteristic of nature which tends to make us doubt our immortality. Of all the things around us, from a pebble to a solar system, science tells us that they are transitory. Each of them arose out of something else, each of them will pass away into something else. What is a man that he should be exempt from this universal law?

'Thus we have three questions to consider: (1) Is my self an activity of my body? (2) Is my present body an essential condition of the existence of my self? (3) Is there any reason to suppose that my self does not share the transitory character which I recognise in all the material objects around me?' (pp. 78-9.)

'The effects of body on mind and of mind on body could be explained on the hypothesis that the self and the body were two separate realities, neither of which was the mere product of the other'—a dualistic hypothesis. But

' Monism, whether it be materialism or idealism, is more attractive to the majority of inquirers than dualism is.' (p. 81.)

Moreover, McTaggart shows how materialistic monism is commonly preferred to idealistic monism, since man finds constant evidence that the nature of matter is all but independent of his will. He cannot create matter, and he is severely limited in the extent to which he can alter it. And from this, by what McTaggart considers an understandable but unwarrantable leap of thought, man infers that whatever is outside the influence of his will must necessarily be altogether independent of him. Matter appears to be far more powerful than spirit; we know more about the one than about the other, and can observe unity and stability in the former and not in the latter. All this encourages belief in matter as sole reality, and to make of spirit merely the behaviour of matter under varying circumstances, an energy transformed into will, thought or emotion, just as in science the same energy can show itself as motion, heat or electricity. (pp. 81-3.)

' These conclusions depend . . . on the proposition that matter can exist independently of spirit. . . . Deeper inquiry will, I think, show us that matter cannot be independent of spirit, that, on the contrary, matter is only an appearance to the mind which observes it, and cannot, therefore, exist independently of spirit. If this is the case we cannot be entitled to consider the self as the activity of its body.' (p. 83.)

As to the second question, McTaggart says:

' It seems to me that the facts only support a very different proposition—namely, that, *while a self has a body,* that body is essentially connected with the self's mental life. . . . It does not follow, because a self which has a body cannot get its data except in connection with that body, that it would be impossible for a self without a body to get data in some other way. It may be just the existence of the body which makes these other ways impossible at present.' (p. 105.)

Considering the third question, McTaggart remarks that:

'When science says that a material object—a planet, or a human body—ceases to exist . . . it does not mean that anything is annihilated. It means that units, which were combined in a certain way, are now combined otherwise. The form has changed. But everything which was there before is there now. . . . The analogy of science does not give us reason to suppose anything to be transitory except combinations.' (pp. 107-8.)

But he finds the self not to be a combination, since if a whole is this, it would be formed of parts which could exist without the combination. And that it is inconceivable that his thoughts and emotions should exist apart from his self. The self, he considers to be complex but not a compound. It has parts but is not built up out of them. (pp. 108-9.)

'The self, therefore, cannot cease by the separation of its parts.' (p. 109.)

But to dispel all doubts on the survival of the self would be, McTaggart considers, the work of a complete metaphysical system. All that he has attempted here is the refutation of the most usual arguments against immortality—a demonstration that those carrying most weight with the majority of men are quite without validity.[1] (p. 110.)

[1] It is obviously impossible in a work of this nature to allow sufficient space to do full justice to McTaggart's theories on human immortality.

Extracts from C. D. Broad's 'Mind and its Place in Nature.'
Note on Bergson's view of the brain.
A Theory of C. E. M. Joad concerning psychic phenomena

In chapter XII of *Mind and its Place in Nature*, Professor Broad observes:

> 'What we must do . . . is to discuss the antecedent probability of survival on data which are common to all men. . . . Now . . . the most striking feature of the world as we know it in daily life is, for our purpose, that it does not present the faintest trace of evidence for survival. . . . Every.. factor making for belief in the continued existence of dead men is lacking in our ordinary experience. Yet . . . such a belief has been all but universal.'[1]

After showing that 'primitive man had simply more *causes*, but no better *reasons* for a belief in survival than we have,' Professor Broad calls attention to the difficulty we experience 'in actually envisaging the cessation of our own conscious life.' (But was it really any easier, I wondered, soberly to imagine our survival of death?) And he considers that 'the belief represents nothing more profound than an easily explicable limit of our powers of imagination. . . . And it obviously provides no evidence for the truth of that belief'[2].

' But the absence of evidence for the belief cannot be

[1] pp. 520-1.   [2] pp. 522-4.

taken as strong evidence against it, in view of what we know about the means by which embodied human spirits have to communicate with each other.'[1]

Discussing two sets of facts which might be interpreted as providing positive evidence against survival, he states that he is inclined to think the one fallacious and the other logically invalid. And he adds:

' The world, then, as it presents itself to common-sense and everyday experience, offers no positive reasons for and no positive reasons against human survival.'[2]

' Science . . . amplifies and elaborates the views of common-sense on the connection of body and mind . . . I think it is fair to say that our ordinary scientific knowledge of the relation of body to mind most strongly suggests epiphenomenalism, though it does not necessitate it: and that epiphenomenalism is most unfavourable to the hypothesis of human survival'.[3]

' It is, however, possible to put forward other theories about the mind and its relation to the body, which are consistent with ordinary experience and with scientific knowledge and are less unfavourable to survival than epiphenomenalism.'[4]

One of these is the Instrumental Theory. This makes a mind a substance independent of the body existentially. This substance may have been in existence before any beginning of the body, and it may continue in existence after the body has perished. Although Professor Broad holds that this theory is not inconsistent with many facts, he finds that in its bare crudity it is untenable.[5] Another theory is the Compound Theory already outlined. This makes the mind a compound of the body and something else; and 'mental events and characteristics

[1] pp. 525-6.   [2] See pp. 526-32.   [3] pp. 532-3.   [4] p. 533.   [5] p. 534.

belong to this compound substance and not to its separate constituents.'[1]

'But . . . it would be foolish to accept it [the Compound Theory] unless there were some facts which it explains and which the Epiphenomenalist Theory does not. Now I do not think that there is anything in the normal phenomena which requires us to suppose that a mind depends for its existence . . . on anything but the body. . . . We must therefore turn to abnormal phenomena'.

'It is very important to begin by drawing a distinction between *survival* and mere *persistence*. . . .'[2]

'On the Compound Theory we can suppose that the psychic factor may persist for a time at least after the destruction of the organism with which it was united to form the compound called "John Jones's mind." This psychic factor is not itself a mind, but it may carry modifications due to experiences which happened to John Jones while he was alive. And it may become temporarily united with the organism of an entranced medium. If so, a temporary "mindkin" . . . will be formed. . . . It will not be surprising if it displays some traits characteristic of John Jones, and . . . many traits which are characteristic of the medium. And the reason why we can get no information about the present life . . . of John Jones is that no such mind is existing at all.'[3]

After further discussion on the Compound Theory and its implications, Professor Broad concludes by saying:

'This Compound Theory seems to be the minimum assumption that will explain certain fairly well-attested abnormal phenomena. . . . Anyone who adopts the view that the mind is existentially dependent on the organism

[1] p. 538.   [2] pp. 538-9.   [3] pp. 540-1.

alone is taking up a position which is not *necessitated* by the facts which everyone admits, and which can hardly be reconciled with the very *possibility* of many alleged facts for which there is at least respectable *prima facie* evidence. . . . It [the theory] is compatible with all the facts which everyone admits; it has nothing against it except a super-stitious objection to dualism, and it leaves open the possibility that these debatable phenomena are genuine.'[1]

Elsewhere, Professor Broad observes that the fact that some claims to knowledge obtained supernormally were seen to be valid would not tend *directly* to demonstrate either the pre-existence of mind or its survival of the destruction of the body; but he considers that it would have an indirect bearing on these questions, since the great difficulty in accepting this conclusion is caused by the dead weight of antecedent improbability which has to be overcome.

This antecedent improbability, he shows, springs chiefly from the belief that every activity of the mind has correlations with processes in the brain and nervous system. Once extra-sensory perception was recognised as a fact, there would be positive ground for questioning this correlation. Thus the antecedent improbability of the existence of mind without body might well be reduced.'[2]

BERGSON'S VIEW OF THE BRAIN

The more extreme materialists, I learned, tend to regard the mind as the aggregate of the nerve cells constituting the brain, or as material substance surrounding the brain. So, too, in psychology a complete parallelism is assumed between the mind and the body, physiological modifications attending all psycho-logical events. On all these views it is always the material which

[1] p. 550.
[2] *Henry Sidgwick and Psychical Research* (S.P.R. *Proceedings*, Vol. 45, 1938-39).

determines and conditions the mental; anything that occurs in the mind must be a result of something which first occurred in the brain.

Against this theory, Bergson advances facts with which he finds it incompatible. Removal of large portions of those very parts of the brain formerly considered indispensable to the causation of mental activity, has resulted in no psychological derangement, whereas if mental activity is the outcome of cerebral activity, disturbances in psychology would inevitably result. No corresponding physiological changes are to be found in the phenomena of abnormal psychology—dual personality, etc., and on the parallelist hypothesis subconscious mental activity is not to be explained. Bergson's inference is that cerebral activity is conditioned by mental activity. The brain is not consciousness, neither is the cause of conscious processes contained within it: it is only the organ of consciousness, that spot where consciousness penetrates matter.[1]

Bergson believes the role of the brain to be the 'acting out' what the mind thinks; it is the organ of pantomime. It is also the organ of attention to life which keeps our consciousness fixed on the world we live in, limiting our awareness. But when this attention is suspended or the defences by the brain are enfeebled, some 'virtual' perceptions may penetrate the margin of consciousness and result in telepathy or other extra-sensory manifestations. Bergson maintains that we perceive unconsciously a great deal more than we realise, and that it is possible that we may be capable not only of retaining all our memories but also of perceiving all that is happening anywhere in the world.[2]

Memory being a psychical function, the storing and recollecting of experiences are not dependent on the brain. Neither memory proper nor extra-sensory perception have any cerebral correlate. The function of the brain is to be an organ of limitation

[1] See C. E. M. Joad, *Guide to Philosophy*, pp. 545-6 (Gollancz, 1938).
[2] H. Habberley Price on Bergson, in S.P.R. *Proceedings*, Vol. 46, 1940-41.

—to prevent the recalling of too much—rather than to be the organ of memory. In loss of memory resulting from damage to the physical brain, memories still exist; but the brain channel between these and the threshold of conscious action fails to work.

In the view of Professor Habberley Price, Bergson's theory of the brain is the only kind able to include the astounding fact of perception of physical objects by clairvoyance as differentiated from awareness of mental states by telepathy.[1]

The characteristic of ESP and memory proper of being without any cerebral correlate led Bergson to consider that it is not upon him who affirms belief in survival of bodily death that the onus of proof will rest, but rather upon him who denies it.[2]

A THEORY OF C. E. M. JOAD CONCERNING PSYCHIC PHENOMENA
(FROM *The Recovery of Belief*)

' The traditional division of the human being is not two-fold but threefold, into mind, body and soul. Mind is brought into being in consequence of the contact of the soul with the natural, temporal order, which results from its incorporation in a physical body. It is brought initially into being in the form of ideas. Ideas emerge on the combination of soul with body much as water emerges on the combination of oxygen and hydrogen, and it is the cluster of these emerging ideas which constitutes a mind.

' Since a mind comes into existence as a by-product of the soul's incarnation in matter, its existence is temporary only. Moreover, it is not in the mind that the unity of the person resides, so that the arguments advanced by Hume and later by William James against the conception of the substantial or unified self, arguments which at the level of

[1] *Ibid.*   [2] *Ibid.*

psychology it is extremely difficult to rebut, are beside the point, seeing that the unity of a self resides elsewhere—in a region which is inaccessible to consciousness. Soul or spirit when brought into contact with matter by incarnation in a body, expresses itself initially in a succession of ideas. A mind is simply the bundle of ideas which constitute it at any given moment. Hence ideas are primitive and mind derivative.

'The "bundle" theory of mind allows for the fact that the unity of a mind is a matter of degree. (Some minds are much more closely knit bundles of ideas than others.) It allows for the cases of dissociated and multiple personalities. (Ideas may cluster not in one system but in two. These two systems may take control at different times. But nevertheless this hypothesis makes provision for the continuance of a person—a unity which is eternal—by locating it not in mind but in soul.) It allows for the fact that ideas may sometimes wander from the bundle to which they normally belong and temporarily form part of another bundle' (as in *telepathy*); 'and directly influence a piece of matter other than the brain' (as in *telekinesis*). 'This hypothesis brings *telepathy* and *telekinesis* under the ægis of a single principle of explanation.'

Again, with reference to the possibility of survival,

' It allows for the fact that ideas may get loose from the "mind," survive for a time, form part of the idea-bundle which would be regarded as another mind, and form a temporary "mindlet" of their own which can animate some other body, e.g., a medium in trance. This theory makes intelligible the low intellectual content of "spirit communications." (Even if ghosts have or are souls, they have no brains.) Also their dual reference. It could also explain ghosts as a temporary association with non-cerebral matter. (Ghosts have objective existence, for animals see them and are not victims of subjectively projected hallucinations.)'

Summing up, Joad says:

'The incarnated soul expresses itself in ideas; these ideas cluster in bundles and are known to us under the name of mind or consciousness. Some ideas may become detached from the bundle to which they normally belong and associate themselves temporarily with other bodies and brains and even non-cerebral matter. It is in this tendency of ideas to wander that the most plausible explanation of many supernormal phenomena is to be found. None of the explanations of science is remotely satisfactory. And science has either to ignore these phenomena or write them off as illusory.' (pp. 201-210.)

Note on Plato's forms, and God in Plato's 'Dialogues'
Extracts from Plato's 'Laws'

There is a 'form' or 'idea' for each of the qualities that is common to a number of things; a single essential nature for every set called by the same name. Thus, for instance, although in this world there are innumerable beds, there is only one form of a bed. And in the same way as the reflection of a bed in a mirror would not be 'real,' so every particular bed is unreal, not in the sense that it does not exist but because the only real bed is the ideal bed.

All Forms or Ideas not only possess complete reality; it is they alone which constitute reality and the real world. They are the source of being of particulars, endowing them with that essence which must be, however imperfectly, embodied in every particular to make it just that thing.

The Forms then constitute the world of being, whereas our world is the world of becoming in which everything strives for a more complete reality. Although sensible things have that degree of reality only as they approximate to the Forms more or less imperfectly, their striving is towards a more complete manifestation of the Forms which are present in them. It could be said that they seek to make themselves real—to realise themselves.

An early reference to God occurs in the *Republic*, Book II, (378-9) where Socrates lays down as first principle that God is the author of good only. And as second principle that God is true; he does not change, neither can he deceive (380). For God and the things of God are absolutely perfect.

We meet here also with the true lie, the 'lie in the soul,' with which 'the sin against the Holy Ghost' might be compared. (381-2.)

From the Dialogues generally we learn also that God is divine beauty, the good, the heavenly pattern, absolute justice, temperance, righteousness. He is free from jealousy, the best of causes, and his deeds the fairest. He is measure, beauty in symmetry, truth, and the measure of all things. We are told, too, that the care of men is natural to the goodness of the Gods; they own us, and are the best of guardians for everything great and small. Moreover, it is by contemplation of the divine that man increases in himself the divine part.

This divine part I saw as the essence of the Form present in its particulars in however imperfect a degree. In the Christian soul this was called the divine spark. And just as the more a particular realised the essence of the Form itself, the greater its approach to reality; so the more the human soul partook of divine contemplation, the more was it rendered capable of real (eternal) life.

EXTRACTS FROM THE LAWS

The predominant idea of the whole dialogue is the priority of the soul to the body. The end of life is declared to be to make the soul as good as possible, and thus to prepare here for communion with the Gods in another world. The soul can only be honoured by being improved.

What interested me the most in the *Laws*, was the state of religious belief amongst the Greeks as seen by Plato; it seemed not unlike that of ours at the present time. Plato found the cause of disbelief to lie in three things which prove even now to be equally strong deterrents to belief. The first he sees in the bad effect of mythological tales. This might be compared with doubts about the scriptures; as when, for instance, Genesis is judged as science rather than poetry, and found lamentably wanting. Secondly, he notes the self-conceit of a younger generation of philosophers who maintain that the heavenly bodies are only earth and stones; and who believe that the Gods are created by the laws of the states, and that religion is a 'cooking-up of words and a make-believe.' Such might be likened to those of us nowadays who have become unbelievers through physical science, or again through the political character of religion.[1] Thirdly, he blames the confusion in men's minds which causes them to misinterpret the appearances in the world around them: the apparent failure of the righteous, the sufferings of the 'innocent,' the flourishing of the unrighteous. These last difficulties appear almost insurmountable to-day.

The Athenian Stranger says:

' When you or I argue for the existence of the Gods and produce the sun, moon and stars, claiming for them a divine being, if we would listen to the aforesaid philosophers we should say that they are earth and stone only, which can have no care at all of human affairs, and that all religion is a cooking-up of words and a make-believe.' (887.)

' " You are young, and the advance of time will make you reverse many of the opinions which you now hold. Wait, therefore, until the time comes, and do not attempt to judge of high matters at present; and that is the highest of which you think nothing—to know the Gods rightly and to live accordingly. You and your friends are not the first to have held this opinion about the Gods. There have always been persons more or less numerous who have had the same disorder. I have known many of them, and can

[1] See Jowett's Introduction to the *Laws*.

tell you that no one who had taken up in youth this opinion, that the Gods do not exist, ever continued in the same until he was old. What may be the true doctrine, if you are patient and take my advice, you will hereafter discover. In the meantime take heed that you do not offend against the Gods." ' (888.)

' " O thou best of men, in believing that there are Gods you are led by some affinity to them, which attracts you towards your kindred and makes you honour and believe in them. But the fortunes of evil and unrighteous men in private as well as public life which . . . are wrongly counted happy in the judgment of men . . . draw you aside from your natural piety." ' (899.)

' " The ruler of the universe has ordered all things with a view to the preservation and perfection of the whole, and you do not seem to be aware that this and every other creation is for the sake of the whole, and in order that the life of the whole may be blessed; and that you are created for the sake of the whole, and not the whole for the sake of you." ' (903.)

' " If a man look upon the world not lightly or foolishly, there was never any one so godless who did not experience the effect opposite to that which the many imagine. For they think that those who handle these matters by the help of astronomy . . . may become godless; because they see, as far as they can see, things happening by necessity, and not by an intelligent will accomplishing good." '

' " No man can be a true worshipper of the Gods who does not know these two principles—that the soul is the eldest of all things which are born, and is immortal and rules over all bodies." ' (966-7.)

Aristotle's argument for God's existence.
Extracts from Aristotle's ' Nicomachean Ethics,' and ' De Anima,' with notes.
Note on the medieval Church and Aristotle's philosophy

(ARISTOTLE 384-323 B.C.)

Aristotle's argument for the existence of his deity did not, I thought, carry much persuasive force.

He says that substances are, of existing things, primary. Therefore, if they are liable to decay, then so are all things. But change and time have neither ever begun nor will ever end, and are therefore indestructible. The one change that can be continuous and without end is circular motion in space. This necessitates an eternal substance, a pure immaterial Form with activity as essence. Since this motion exists in the heavenly spheres it can only be due to such a substance: pure and active Form, the Unmoved Mover.

In the *Nicomachean Ethics*, speaking of the highest virtue of contemplation as the activity of the divine in man, Aristotle says:

' Yet must we not give ear to those who bid one as man to mind only man's affairs, or as mortal only mortal things; but, so far as we can, to make ourselves like immortals, and do all with a view to living in accordance with the highest Principle in us. . . .' (Book X, 1178a.)

' Now he that works in accordance with, and pays observance to, Pure Intellect, and tends this, seems likely

282

to be both in the best frame of mind, and dearest to the Gods: because if, as is thought, any care is bestowed on human things by the Gods, then it must be reasonable to think that they take pleasure in what is best and most akin to themselves (and this must be Pure Intellect); and that they requite with kindness those who love and honour this most.' (Book X, 1179a.)[1]

This seemed a little hard on those whose strength of intellect might not be the salient characteristic; but I saw in Aristotle's pronouncement only another exhortation to men to transcend what is finite in their natures by a continuous striving to 'play the immortal.' It has, however, been suggested that his admonishments may fail in their purpose since it is doubtful whether this Final Cause, pure form without matter, carries any more conviction than the opposite abstraction of pure matter without form.[2] And elsewhere Cornford admits to finding Aristotle's system a monument of rationalism with charity left out: a sepulchral monument rather than an abiding shelter for the spirit. For him the Being that Aristotle describes as the object of desire is no longer one that can elicit anything remotely connected with such an emotion.[3]

In the *de Anima*, Aristotle says:

' Now reason seems to be an entity implanted in the soul and which is incapable of being destroyed.' (408b.)
' Now concerning reason and the speculative faculty, we have as yet no sure evidence, but it appears to be a generically separate type of soul, and it alone is capable of existing in a state of disconnection from the body, as the eternal is separable from the mortal. The remaining parts

[1] Translations by D. P. Chase (Whitaker, 1847).
[2] Francis M. Cornford, *Greek Religious Thought*, p. xxvi.
[3] *Before and after Socrates.*

of the soul, however, are . . . evidently not separable, as some declare.' (413b.)

Lord Russell insists that in order to understand Aristotle's doctrine of the soul it is necessary to remind ourselves that Aristotle says 'the soul is the form of the body,' and that here form does not indicate 'shape.' To Aristotle the soul was that which made the body *one* thing through unity of purpose, an organic whole; e.g. the eye in isolation cannot see—it is the soul that sees.[1]

NOTE ON THE MEDIEVAL CHURCH'S CHOICE OF ARISTOTLE'S PHILOSOPHY AS A BASIS OF ITS THEOLOGY

Professor A. E. Taylor tells us that the Church rejected Platonism as a philosophy on which it could openly build medieval theology because of Plato's denial of the resurrection of the body.[2] And Fr. Victor White states that Tertullian and others had seen an incompatibility between the Gospel and Plato's psychology which led inevitably to the contempt of the flesh of the Manichees and the Gnostics, with a drive towards release from its fetters. Whereas Aristotle's energetic insistence on the flesh as being of man's essence, and his belief in matter as first cause of the universe, were more readily compatible with a Gospel which preached salvation in and through the flesh, and resurrection of the body hereafter. This affirmation of the flesh, we are told, far outweighed Aristotle's inconclusiveness concerning immortality, his denial of individuality to *nous* and the lack of religious qualities in his later works.[3]

---

[1] *History of Western Philosophy*, pp. 188 and 193.
[2] *Aristotle*, p. 92 (Nelson, 1943).
See the *Phaedo* 66D where Plato speaks of being wholly freed from the body.
[3] *God and the Unconscious*, p. 97.

TEXT 6 *Extracts from Descartes, 'Discourse on Method' and the 'Meditations'*

(DESCARTES 1585-1660)

Descartes, having decided to doubt everything he possibly could in order to find a firm basis for his philosophy, and having arrived at his *Cogito, ergo sum,* says:

'From reflecting on the circumstance that I doubted, and that consequently my being was not wholly perfect (for I clearly saw that it was a greater perfection to know than to doubt), I was led to inquire whence I had learned to think of something more perfect than myself; and I clearly recognised that I must hold this notion from some nature which in reality was more perfect.

'It but remained that it had been placed in me by a nature which was in reality more perfect than mine, and which even possessed within itself all the perfections of which I could form any ideas; that is to say, in a single word, which was God. There was of necessity some other more perfect Being upon whom I was dependent, and from whom I had received all that I possessed; for if I had existed alone, and independently of every other being, so as to have had from myself all the perfection, however little which I actually possessed, I should have been able, for the same reason to have had from myself the whole remainder of perfection, of the want of which I was conscious, and thus could of myself have become infinite, eternal, immutable, omniscient, all-powerful, and, in fine, have possessed all the perfections which I could recognise in God.'[1]

MEDITATION III, *Of God, that He Exists*
(TRANSLATED BY JOHN VEITCH)

' By the name God, I understand a substance infinite, eternal, immutable, independent, all-knowing, all-powerful, and by which I myself, and every other thing that exists, if any such there be, were created. But these properties are so great and excellent, that the more attentively I consider them the less I feel persuaded that the idea I have of them owes its origin to myself alone. And thus it is absolutely necessary to conclude, from all that I have before said, that God exists; for though the idea of substance be in my mind owing to this, that I myself am a substance, I should not, however, have the idea of an infinite substance, seeing I am a finite being, unless it were given me by some substance in reality infinite.

' And it cannot be said that this idea of God is perhaps materially false, and consequently that it may have arisen from nothing: for on the contrary, as this idea is very clear and distinct, and contains in itself more objective reality than any other, there can be no one of itself more true, or less open to the suspicion of falsity.

' The idea, I say, of a being supremely perfect, and infinite, is in the highest degree true. It is likewise clear and distinct in the highest degree, since whatever the mind clearly and distinctly conceives as real or true, and as implying any perfection, is contained entire in this idea. And this is true nevertheless, although I do not comprehend the infinite and although there may be in God an infinity of things that I cannot comprehend, nor perhaps even compass by thought in any way; for it is of the

---

[1] *Discourse*, Part I. Translated by John Veitch.

nature of the infinite that it should not be comprehended by the finite.

'I am here desirous to inquire further, whether I, who possess this idea of God, could exist supposing there were no God. And I ask, from whom could I, in that case, derive my existence? Perhaps from myself or from my parents, or from some other causes less perfect than God. But if I were myself the author of my being, I should doubt of nothing, I should desire nothing, and, in fine, no perfection would be awanting to me; for I should have bestowed upon myself every perfection of which I possess the idea, and I should thus be God.

'There remains only the inquiry as to the way in which I received this idea from God; for I have not drawn it in from the senses; it is innate in the same way as is the idea of myself. And, in truth, it is not to be wondered at that God, at my creation, implanted this idea in me, that it might serve, as it were, for the mark of the workman impressed on his work; and it is not also necessary that the mark should be something different from the work itself; but considering only that God is my creator, it is highly probable that he in some way fashioned me after his own image and likeness, and that I perceive this likeness, in which is contained the likeness of God, by the same faculty by which I apprehend myself. I perceive that I could not possibly be of such a nature as I am, and yet have in my mind the idea of God, if God did not in reality exist.'

Spinoza 'transformed the Cartesian dualism into a pantheism, whose fundamental conception was the unity of substance. By substance Spinoza understands that which is in itself and is to be conceived by itself. There is only one substance, and that is God. This substance has two fundamental qualities or attributes cognisable by us, namely, thought and extension; there is no extended substance as distinct from thinking substance. Among the unessential, changing forms or modes of these attributes is included individual existence. Such existence does not belong to God, since, were it otherwise, he would be finite, and not absolute; all determination is negation. God is the immanent cause (a cause not passing out of itself) of the totality of finite things or the world. God works according to the inner necessity of his nature; in this consists his freedom. God produces all finite effects only indirectly, through finite causes; there is no such thing as a direct working of God in view of ends, nor as human freedom independent of causality. It can only be said that one mode of extension works upon another mode of extension, and one mode of thought on another mode of thought. Between thought and extension, on the contrary, there exists, not a causal nexus, but a perfect agreement. The order and connection of thought is identical with the order and connection of things, each thought being in all cases only the idea of the corresponding mode of extension. Human ideas vary in clearness and value from the confused representations of the imagination to the adequate knowledge of the intellect, which conceives all that is particular from the point of view of the whole which contains it, and comprehends all things under the form of eternity (*sub specie aeternitatis*), not as accidental, but as necessary. From confused mental representations, which cannot rise above the finite, arise passions and the bondage of the will, while intellectual knowledge gives rise to the intellectual love of God, in which our happiness and our freedom consist. Beatitude is not a reward of virtue, but virtue itself.'[1]

In Part V of the Ethics, Spinoza writes a great deal on love. And Mr. Stuart Hampshire warns us that 'the intellectual love of God' can only be grasped in relation to Proposition XXIV which tells us that 'the more we understand individual things, the more we know God.'[2] Moreover, it is necessary constantly to bear in mind that if 'Nature' is substituted for the word 'God' throughout the following quotations, we reach the conclusion that this 'intellectual love' denotes a complete subservience of the individual self to a passionate desire to know and understand Nature, the system of things as they are.

And it is in the light of Spinoza's views on the mind in general and of Definition VI of Part III in particular, where it is stated that it is a property of love that the lover should wish to unite himself with the loved object, that his remarks on the possible eternity of the human mind must be understood. The self as a distinct personality, we are told, does not survive; for with the attainment of real knowledge the mind becomes united with God and Nature conceived under the attribute of thought, and individuality as a distinguishable entity vanishes.[3]

[1] Ueberweg, *op. cit.*, Vol. II, p. 55.   [2] *Op. cit.*, pp. 168-9.
[3] *Ibid.*, pp. 174-5.

PROPOSITIONS FROM PART V OF THE ETHICS

XXI   'The mind can imagine nothing, neither can it remember anything that is past, save during the continuance of the body.'

XXII   'In God, however, there must necessarily exist an idea which expresses the essence of this or that human body under the form of eternity.'

Demonst.   'God is not only the cause of the existence of this or that human body, but also of its essence which must therefore be necessarily conceived by the very essence of God, and this in virtue of a certain eternal necessity; a conception which indeed must necessarily have place in God.'

XXIII   'The human mind cannot be absolutely destroyed along with the body; something of it remains which is eternal.'

Demonst.   'As there is necessarily a something which by a certain eternal necessity is conceived by the very essence of God, this something pertaining to the essence of the mind will necessarily be eternal.'

Schol.   '. . . We feel and are persuaded that we are eternal. . . . Although we have no remembrance of any existence previous to the existence of the body, we are yet persuaded that our mind, inasmuch as it involves the essence of the body under a form or aspect of eternity, is eternal, and that this existence cannot be defined by time or explained by duration.'

XXX   'Our mind in so far as it knows itself and the body under the form of eternity, in so far has it necessarily a knowledge of God, and knows that it is in God and is conceived through God.'

XXXI (Schol.)	'The mind is eternal in so far as it conceives things under the form of eternity.'
XXXIII	'The intellectual love of God which arises from the third kind of intellectual is eternal.'
XXXIV (Coroll.)	'No other than intellectual love can be eternal.'
XXXV	'God loves himself with an infinite intellectual love.'
XXXVI	'The intellectual love of the mind for God is the very love of God—the love wherewith God loves himself, not as he is infinite, but as he can be interpreted by the essence of the human mind considered under a species of eternity; in other words, the intellectual love of the mind towards God is part of the infinite love wherewith God loves himself.'
Coroll.	'Hence it follows that God, in so far as he loves himself, loves mankind, and consequently that the love of God for man and the intellectual love of the mind of man for God, are one and the same.'
XXXVIII (Schol.)	'Death is by so much the less destructive as the clear and distinct cognition of the mind is greater, and as God consequently is loved the more. It follows that the human mind may be of such a nature that what we have shown as liable to pass away or to perish with the body, when contrasted with that which remains unchanged, may be of no significance.'
XL (Coroll.)	'Now the eternal part of the mind is the understanding by which alone we say we act; but the part that perishes we have shown to be that wherewith imagination is connected; by this part alone do we suffer.'

TEXT 8   *Extracts from Leibniz's ' Monadology,' with notes*

(LEIBNIZ 1646-1716)

After I had read the *Monadology* I learnt that in Lord Russell's opinion it contains only the popular philosophy of Leibniz which must be considered shallow, incredible and orthodox. His true thought not being such as would secure him the approval he found so necessary, was left unpublished and is only now being brought to light. This philosophy, says Lord Russell, is largely influenced by Spinoza, and is deep, utterly logical and unorthodox.[1]

It is said, further, that Leibniz concealed his great debt to Spinoza, minimising the extent of his discussion with the Jewish heretic. A courtier and a politician, loving power, money, position and adulation, Leibniz unlike Spinoza was in the thick of public life. A man of wide attainments and tremendous knowledge, he has been considered the finest intellect of his time in Europe, barring Newton,[2] and even one of the superlative minds of all time.[3]

Of his character it has been observed that 'although intellectually great, he was something of a moral poltroon, doubtless made so through his vanity—for he was extremely vain, eager for distinction and living for the smiles of the great. He was of a

[1] *Op. cit.*, p. 604.
[2] S. Hampshire, *op. cit.*, p. 233.
[3] B. Russell, *op. cit.*, p. 604.

contentious and jealous character . . . and while ignoring Spinoza or speaking of him disparagingly, he derived from him the germs of his own philosophy.'[1] (I record this bad press merely to suggest the strong incentives Leibniz may indeed have had for suppressing his real philosophy.)

The monads Leibniz calls 'windowless,' since they neither know nor are affected by each other. They tick 'in time' together through the benevolence of the Creator of the best of all possible worlds. But the argument for God's existence from Pre-established Harmony—that since all the clocks are synchronised without any casual interaction, it must be a Cause outside that wound and set them—can be valid only for those who accept the non-interaction of the monads which reflect the universe.

This argument, moreover, can be converted into the argument from design, the Physico-Theological argument dismissed by Kant. The interesting point about this is the theory it advances that the God it postulates may be neither omnipotent nor omniscient, and that the defects of creation and the presence of evil in the world may be due to the limitations of his power.

Whitehead has told us that with the monads which constituted a fresh version of an atomic interpretation of the Universe, Leibniz approached cosmology subjectively, showing what it must be like to be an atom. Each individual monad was directly in communication with God; and therefore there was an indirect communication between monads through God. But why is the supreme monad, God, immune from the decree of isolation? How do the windowless monads come to have windows towards God, and vice versa? Leibniz, we are told, was the first and far away the greatest philosopher to allow communication between the experiencing subject and the mysterious reality in the background whilst facing the inherent difficulty.[2]

[1] R. D. Willis, *op. cit.*, p. 138.   [2] *Adventures of Ideas*, p. 131.

Early in the *Monadology*, we meet with the principle of sufficient reason' which demonstrates that everything in the universe must be just as it is. Leibniz affirms that nothing which happens can do so without a reason, and that no fact or statement can be true unless it has a sufficient reason why it should be so and not otherwise. This principle is deduced from the existence of God. But he merely invokes the principle of sufficient reason to postulate a First Cause. He offers no satisfactory proof of God's existence.

Thus we read:

38. 'The final reason of things must be found in a necessary substance, in which the detail of change exists eminently as their source. And this substance we call God.

39. 'Now this substance being a sufficient reason of all this detail, which also is everywhere linked together, *there is only one God, and this God suffices.*

40. 'We may also conclude that this supreme substance, which is unique, universal, and necessary—having nothing outside of it—and which is a simple series of possible being, must be incapable of limits, and must contain as much of reality as possible.

41. 'Whence it follows that God is perfect, perfection being nothing but the magnitude of positive reality taken exactly, setting aside the limits or bounds in that which is limited. And where there are no bounds, that is to say, in God, perfection is absolutely infinite.

42. 'It follows also that the creatures have their perfections from the influence of God, but they have their imperfections from their own nature, which is incapable of existing without limits. For it is by this that they are distinguished from God.'

Besides bringing into their ultimate form the metaphysical proofs of the existence of God, Leibniz advances his own original argument from eternal truths. It is fundamentally a form of the cosmological proof.

Leibniz holds that there are two kinds of truths, necessary and contingent. All statements of truths which are such as their opposite is neither possible nor even conceivable, are necessary truths. They deal with essence only; as, for example: 'If A is smaller than B, and B is smaller than C, then A is smaller than C;' is always true. Whereas truths dealing with existence, such as 'the sun is shining' may be true sometimes but not at others. These are contingent truths.

Necessary or eternal truths, Leibniz says, must belong to eternal minds. And he terms God's thought the 'region of eternal truths,' for the necessity of necessary truths was explicable on the hypothesis that they are being thought by God. Leibniz sees in necessary truths the ultimate explanation of contingent truths.

43. 'It is true, moreover, that God is not only the source of existences, but also of essences, so far as real, or of that which is real in the possible. For the divine understanding is the region of eternal truths, or of the ideas on which they depend, and without him there would be nothing real in the possibilities of things, and not only nothing existing, but also nothing possible.

44. 'At the same time, if there be a reality in the essence or possibilities or in the eternal truths, this reality must be founded in something existing and actual, consequently in the existence of the necessary Being, in whom essence includes existence, or with whom it is sufficient to be possible in order to be actual.'

It has been observed:

'As each monad is confined to itself, we can know the harmony of existence with our perceptions only through our knowledge of God. Yet it would seem that the knowledge of God cannot be attained by a being who is an individual substance, unless he transcends the limits of his individuality—i.e. unless he goes beyond representations or perceptions, which are merely modifications of his own being, and rises to a representation or perception which includes existence in itself. And this, indeed, is implicitly acknowledged by Leibniz himself when he defines God as the Being, the possibility or thought of whom involves his existence.'[1]

45. ' Thus God alone (or the necessary Being) possesses this privilege, that he must exist, if he is possible; and since nothing can hinder the possibility of that which includes no limits, no negation, and consequently no contradiction, that alone is sufficient to establish the existence of God *a priori*. We have likewise proved it by the reality of eternal truths. But we have also just proved it *a posteriori* by showing that, since contingent beings exist, they can have their ultimate and sufficient reason only in some necessary Being, who contains the reason of his existence in himself.'

We are further told:

46. ' Nevertheless, we must not suppose, as some do, that eternal verities, being dependent upon God, are arbitrary, and depend upon his will, as Descartes, and afterwards M. Poiret, appear to have held. This is true only of contingent truths, the principle of which is fitness, or the choice of the best; whereas necessary truths depend solely on his understanding, and are its inner object.

47. ' Thus God alone is the primitive unity, or the original simple substance of which all the created or derived monads are the products; and they are generated so to speak, by continual fulgurations of the Divinity, from moment to

[1] E. Caird, *Philosophy of Kant*, p. 77 (Maclehose, 1877).

moment, bounded by the receptivity of the creature, of whose existence limitation is an essential condition.

48. ' In God is *Power*, which is the source of all; also *Knowledge*, which contains the detail of ideas; and, finally, *Will*, which generates changes or products according to the principle of optimism.

84. '. . . Spirits are able to enter into a kind of fellowship with God. In their view he is not merely what an inventor is to his machine (which is the relation of God to other creatures), but also what a prince is to his subjects, and even what a father is to his children.

89. ' We may say, furthermore, that God as architect satisfies entirely God as legislator, and that accordingly, sins must carry their punishment with them in the order of nature, and by virtue even of the mechanical structure of things; and that good deeds in like manner will bring their recompense, through their connexion with bodies, although this cannot, and ought not always to happen immediately.

90. ' Finally, under this perfect government, there will be no good deed without its recompense, and no evil deed without its punishment, and all must redound to the advantage of the good, that is to say, of those who are not malcontents, in this great commonwealth, who confide in Providence after having done their duty, and who worthily love and imitate the Author of all good, pleasing themselves with the contemplation of his perfections, following the nature of genuine "pure love" which makes us blest in the happiness of the loved. In this spirit the wise and good labour for that which appears to be conformable to the divine will . . . contented the while with all that God brings to pass . . . recognising that if we were sufficiently acquainted with the order of the universe we should find that it surpasses all the wishes of the wisest, and that it

could not be made better than it is, not only for all in general, but for ourselves in particular, if we are attached . . . to the Author of All, not only as the architect and efficient cause of our being, but also as our master and final cause, who ought to be the whole aim of our volition, and who alone can make us blest.'

From the *Monadology of Leibniz*, translated by Frederic Henry Hedge (*Journal of Speculative Philosophy*, ed. W. T. Harris, I, 1867, pp. 129-137; id., F. H. Hedge's *Atheism in Philosophy, and Other Essays*, Boston, Roberts Bros., 1884, pp. 245-273).

Note on Kant's three postulates.
Kant on the arguments for God's existence

(KANT 1724-1804)

The supreme good is realisable only if there is postulated a Being who is the cause of nature and who effects conformity between nature and the moral character of the agent. Such a Being must act from the consciousness of law and be a rational intelligence, and a will. Therefore the supreme good implies the existence of God. But God's nature is not brought within range of our knowledge when we conceive of him as having intelligence and will; for we do not attribute to him psychological characteristics peculiar to human intelligence and will, such as would be incompatible with the nature of a Supreme Being. We have that apprehension of God only as is requisite for moral action. Thus although the predicates arise from the nature of man, no anthropomorphism is intended.

The realisation of the supreme good would not be possible apart from the three postulates. We are morally bound to promote the supreme good; and in the influence on the agent by the moral law the possibility of the realisation of the supreme good is presupposed. Thus, on the immortality of the soul, Kant says that Reason demands the union of felicity and virtue, the *summum bonum*. But for man whose desires conflict with his reason, virtue is obtainable only by infinite progress. Thus pure, practical reason demands our postulating this infinite progress.

And this is possible only on the supposition that life is prolonged infinitely. Further, a man must preserve his personality since without it he could not be a free agent willing the moral law. Thus immortality is a logical presupposition indispensable to the realisation of the highest good. What speculative reason failed to prove theoretically, practical reason has established: that man is immortal because his duration, as a moral agent, must be sufficient for the total realisation of the moral law.

ARGUMENTS FOR GOD'S EXISTENCE

The Ontological Proof argues that
' because the idea of God includes existence, therefore he necessarily exists. It is to be observed that the predicate is asserted only on condition of the assertion of the subject. If a triangle exists, it cannot but have three angles; and so if God exists, he is, in the case supposed, a necessary Being, i.e., he exists by the necessity of his nature. There is a contradiction in supposing the existence of a triangle without three angles, or the existence of a God who is not necessarily existent. There is a contradiction, in other words, in supposing the existence of the subject without the predicate; but there is no contradiction in supposing that both are nonexistent, or denied together. There may be no such thing as a triangle, why should there be such a Being as God?'[1]

Kant points out that a judgment that the predicate is inseparable from the subject fails to prove the real existence of the subject. He finds in this confusion of a purely logical necessity with necessary existence, a fertile cause of illusion.

Of the *Cosmological Proof*, Kant says:
' If something exists, an absolutely necessary Being

[1] E. Caird, *Philosophy of Kant*, pp. 630-1.

exists. Now I, at least, exist myself; therefore an absolutely necessary Being exists. The minor proposition contains an experience; and the major the existence of the necessary Being from experience in general. (Every thing contingent has its cause, which if it is again contingent, must likewise have a cause, till the series of causes subordinate to one another must terminate in an absolutely necessary Cause, without which it [this series] would not be complete. . . .)

' And thus the second way, which speculative reason takes to prove the existence of the Supreme Being, is not only alike fallacious with the first, but has this blamable in it, that is, by promising us a new path, but after a short circuitous course, bringing us back again to the old one, which we left on its account, is guilty of an *ignoratio elenchi*.' [1]

The Physico-Theological Proof [2]

'will always deserve to be treated with respect. It is the oldest, the clearest, and most in conformity with human reason.

' First, there are everywhere in the world clear indications of an intentional arrangement carried out with great wisdom, and forming a whole indescribably varied in its contents, and infinite in extent.

' Secondly, the fitness of this arrangement is entirely foreign to the things existing in the world, and belongs to them contingently only; that is, the nature of different things could never spontaneously, by the combination of

---

[1] Argument that whilst appearing to refute an opponent actually disproves something not advanced by him.
From *An Enquiry, Critical and Metaphysical into the Grounds of Proof for the EXISTENCE OF GOD, and into the THEODICY, a Sequel to the Logic and the Prolegomena*, translated by John Richardson, printed in 1819, but now first published, MDCCCXXXVI.
[2] *Critique of Pure Reason*, translated by Max Muller.

so many means, co-operate towards definite aims, if these means had not been selected and arranged on purpose by a rational disposing principle, according to certain fundamental ideas.

' Thirdly, there exists, therefore, a sublime and wise cause (or many), which must be the cause of the world, not only as a blind and powerful nature by means of unconscious fecundity, but as an intelligence, by freedom.

' Fourthly, the unity of that cause may be inferred with certainty from the unity of the reciprocal relation of the parts of the world, as portions of a skilful edifice, so far as our experience reaches, and beyond it, with plausibility, according to the principles of analogy.

' We see that the Physico-Theological Proof, baffled in its own undertaking, takes suddenly refuge in the Cosmological Proof, and as this is only the Ontological Proof in disguise, it really carries out its original intention by means of pure reason only; though it so strongly disclaimed in the beginning all connection with it, and professed to base everything on clear proofs from experience.

' Thus we have seen that the Physico-Theological Proof rests on the Cosmological, and the Cosmological on the Ontological Proof of one original Being; and as besides these three, there is no other path open to speculative reason, the Ontological Proof, based exclusively on pure concepts of reason, is the only possible one, always supposing that any proof of a proposition, so far transcending all empirical use of the understanding, is possible at all.'

Extracts from Hegel's ' Philosophy of Religion,' together with notes from J. M. Sterrett's ' Studies' in the same

(HEGEL 1770–1831)

To say that God is Absolute is not to discover him to thought. If it is added that he is the Absolute Substance and that everything else is phenomenal and relative, we arrive only at Spinoza's pantheism.

> ' The defect attaching to this . . . Substance . . . of Spinoza, lies in the categories of origination and perishing. Substance is not conceived of as the active agent within itself, as subject and as activity in accordance with ends; not as wisdom but only as power. It is essentially purposeless, empty power, which merely staggers about, so to speak.' (I, p. 333.)[1]
> ' This abstract Substance, which is the ultimate principle of the philosophy of Spinoza, this Substance which is *thought of,* which is only for thought, cannot be the content of the religion of a people, cannot be the faith of a concrete Spirit.' (II, p. 56.)[2]

Further we read:

---

[1] In this section the references to Hegel's *Philosophy of Religion* have been placed immediately after each extract, and those to J. M. Sterrett's *Studies in Hegel's Philosophy of Religion* given in footnotes as this makes for easier reading.

[2] Hegel uses the term *abstract* for the kind of knowing that isolates a part

303

' In the spirit, as such, the consciousness of God exists immediately with the consciousness of its self.' (I, pp. 42-3.)

' According to the philosophical conception, God is Spirit, is concrete; and ... the whole of religious doctrine consists in the development of the fundamental conception of Spirit . . . Spirit is essentially self-manifestation—its nature is *to be for Spirit* . . . It has been said that the . . . material universe must have spectators, and must be for Spirit or mind; how much more, then, must God be for Spirit? ' (I, p. 46.)

' The fact of the fellowship of God and Man with each other involves a fellowship of Spirit with Spirit. It is a fellowship, and this very circumstance involves the difficulty of at once maintaining the fact of difference and of defining it in such a way as to preserve the fact of fellowship. That Man knows God implies, in accordance with the essential idea of communion or fellowship, that there is a community of knowledge; that is to say, Man knows God only in so far as God himself knows himself in Man. This knowledge is God's self-consciousness, but it is at the same time a knowledge of God on the part of Man, and this knowledge of God by Man is a knowledge of Man by God. The spirit of Man whereby he knows God is simply the Spirit of God himself.' (III, pp. 303-4.)

God is eternally self-conscious. And as men recognise God as their Father and adopt his will as their own, their consciousness of him rises to self-consciousness. Only as God is known as him in whom we live and move and have our being do we attain fully

---

or element from its organic connection of thought; it is thus a one-sided view. *Concrete* he uses for the kind that grips together these elements in indestructible unity; it is thus a catholic view. Science and sense are examples of the first kind of knowledge, philosophy an example of the second. The reason concretes, whilst the mere understanding abstracts.

to this. The ultimate purpose of men's creation is to be the perfect reflection of God and thus complete his self-conscious ness.[1]

Hegel uses the term *consciousness* to signify the phenomenal part of the mind in which external things are known. Professor Sterrett warns us that we must not misinterpret Hegel's assertion that the self-consciousness of man is the complement of the Divine self-consciousness, as meaning that God first came to consciousness in man. That would be pantheism, and is the doctrine of Schopenhauer and the left-wing Hegelians. The similar charge that Hegel makes the finite spirit one with Deity is, according to Sterrett, also unfounded.[2] Certainly Hegel says:

> ' I and God are different from one another; if both were One, there would then be immediate relation, free from any mediation; relationless unity, that is to say, unity without differentiation.' (I, pp. 166-7.)

And again:

> ' If man be immediately God . . . that is the doctrine of Pantheism. The Church declares that it is only through the abrogation of this naturalness that man becomes united with God.' (I, p. 217.)

This is Hegel's ' Die to live.' Further, Sterrett declares that to Hegel no man is divine; but through the *Theios paidagogos* in an age-long struggle, man as man is made capable of the Divine.[3]

Hegel holds that it is from the inadequacy of the commonplace conception of the finite and the Infinite, that the majority of our intellectual troubles arise, giving birth to relativism,

[1] See Sterrett, *op. cit.*, pp. 205-7 (Swan Sonnenschein, 1891).
[2] *Ibid.*, p. 205.   [3] *Ibid.*, p. 206.

scepticism and doubtful theology. It was his great endeavour to demonstrate how thought could, in the form of the dialectic, force such inadequate conceptions of the Infinite and the finite out of an unnatural separation, into fulfilment in each other with the emergence of the true concrete Infinite.[1] It is in the rationality of the real, binding together God and man in no fortuitous or arbitrary relationship, that Hegel finds his basis for the Philosophy of Religion: the fundamental notion of the fact of an Infinite which is concrete, and unites the earth in kinship. God and man are parts of one system of thought, and not irreconcilable elements.[2]

' It is sufficient here merely to observe regarding the supposed opposition of the Philosophy of Religion and positive religion, that there cannot be two kinds of reason and two kinds of Spirit; there cannot be a Divine Spirit and a human which are absolutely different. Human reason —the consciousness of one's being—is indeed reason;[3] it is the divine in man; and Spirit, in so far as it is the Spirit of God, is not a spirit beyond the world. On the contrary, God is present, omnipresent, and exists as Spirit in all spirits. God is a living God, who is acting and working. Religion is a product of the Divine Spirit; it is not a discovery of man, but a work of divine operation and creation in him.' (I, p. 33.)

' God is infinite, I am finite; these are false, bad expressions, forms which do not adequately correspond to

---

[1] By *dialectic* is meant that self-imposed criticism which rejects partial conceptions of the understanding, and by annulling abstractions moves towards a whole, concrete unity.

[2] *Ibid*, p. 52.

[3] It is necessary to distinguish between Reason (*Vernunft*) and Reason (*Verstand*). The former is the unifying faculty of comprehension, speculative and synthesising, whilst the latter is the understanding which analyses and defines separate constituents as independent and ultimate data.

that which the Idea, the nature of the real object is.[1] The finite is not that which is, in like manner the infinite is not fixed; these determinations are only moments of the process.[2] It is equally true that God exists as finite and the Ego as infinite. . . . What is true, what is the Idea exists only as a movement. Thus God is this movement within himself, and thereby alone is he the living God—God is movement towards the finite, and owing to this he is, as it were, the lifting up of the finite to himself. In the Ego, as in that which is annulling itself as finite, God returns to himself, and only as this return is he God. Without the world God is not God.'

' We must get rid of this bugbear of the opposition of the finite and the infinite. It is customary to frighten us out of the wish to know God and to have a positive relation to him, with the bugbear that to seek to take up any such attitude towards God is presumption, while the objections are brought forward with much unction and edifying language, and with vexatious humility. This presumption, however, is undoubtedly an essential part of philosophy as well as of religion.' (I, pp. 199-200.)

Religion for Hegel is a living, mutual communion between God and man, in which the seeking and finding are utterly real.

[1] Of this *Idea*, Hegel says: ' We have, speaking generally, to consider the Idea as divine self-revelation . . .' (III, p. 4). It is the essential relation of finite and Infinite as the organic, concrete system of thought. It is Divine self-consciousness. It can be thought of as God in—and for—himself before the creation, in his eternity, outside the world; in the creation of the world (where God because of his very essence, reconciles the externality and alienism of creation to himself); and as the process of reconciliation, the work of the Holy Spirit in his Church. (See Sterrett, *op. cit.*, pp. 288-9.)

[2] *Moment* is a constituent factor in a unity. Thus e.g. the Three Persons of the Trinity are moments in the Godhead.

For him, to know God *is* eternal life. And although religion can never be merely intellectual, he claims for human thought the power to know reality, maintaining the ultimate identity of thought and being. But because God for him is no unknowable *Ding-an-sich* deity whose very nature involves a perpetual game of hide-and-seek, Hegel we are told, has often been considered impious.[1]

' At the present time we only hear religion spoken of, and do not find that investigation is made regarding the nature of God, what he is in himself, and how the nature of God must be determined. God, as God, is not even made an object of thought.' (I, p. 45.)

' On God's part there can be no obstacle to a knowledge of him through men. The idea that they are not able to know God must be abandoned when it is admitted that God has a relation to us . . . communicates himself and has revealed himself. . . . If there is no hindrance on God's side to the knowledge of him, then it is owing to human caprice, to an affectation of humility, or whatever you like to call it, that the finitude of knowledge, the human reason, is put in contrast to the divine knowledge and the divine reason, and that the limits of human reason are asserted to be immovable and absolutely fixed. What is here suggested . . . is the more definite thought that it is not the so-called human reason with its limits which knows God, but the Spirit of God in Man.' (III, pp. 194-5.)

' The object of theology as generally understood is to get to know God as the merely objective God, who is absolutely separated from the subjective subconscious and is thus an outward object, just as the sun, the sky, etc., are objects of consciousness, and here the object is permanently characterised as an Other, as something external. In

[1] Sterrett, *op. cit.*, p. 75.

contrast to this the Notion[1] of the absolute religion can be so presented as to suggest that what we have got to do with is not anything of the external sort, but religion itself, i.e., the unity of this idea which we call God with the conscious subject.'[2] (II p. 330.)

' It no longer gives our age any concern that it knows nothing of God; on the contrary, it is regarded as a mark of the highest intelligence to hold that such knowledge is not even possible. What is laid down by the Christian religion as the supreme, absolute commandment, "Ye shall know God," is regarded as a piece of folly. The wisdom of our time has made of God an infinite phantom, which is far from us, and in like manner has made human knowledge a futile phantom of finiteness, or a mirror upon which fall only shadows, only phenomena. How, then, are we to respect the commandment, and grasp its meaning, "Be ye perfect, as your Father in heaven is perfect" since we know nothing of the Perfect One, and since our knowing and willing are confined solely and entirely to appearance, and the truth is to be and to remain absolutely and exclusively a something beyond the present? And ... what else would it be worth while to comprehend, if God is incomprehensible?' (I, p. 36.)

' Religion must be something for all men; for those who have so purified their thought that they know what exists in the pure element of thought, and who have arrived at a philosophical knowledge of what God is, as

---

[1] Of the *Notion*, Hegel says: 'The Notion is the inner element, the Potentiality' (I, p. 275). 'The unity of man with God, with nature in the general sense as Potentiality' (I, p. 274). Generally speaking Notion is 'what has life, what is self-mediating' (III, p. 356).

[2] It is necessary to distinguish between *idea* (*Begriff*) meaning a grasping together of constituent parts of a concrete thought, a comprehension; and *Idea* (*Idée*).

well as for such as have not got beyond feeling and ordinary ideas.' (III, p. 366.)

'Scientifically considered, God is at first a general, abstract name, which as yet has not come to have any meaning. For it is the Philosophy of Religion which is the unfolding, the apprehension of that which God is, and it is only by means of it that our philosophical knowledge of his nature is reached.' (I, p. 90.)

That Hegel teaches both the personality of God and the immortality of man is strongly upheld, says Professor Sterrett, by Hegel's recognised exponent Dr. Erdmann. The personality of God is in substance the same as in man, but it is infinite. Lotze, we are told, even says that 'perfect personality can be found only in God, and that in all finite spirit there exists only a weak simulacrum.' Sterrett holds that any interpretation of Hegel which fails to attribute to him belief in the personality and freedom of both God and man is valueless.[1]

For Hegel, the postulating of a *deus ex machina*, a First Cause, can give us only a God in name, an unknowable *noumenon*, such as e.g., Kant's *Ding-an-sich*, which Jacobi described as 'enjoying a position of *otium cum dignitate*, which is the next thing to non-existence.' Only if God is a living God in living relation with his creatures, can man know him, and perceive his manifestations. In his essential process of creating and transcending the finite, is he thus in relation to it.[2]

The Idea, the First Principle, is God as Self-conscious Reason, the absolute reason and will, free metaphysically but necessitated morally through the necessity of Divine Love.[3] Here, the immanent Deity is 'at home' in all that he has created, and is not merely the *deus ex machina* above the world

---

[1] *Op. cit.*, p. 180.   [2] *Ibid.*, p. 31.

[3] Necessity, *Nothwendigkeit*, is found only in the concrete; its true significance in the ethical and spiritual. Thus 'the truth of necessity is freedom.'

who but rarely reaches out a helping hand from above the skies.[1]

God is not only immanent; he is transcendent: but in place of the substance of Aristotle, Hegel substitutes the complete concrete Christian conception of Spirit, of Subject, that Essence which impels itself into phenomenal being. And not only does he maintain that such a conception is absolutely required for Personality in the Godhead, but that that Personality itself requires that the nature of God should be triune. Thus, he regards the doctrine of the Holy Trinity as the living core of all Christian theology. For him religion is immanent in the triune divine nature, and he finds in the relationship of the Three Persons of the Trinity, all that is the essence of religion—the absolute form of love, communion and atonement.[2]

Viewed by the mere understanding, the Trinity is a mystery and contradiction. The mental picturing of the invisible in the visible, metaphorical finite thought, the Absolute truth conceived in terms of understanding, sense and imagination, is what Hegel calls *Vorstellung*. He sees in this picture-thinking or representation a device of thought used by the greatest part of mankind, in order to get above sense and bring an object before the mental eye. Conceptions resulting from such a method derive partly from sense and partly from the self-conscious, and they ' half-conceal and half-reveal.' Philosophy is thus necessary to convert conceptual into organic thought.[3]

Spiritual truth appears primarily to everyone in the form of representative knowledge. And metaphors are used, then abused. From infancy to old age it is metaphors which feed and foster our religious life. As metaphor, the language of biblical and devotional literature is anthropomorphic, and it is necessary to struggle ceaselessly with worn-out conceptions which distort the truth.[4]

The Incarnation, Hegel considers, is the fundamental doctrine of Christianity from the historical, temporal side, as he finds in

[1] *Ibid.*, pp. 161 and 163.   [2] *Ibid.*, p. 165.   [3] *Ibid.*, pp. 88-9.   [4] *Ibid.*, p. 90.

the doctrine of the Holy Trinity the fundamental one on the Godward side.

It is in the most forcible terms that Hegel expresses his view of the necessity not only of the Incarnation, but that this should have taken place at a certain time and in a certain place, once and for all, in one special human being. Unlike the oriental *Avatars*, this Incarnation can occur once only and is absolutely unique.[1]

Jesus Christ is not simply a great man or a sublime teacher, or the greatest of the prophets. He is absolutely the incarnate Son of God, and thus is he beyond all human categories and relative definitions. The God-Man cannot be properly defined otherwise; and this is the doctrine as taught by the Church. But the complete and endless differentiation between the divine and the human spirit renders the thought of the Incarnation monstrous to us.[2]

On the Divine side ' It is finished,' once and for ever. On the manward side the reconciliation is a continual doing, a working out in humanity and in the individual man.[3]

Of Hegel's few statements on immortality in the *Philosophy of Religion*, these appeared to me as the most significant:

' The idea which a man has of God corresponds with that which he has of himself, of his freedom. Knowing himself in God, he at the same time knows his imperishable life in God; he knows of the truth of his Being, and therefore the idea of the *immortality of the soul* here enters as an essential moment into the history of religion. The ideas of God and of immortality have a necessary relation to each other; when a man knows truly about God, he knows truly about himself too: the two sides correspond with each other.' (I, pp. 79-80.)

' The idea of immortality hangs together with the idea

---

[1] *Ibid.*, p. 293. [2] *Ibid.*, pp. 293-4. [3] *Ibid.*, p. 294.

of God. It always corresponds, in short, with the stage at which the metaphysical conception of God has arrived. The more the power of spirituality is conceived of in accordance with its content in an eternal form, the worthier is the idea of God, as well as the idea of the spirit of the human individual and of the immortality of the spirit.' (I, pp. 313-14.)

' Man as Spirit is immortal, is an object of God's interest, is raised above finitude and dependence, above external circumstances; he has freedom to abstract himself from everything, and this implies that he can escape mortality.' (III, p. 57.)

' What is mortal is what can die; what is immortal is what can reach a state in which death cannot enter.' (III, p. 57.)

' The soul, the individual soul, has an infinite, an eternal quality, namely, that of being a citizen in the Kingdom of God. This characteristic contains the reason why the immortality of the soul becomes a definite doctrine in the Christian religion. The infinite demand to see God, i.e., to become conscious in spirit of his truth, is in this temporal Present not yet satisfied so far as consciousness in its character as ordinary consciousness is concerned. (III, p. 105.)

For Hegel, feeling, intuition and faith are essential elements of religion, and his aim is to translate their content into thought-forms so that it may be preserved.[1] To him pectoral theology is true theology since he believes that the heart is not self-moved and the feelings not self-inspired.[2] Yet theology must also be thought.[3] An 'Age of Reason', however, seemed to him as foolish as it was odious. Knowledge of God was not to be attained through reasons *pro* and *con*; there must be vital

[1] *Ibid.*, p. 12. [2] *Ibid.*, p. 84. [3] *Ibid.*, pp. 44-5.

experience of communion with God. And to know him is eternal life.[1]

If he was impatient with agnosticism, he was even more so with mysticism. He believed that one devitalised thought whilst the other flooded it with more than the unprepared mind was able to receive.[2]

It is in the true *cultus* or worship that the real reconciliation of the two conceptions of God as immanent and transcendent is to be found.[3] The unity of God and man is represented in the Incarnation.[4] The transcendental God is manifested immanence. And the at-one-ment of God and man is effected through the twofold actions of God's grace and of man's self-sacrifice—actions which involve each other mutually—the death of the old Adam and the birth of the new. Man is truly man only when united to God. And it is in 'Die to live' that Hegel finds the ultimate law of being.[5]

It has been said that

> 'what Christianity teaches is only that the law of the life of the spirit—the law of self-realisation through self-abnegation—holds good for God as for man, and, indeed, that the spirit that works in man to 'die to live' is the Spirit of God. For Hegel such a doctrine was the demonstrated result of the whole idealistic movement which is summed up in his Logic.'[6]

Thus, for Hegel, ' He that saveth his life shall lose it, and he that loseth his life shall save it' is the fundamental truth of the nature of all Spirit. And worship is a giving up of the self and a receiving of God.[7]

Dogma, he said, was necessary and must be taught as valid truth and as being the work of the Holy Spirit. And since it must

---

[1] *Ibid.*, p. 34.   [2] *Ibid.*, p. 74.   [3] *Ibid.*, p. 55.   [4] *Ibid.*, p. 57.
[5] *Ibid.*, pp. 157-8.   [6] E. Caird, *Hegel*, p. 218 (Blackwood, 1883).
[7] See Hegel, *Philosophy of Religion*, Vol. I, pp. 227-8.

be preserved and taught, the ministry is an essential part of the Church. The Church is in general the communion of worshippers and is possible only through definite teaching. Christian consciousness is by the immanent Holy Spirit led into all truth.[1] And it is important, Hegel says, that the Christian religion should not be confined to the literal words of Christ himself; for it is in the Apostles that the developed and completed truth is first shown.[2]

For Hegel personality is immortality. Man's goal is the realisation of self-consciousness in his reflection of God. This, we are told, is the subject matter of Hegel's entire philosophy. And that anyone should doubt this is accounted for by the fact that Hegel is known better through the traditions of his opponents than through a careful study of his own philosophy.[3]

Clement, it is said, opposed those who pronounced all paganism to be entirely false, and declared that everything that was good in heathen religions must be included in God's plan of education for the human race; that Greek philosophy as well as Judaism was a preparation for Christianity.[4] It is in the *Logos* that God has revealed himself to every nation, Christianity being the highest revelation. Moreover, in spite of its profundity the Christian religion is easily understandable in its outward aspect although calling us always to penetrate to greater depths of inner truth. Thus is it adapted to every stage of culture whilst satisfying the highest requirements.[5]

---

[1] See *Ibid.*, Vol. III, pp. 123-6 and 97-8; and Sterrett, *op. cit.*, pp. 296-7.
[2] Sterrett, *op. cit.*, p. 296. [3] *Ibid.*, p. 208. [4] *Ibid.*, p. 26.
[5] *Philosophy of History*, p. 344, quoted by Sterrett, *op. cit.*, p. 300.

Extracts from Kierkegaard's 'Journals,' 'For Self-Examination,' 'The Point of View,' 'Training in Christianity,' 'Concluding Unscientific Postscript,' etc.

(KIERKEGAARD 1813-1855)

'If man is to receive any knowledge about the Unknown, he must be made to know that it is unlike him, absolutely unlike him.' (*Philosophic Fragments*, pp. 36-7.)

'The majority of men live all too safely in life, that is why they learn to know God so little.' (*Journals*, 627.)

'. . . Only think what it means to dare to believe that God came into the world, and for my sake too. . . . If it were not God himself who said it . . . of all blasphemies it would be the most terrible. It is therefore not invented to show how important man is to God—but in order to show how infinite is the love of God.' (*Ibid.*, 752.)

'The fact that God lived here on earth as an individual man is infinitely noteworthy . . . infinitely more noteworthy than all consequences. . . . How could it be noteworthy that God's life had noteworthy consequences? To talk in such a way is to twaddle.' (*Training in Christianity*, p. 34.)

'Christianity did not come into the world as an admirable example of the gentle art of consolation—but as the *absolute*. It is out of love that God wills it so. . . . He will not suffer himself to be transformed by men and be a nice . . . human God: he will transform men, and that he wills out of love. . . . God presumably does not understand men, his requirements are exorbitant. . . . Relatively understood, the absolute is the greatest plague. . . . Christianity seems madness, since it is incommeasurable with any finite wherefore.' (*Ibid.*, p. 66.)

' The God-Man is the paradox, absolutely the paradox; hence it is quite clear that the understanding must come to a standstill before it.' (*Ibid.*, p. 85.)

'. . . Every individual . . . needs and craves to have something which stands and shall stand unconditionally fast. . . . Let the race, let each individual make the experiment of doing without the unconditional . . . it may seem like stability and security. But at bottom it is . . . a whirlpool. Even the greatest events and the most laborious lives are . . . like sewing without knotting the thread—until the end is once again made fast by the fact . . . that the individual comes to relate himself to the unconditional. Without [which] man cannot in the deepest sense be said to " live." ' (*Supplement* to *On My Work as an Author*, pp. 163-4.)

' Faith is precisely the contradiction between the infinite passion of the individual's inwardness and the objective uncertainty. If I am capable of grasping God objectively, I do not believe, but precisely because I cannot do this I must believe.' (*Concluding Unscientific Postscript*, p. 182.)

' The object of faith is not a doctrine, but God's reality in existence as a particular individual.' (*Ibid.*, p. 290.)

' The man who never let go of probability never committed himself to God. All religious (not to say Christian) adventure is on the farther side of probability, is by letting go of probability.' (*For Self-Examination*, p. 116.)

' As thou believest, so art thou; to believe is to be.'

317

Christianly understood, sin lies in the will, not in the intellect.'
(*The Sickness unto Death*, p. 132.)

'A true sentence of Hugo de St Victor (Helfferich: *Mystik*, Vol. I, 368): "In things which are above reason faith is not really supported by reason, because reason cannot grasp what faith believes; but there is also a something here as a result of which reason is determined, or which determines reason to honour faith which it cannot perfectly understand." That is what I explained (e.g. in the *Final Postscript*); not every absurdity is "the absurd" or the paradox. The effect of reason is in fact to know the paradox negatively—but not more.' (*Journals*, 1033.)

'Imitation must be introduced, to exert pressure in the direction of humility. We must get rid of all the bosh about this being said only to the Apostles and this only to . . . the first Christians, etc. Christ no more desires now than he did then to have admirers (not to say twaddlers). The "disciple" is the standard. It shall not be so that we men are permitted to abrogate the ideal requirement, saying that the thing is not for us, and then to hunt up a certain mediocrity, and then begin to make that the standard, and then become distinguished . . . merely because the standard has been altered to suit us.'
(*For Self-Examination*, p. 207.)

'Everyone who has not suffered for the doctrine has in one way or another been guilty of using his shrewdness to spare himself.' (*Ibid.*, p. 215.)

'The same thing happens to Christianity, or to becoming a Christian, as to all radical cures; one puts it off as long as possible.'
(*Journals*, 27.)

'Christ certainly died for all men, and also for me; but that "for me" must be understood in the sense that he only died for me in so far as I belong to the many.' (*Ibid.*, 192.)

'. . . The consciousness of sin is the *conditio sine qua non* of Christianity.' (*Ibid.*, 479.)

'People try to persuade us that the objections against Christianity spring from doubt. That is a complete misunderstanding. The objections . . . spring from insubordination, the dislike of obedience, rebellion against all authority. As a result people have hitherto been beating the air . . . because they have fought intellectually with doubt instead of fighting morally with rebellion.' (*Ibid.*, 630.)

'Most people really believe that the Christian commandments (e.g. to love one's neighbour as oneself) are intentionally a little too severe—like putting the clock on half an hour to make sure of not being late in the morning.' (*Ibid.*, 762.)

'The pagans had after all far more feeling for what is fitting in everyday religion than we Protestants in particular. One need only recall how they thought of the gods *first* at meal times, at festivities, almost everywhere indeed.' (*Ibid.*, 934.)

'Christianity has been made too much into a *consolation*; people have forgotten that it is a *demand*.' (*Ibid.*, 999.)

'. . . Of one fault we are all guilty more or less: of loving too little.' (*For Self-Examination*, p. 13.)

The *Journals* are translated by Alexander Dru; the *Concluding Unscientific Postscript* and *Philosophical Fragments* by David Swenson. The remaining works are translated by Walter Lowrie, D.D. In every case the publishers are the Oxford University Press.

NOTE ON KIERKEGAARD'S THOUGHT

It has been said that in dialectics, the talent of Kierkegaard fell little short of that of Plato; whilst for Wittgenstein Kierkegaard was of all nineteenth century philosophers the greatest.[1] In the philosophy of both, we are told, there is the same appreciation of a Socratic ignorance felt to be so necessary as a corrective to the thought of our time.[2]

Just as Spinoza sought that which would give him joy eternal, so Kierkegaard, I read, sought the truth for which he could live and die.[3]

Existence for him was the offspring of the conflict between the finite and the infinite, of time and eternity, and thus was a continual struggle to become in the 'tension of reality.' All real thinking must concern itself only with such existence and be conditioned by it—truth inseparable from the existence of the knower.[4]

For Kierkegaard, the God-Man is himself the existential.[5] And existential thinking is as passionate as philosophy is dispassionate. (Faith and truth are passions.) Therefore, it is open to the whole of humanity, since all can feel and suffer whilst few are able to reason. It cannot be that truth should be within reach of a learned minority only. The world of qualities, of reality, is open to the eye of the heart.[6] ' By love may he be gotten; but by thought never.'[7]

The existential, the Paradox, confronts a man with a deliberate choice. But the individual venturing wholly to be himself alone and confronting God, is not born until the death of the 'first immediacy.' This utter self-naughting includes the denial of romantic imagination and of the speculative wisdom of the world, of a merely æsthetic attitude to life, of the cozy delights of intellectual occupation, all of which usurp the rightful place of religion in a man's life.[8]

[1] M.O'C. Drury in *The Listener*, Jan. 28, 1960.
[2] *Ibid.* See also Kierkegaard's *Journals*, 962.
[3] M. Chaning-Pearce, *Sören Kierkegaard, a Study*, p. 29 (James Clarke, 1946).
[4] *Ibid.*, p. 30.   [5] Kierkegaard, *Journals*, 1054.
[6] Chaning-Pearce, *op. cit.*, p. 37.   [7] *The Cloud of Unknowing*.
[8] Chaning-Pearce, *op. cit.*, p. 47.

In his ferocious attacks on the romantic poet, the desiccated don, the abstract philosopher, the unrealist clergyman, we are told that Kierkegaard was chastising himself. That *trahison des clercs*, the treachery to life and the unlearned by the intellectuals which lies in this romantic, philosophic, æsthetic and religious detachment from real life, is a detachment to which Kierkegaard himself was particularly liable, and which he attacked therefore the more mercilessly.[1]

The Christianity of Kierkegaard is rooted in a realism entailing an inwardness which grows always more intense and more probing. ' The Kingdom of Heaven is *within*.' But for most men, as Mr. Chaning-Pearce declares, the inward is so unfamiliar and so obscure that nothing short of disaster can compel a man to face it. It is a realism uncongenial to those for whom the outward life alone holds the security of familiarity.[2]

Kierkegaard's doctrine of faith appears to Mr. Chaning-Pearce as nothing new, but a harking back to the conception of it found in the Bible, where faith is the very foundation of life and thought. To an age, however, that has turned away from faith as a creative force and has pursued the gods of humanism, Kierkegaard's reassertion comes as an 'offence,' a stumbling-block to man's unregenerate understanding.[3]

Although he derided the false gentleness that he found in Victorian Christianity, that sickly sentimental attitude, and although he urged severity as the only hope for a Christianity that has been abolished by gentleness,[4] in the *Journals* he shows how his own life has taught him the true gentleness of God, and that God's love is a spring that never runs dry.[5]

---

[1] *Ibid.*, p. 56. [2] *Ibid.*, p. 62. [3] *Ibid.*, p. 79.
[4] *Training in Christianity*, p. 222. [5] 1102 and 1105.

TEXT 12 *Extracts from the 'Upanishads,' and from the*
          'Bhagavadgîta,' with notes

The following are extracts from the *Katha*, the *Bridhadâranyka*, the *Svetâsvatara* and the *Maitrayana-brahmana Upanishads*. They are translated by Professor Max Muller, Oxford, Clarendon Press, 1884.

Of the *Katha-upanishad* he tells us that it is probably more widely known than any other Upanishad and has been frequently quoted as one of the most perfect specimens of the mystic philosophy and poetry of the ancient Hindus.

KATHA-UPANISHAD

1ST ADHYÂYA, 2ND VALLÎ:

2. 'The good and the pleasant approach man: the wise goes round about them and distinguishes them. Yea, the wise prefers the good to the pleasant, but the fool chooses the pleasant through greed and avarice.'

6. 'The Hereafter never rises before the eyes of the careless child, deluded by the delusion of wealth. "This is the world," he thinks, "there is no other" . . .'

20. 'The Self, smaller than small, greater than great, is hidden in the heart of that creature. A man who is free from desires and free from grief, sees the majesty of the Self by the grace of the Creator.'

IST ADHYÂYA, 3RD VALLÎ:

7. 'He who has no understanding, who is unmindful and always impure, never reaches that place, but enters into the round of births.'

8. 'But he who has understanding, who is mindful and always pure, reaches indeed that place, from whence he is not born again.'

2ND ADHYÂYA, 5TH VALLÎ:

13. 'There is one eternal thinker, thinking non-eternal thoughts, who, though one, fulfils the desires of many. The wise who perceive him within their Self, to them belongs eternal peace, not to others.'

2ND ADHYÂYA, 6TH VALLÎ:

14. 'When all desires that dwell in his heart cease, then the mortal becomes immortal, obtains Brahman.'

BRIDHADÂRANYKA-UPANISHAD
IST ADÂHYYA, 4TH BRÂHMANA:

1. 'In the beginning this was Self alone, in the shape of a person (*purusha*). He looking round saw nothing but his Self. He first said, "This is I"; therefore he became I by name. Therefore even now, if a man is asked, he first says, "This is I," and then pronounces the other name which he may have.'

2. 'He feared, and therefore any one who is lonely fears. He thought, "As there is nothing but myself, why should I fear?" Thence his fear passed away. For what should he have feared? Verily fear arises from a second only.'

3. 'But he felt no delight, therefore a man who is lonely feels no delight. He wished for a second. He was so large as man and wife together. He then made this his Self to fall in two, and thence arose husband and wife. Therefore Yâgnavalkya said: "We two are thus (each of us) like half a shell." Therefore the

void which was there, is filled by the wife. He embraced her, and men were born.'

Of the *Svetâsvatara-upanishad*, Muller says that it ranks very high amongst the *Unpanishads* and is one of the most interesting, with its strong stress upon the personality of its God, creator and ruler of the world. But he is *Brahma* under a semblance of a personal and creating God; the office of creator being an office too low, it was supposed, for *Brahmā*.

(The Universal Spirit, we have been told, is 'the only real Entity—which when unmanifested and impersonal is called *Brahma* (neuter): when manifested as a personal creator, *Brahmā* (masculine); and when manifested in the highest order of men is called *Brāhmana* (The Brāhmans).')[1]

THE SVETASVATARA-UPANISHAD

6TH ADHÂYA:

1. 'Some wise men, deluded, speak of Nature, and others of Time [as the cause of everything]; but it is the greatness of God by which the Brahma-wheel is made to turn.'
2. 'It is at the command of him who always covers this world, the knower, the time of time [destroyer of time], who assumes qualities and all knowledge, it is at his command that this work [creation] unfolds itself, which is called earth, water, fire, air and ether.'
5. 'He is the beginning, producing the causes which unite [the soul with the body], and, being above the three kinds of time [past, present, future], he is seen as without parts, after we have first worshipped that adorable god, who has many forms, and who is the true source [of all things], as dwelling in our own mind.'
11. 'He is the one God, hidden in all beings, all-pervading, the self within all beings, watching over all works, dwelling in all

---

[1] Monier Williams, *Brahmanism and Hinduism*, p. 2.

beings, the witness, the perceiver, the only one, free from qualities.'

18. 'Seeking for freedom I go for refuge to that God who is the light of his own thoughts, he who first creates Brahman and delivers the Vedas to him.'

22. 'This highest mystery in the Vedânta, delivered in a former age, should not be given to one whose passions have not been subdued, nor to one who is not a son, or who is not a pupil.'[2]

Writing of the *Maitrayana-upanishad*, Muller tells us that here we have a warning against doctrines which we should identify with those of Buddha. He considers the *Upanishads* to be the 'germs of Buddhism, while Buddhism is in many respects the doctrine of the *Upanishads* carried out to its last consequences.' He assigns the genuine and classical *Upanishads* to about the sixth century B.C.

MAITRAYANA-BRAHMANA-UPANISHAD

6TH PRAPÂTHAKA.

28. '. . . And thus it is said:

'"If a man practises Yoga for six months and is thoroughly free [from the outer world], then the perfect Yoga [union], which is endless, high and hidden, is accomplished.

'"But if a man, though well enlightened [by instruction], is still pierced by [the gunas of] passion and darkness, and attached to his children, wife and house, then perfect Yoga is never accomplished."'

7TH PRAPÂTHAKA.

9. 'By it [false knowledge] they show that good is evil, and that evil is good. They say that we ought to ponder on the [new] law,

---

[2] This is similar to the saying of Aristotle: 'Young men are no fit auditors of moral philosophy, because they are not settled from the boiling heat of their affections, nor attempered with time and experience.' (*Ethics*, Nic. I, 3) quoted by Bacon, '*Advancement of Learning*.'

which upsets the Veda and the other sacred books. Therefore let
no one ponder on that false knowledge: it is wrong, it is as it
were, barren. Its reward lasts only as a long as the pleasures last,
as with one who has fallen from his caste.'

It is no easy task to understand the Gîta aright. For we are
told that it is a collection of treatises which have been more or
less adapted to the Krishna theology. And the use of the word
Brahman introduces great confusion, since from the cosmological
point of view it is primal matter, whilst psychologically it
means the realisation of immortality.[1] Again, there are Vedantin
interpolations which use the word *Brahman* as the Absolute and
identify it with the human *atman*.[2]

In the Gîta we have a fully developed divine figure prefigured
by Isvara in the Upanishads. Transcendence and immanence
meet in Krishna, and the Gîta is the crowning glory of that
process of separating out God from Nature which, we are told,
began in the *Katha* and *Mundaka-upanishads*.[3] God is recognised
as someone distinct from man with whom union may yet be
possible, once the human soul has overcome attachment to the
world and the flesh.

Arjuna the warrior chief of the Pandavas, scruples to fight
against his kinsmen the Kurus in a battle undertaken from motives
of ambition. But the Lord Krishna, acting as his charioteer, argues
that the self of each man, as one with essential reality, cannot be
affected by physical death. Moreover, Arjuna as a member of
the *Kshatriya* (warrior) caste must fulfil his duty to kill. He must
cultivate indifference in order to pass into the highest state of
freedom and union with the One Reality. If he fails to fight,
dishonour will be his, and honour pass to the enemy.

Arjuna remaining unconvinced, Krishna now speaks of the

---

[1] Zaehner, *op. cit.*, p. 126.   [2] *Ibid.*, p. 118.
[3] *Ibid.*, p. 118.

incarnations of the Supreme Being. As Krishna-Vasudera he can be approached by men through *Bhakti* (faith and devotion). Even an evil-doer, as long as he worships Krishna wholeheartedly will be deemed good.

Krishna then reveals himself in response to Arjuna's request in his body, the universe. This, says Professor Zaehner, describes a direct experience comparable to those of the prophets of the Old Testament and to that of Mohammed in the Koran.[1]

After this tremendous vision, Arjuna prostrates himself in loving obedience before Krishna, crying out for grace and praying for a relationship as between father and son, lover and beloved.

The essential teaching of the Gîta is summed up at the end of the eighteenth chapter with the telling of the sublime secret— God's love for man.

EXTRACTS FROM THE BHAGAVADGITA
(TRANSLATION BY SIR EDWIN ARNOLD)

Krishna reminds Arjuna that death for the soul is an impossibility: it is a natural inhabitant of Brahman, the eternal world. It is therefore unaffected by the slaying of the body. (Chapter II.)

' Thou grievest where no grief should be, thou speakest
Words lacking wisdom, for the wise in heart
Mourn not for those that live, nor those that die.
Not I, nor thou, nor anyone of these,
Ever was not, nor ever will not be,
For ever and for ever afterwards.
All, that live, lives always. . . .

The soul that with a strong and constant calm
Takes sorrow and takes joy indifferently
Lives in the life undying; that which is
Can never cease to be; that which is not

[1] *Ibid.*, p. 118.

Will not exist. To see this truth of both
Is theirs who part essence from accident,
Substance from shadow. Indestructible,
Learn thou, the Life is, spreading life through all: . . .

How, if thou hearest that the man new-dead
Is, like the man new-born, still living man—
One same, existent Spirit, wilt thou weep ?
The end of birth is death; the end of death
Is birth; this is ordained . . .'

The state of Brahman is to be reached through detachment. Right-thinking is extolled even more than the right act. (Chapter III.)

' Yet, the right act
Is less, far less, than the right-thinking mind.
Seek refuge in thy soul; have there thy heaven.

In sorrows not dejected, and in joys
Not overjoyed; dwelling outside the stress
Of passion, fear and anger; fixed in calms
Of lofty contemplation;—such an one
Is Muni, is the Sage, the true Recluse . . .
. . . That man alone is wise
Who keeps the mastery of himself.'

The Religion of Knowledge; Approach to Krishna is described.
(Chapter IV.)

' Many there be who come, from fear set free,
From anger, from desire; keeping their hearts
Fixed upon me—my Faithful—purified
By sacred flame of knowledge. Such as these
Mix with my being. Whoso worship me,
Them I exalt; but all men everywhere
Shall fall into my path; albeit, those souls

Which seek reward for works, make sacrifice
Now, to the lower gods. I say to thee
Here have they their reward. But I am He
Made the Four Castes, and portioned them a place
After their qualities and gifts.'

The Search for Truth is the greatest good. (Chapter IV.)

'. . . The sacrifice
Which knowledge pays is better than great gifts
Offered by wealth, since gifts' worth—O my Prince,
Lies in the mind which gives, the will that serves;
And these are gained by reverence, by strong search,
By humble heed of those who see the Truth
And teach it . . .
There is no purifier like thereto
In all this world, and he who seeketh it
Shall find it—being grown perfect—in himself.
Believing, he receives it when the soul
Masters itself, and cleaves to Truth, and comes—
Possessing knowledge—to the higher peace,
The uttermost repose.'

Krishna speaks of the doctrine of Renouncing the Fruit of Works.
(Chapter V.)

' That is the true Renouncer, firm and fixed,
Who—seeking nought, rejecting nought—dwells proof
Against the "opposites" '[joy and sorrow, success and failure
    heat and cold].

' Whoso is fixed in holiness, self-ruled,
Pure-hearted, lord of senses and of self,
Lost in the common life of all which lives—
A " Yôgayukt"—he is a Saint who wends

Straightway to Brahm. Such an one is not touched
By taint of deeds. " Nought of myself I do,"
Thus will he think—who holds the truth of truths.'

Self-disciplined by Yoga (integration), the sage attains to Brahman, the innermost soul of the law pervading all nature. (Chapter VI.)

'. . . The sovereign soul
Of him who lives self-governed and at peace
Is centred in itself, taking alike
Pleasure and pain; heat, cold; glory, shame.
. . . loving, all alike,
Evil or good.
        Sequestered should he sit,
Steadfastly meditating, solitary,
His thought controlled, his passions laid away,
Quit of belongings.

. . . And whoso thus
Discerneth Me in all, and all in Me,
I never let him go; nor looseneth he
Hold upon Me . . .
. . . if a man sees everywhere—
Taught by his own similitude—one life,
One Essence in the Evil and the Good,
Hold him a Yôgi, yea, well perfected.'

Devotion to the One supreme God. (Chapter VIII.)

' For who, none other Gods regarding, looks
Ever to Me, easily am I gained
By such a Yôgi; and attaining Me,
They fall not, those Mahatmas, back to birth,
To life, which is the place of pain. . . .'

The Kingly Knowledge and the Kingly Mystery. (Chapter IX.)

' If one of evil life turn in his thought
Straightly to Me, count him amidst the good;
He hath the high way chosen; he shall grow
Righteous ere long: He shall attain that peace
Which changes not. Thou Prince of India
Be certain none can perish, trusting Me . . .
Though they be born from the very womb of Sin,
Woman or man; sprung of the Vaisya caste
Or lowly disregarded Sudra,—all
Plant foot upon the highest path. . . .'

The separateness of the Divine and the Undivine. (Chapter XVI.)

' Two stamps there are marked on all living men,
Divine and Undivine; I spake to thee
By what marks thou shouldst know the Heavenly Man,
Hear from me now of the Unheavenly. . . .

               . . . " This world
Hath not a law, nor Order, nor a Lord,"
So say they: "nor hath risen up by Cause
Following on Cause, in perfect purposing,
But is none other than a House of Lust. . . ,"
Surrendered to desires insatiable,
Full of deceitfulness, folly, and pride,
In blindness cleaving to their errors, caught
Into the sinful course, they trust this lie
As it were true—this lie which leads to death—
Finding in Pleasure all the good which is,
And crying " Here it finisheth."

               Ensnared
In nooses of a hundred idle hopes,

Slaves to their passion and their wrath, they buy
Wealth with base deeds, to glut hot appetites;
" Thus much, to-day," they say, " we gained; thereby
Such and such wish of heart shall have its fill;
And this is ours, and th' other shall be ours."
    . . . So they speak
Darkened by ignorance; and so they fall—
Tossed to and fro with projects, tricked, and bound
In net of black delusion, lost in lusts—
Down to foul Maraka. Conceited, fond
Stubborn and proud, dead drunken with the wine
Of wealth . . . Thus vowed
To self-hood, force, insolence, feasting, wrath,
These My blasphemers, in the form they wear
And in the forms they breed, my foemen are,
Hateful and hating; cruel, evil, vile,
Lowest and least of men, whom I cast down again, at end
    of lives,
Into some devilish womb, whence—birth by birth—
The devilish wombs re-spawn them, all beguiled;
And till they find and worship me, sweet Prince.'

The doctrine of Deliverance and Renunciation. (Chapter XVIII.)

' The work of Brahmans, Kshatriyas, Vaisyas,
And Sudras, O thou Slayer of thy Foes,
Is fixed by reason of the Qualities
Planted in each:

Whoso performeth—diligent, content—
The work allotted him, whate'er it be,
Lays hold of perfectness. . . .

Better thine own work is, though done with fault,
Than doing others' works, ev'n excellently.

332

He shall not fall in sin who fronts the task
Set him by Nature's hand.

Devoted—with a heart grown pure, restrained
In lordly self-control, forgoing wiles
Of song and senses, freed from love and hate,
Dwelling 'mid solitudes, in diet spare,
With body, speech, and will tamed to obey,
Ever to holy meditation vowed,
From passions liberate, quit of the Self,
Of arrogance, impatience, anger, pride;
Freed from surroundings, quiet, lacking nought—
Such an one grows to oneness with the BRAHM; . . .
Sorrows no more, desires no more; his soul,
Equally loving all that lives, loves well
Me, Who have made them, and attains to Me.
And Whatsoever deeds he doeth—fixed
In Me, as in his refuge—he hath won
For ever and for ever by My grace
Th' Eternal Rest. So win thou. In thy thoughts
Do all thou dost for Me. Renounce for Me.
Sacrifice heart and mind and will to Me.
Live in the faith of Me. In faith of Me
All dangers thou shalt vanquish, by My grace; . . .

There lives a Master in the hearts of men
Maketh their deeds, by subtle pulling-strings,
Dance to what tune He will. With all thy soul
Trust Him, and take Him for thy succour, Prince. . . .

Give me thy heart; adore Me; serve Me; cling
In faith and love and reverence to Me.
So shalt thou come to Me. I promise true,
For thou are sweet to Me. . . .'

TEXT 13   *Extracts from the 'Dhammapada' (one of the Canonical Books of the Buddhists), translated from the Pali by Professor Max Muller (Clarendon Press, Oxford, 1881)*
The Buddhist Creed
Extracts from 'The Book of the Great Decease,' translated from the Pali by Sir Monier Monier Williams
The Four Noble Truths and The Noble Eightfold Path

THE DHAMMAPADA

CHAPTER I. THE TWIN-VERSES

1. 'All that we are is the result of what we have thought: it is founded on our thoughts. If a man speaks or acts with an evil thought, pain follows him, as the wheel follows the foot of the ox that draws the carriage.'

4. ' " He abused me, he beat me, he defeated me, he robbed me,"—in those who do not harbour such thoughts hatred will cease.'

5. 'For hatred does not cease by hatred at any time: hatred ceases by love, this is an old rule.'

CHAPTER II. ON EARNESTNESS

21. 'Earnestness is the path of immortality (Nirvāna), thoughtlessness the path of death. Those who are in earnest do not die, those who are thoughtless are as if dead already.'

CHAPTER III. THOUGHT

35. 'It is good to tame the mind, which is difficult to hold in

and flighty, rushing wherever it listeth; a tamed mind brings happiness.'

42. 'Whatever a hater may do to a hater, or an enemy to an enemy, a wrongly directed mind will do us greater mischief.'

CHAPTER IV. FLOWERS

50. 'Not the perversities of others, not their sins of commission or omission, but his own misdeeds and negligence should a sage take notice of.'

CHAPTER V. THE FOOL

64. 'If a fool be associated with a wise man even all his life, he will perceive the truth as little as a spoon perceives the taste of soup.'

69. 'As long as the evil done does not bear fruit, the fool thinks it is like honey: but when it ripens, then the fool suffers grief.'

CHAPTER VI. THE WISE MAN (*Pandita*)

85. 'Few are there among men who arrive at the other shore [become *Arhats*]: the other people here run up and down the shore.'

89. 'Those whose mind is well grounded in the [seven] elements of knowledge, who without clinging to anything, rejoice in freedom from attachment, whose appetites have been conquered, and who are full of light, are free [even] in this world.'

CHAPTER IX. EVIL

121. 'Let no man think lightly of evil, saying in his heart, it will not come nigh unto me. Even by the falling of water-drops a water-pot is filled; the fool becomes full of evil, even if he gather it little by little.'

124. 'He who has no wound in his hand, may touch poison with his hand; poison does not affect one who has no wound; nor is there evil for one who does not commit evil.'

CHAPTER X. PUNISHMENT

133. 'Do not speak harshly to anybody; those who are spoken to will answer thee in the same way. Angry speech is painful, blows for blows will touch thee.'

143. 'Is there in this world any man so restrained by humility that he does not mind reproof, as a well-trained horse the whip?'

CHAPTER XI. OLD AGE

152. 'A man who has learnt little, grows old like an ox; his flesh grows, but his knowledge does not grow.'

155. 'Men who have not observed proper discipline, and have not gained treasure in their youth, perish like old herons in a lake without fish.'

CHAPTER XII. SELF

157. 'If a man hold himself dear, let him watch himself carefully. . . .'

CHAPTER XIII. THE WORLD

174. 'This world is dark, few only can see here; a few only go to heaven, like birds escaped from the net.'

CHAPTER XVI. PLEASURE

211. 'Let no man love anything; loss of the beloved is evil. Those who love nothing, and hate nothing, have no fetters.'

CHAPTER XVII. ANGER

223. 'Let a man overcome anger by love, let him overcome evil by good; let him overcome the greedy by liberality, the liar by truth.'

CHAPTER XVIII. IMPURITY

246. 'He who destroys life, who speaks untruth, who in this world takes what is not given him, who goes to another man's wife,

247. And the man who gives himself to drinking intoxicating liquors, he, even in this world, digs up his own root.'

252. 'The fault of others is easily perceived, but that of oneself is difficult to perceive; a man winnows his neighbour's faults like chaff, but his own fault he hides, as a cheat hides the bad die from the gambler.'

CHAPTER XIX. THE JUST

271, 272. 'Not only by discipline and vows, not only by much learning, not by entering into a trance, not by sleeping alone, do I earn the happiness of release which no worldling can know. *Bhikshu*, be not confident as long as thou hast not attained the extinction of desires.'

CHAPTER XX. THE WAY

273. 'The best of ways is the eightfold; the best of truths the four words; the best of virtues passionless; the best of men he who has eyes to see.'

278. '"All created things are grief and pain," he who knows and sees this becomes passive in pain; this is the way that leads to purity.'

284. 'So long as the love of man towards women, even the smallest, is not destroyed, so long is his mind in bondage, as the calf that drinks milk is to his mother.'

285. 'Cut out the love of self, like an autumn lotus, with thy hand! Cherish the road of peace. Nirvāna has been shown by *Sugata* (Buddha).'

CHAPTER XXII. THE DOWNWARD COURSE

306. 'He who says what is not goes to hell; he also, who, having done a thing says I have not done it. After death both are equal, they are men with evil deeds in the next world.'

CHAPTER XXIV. THIRST

338. 'As a tree, even though it has been cut down, is firm so

long as its root is safe, and grows again, thus, unless the feeders of thirst are destroyed, this pain [of life] will return again and again.'

CHAPTER XXVI. THE BRĀHMAN (*Arhat*)

394. 'What is the use of platted hair, O fool! what of the raiment of goatskins? Within thee there is ravening, but the outside thou makest clean.'

418. 'Him I call indeed a *Brāhman* who has left what gives pleasure and what gives pain, who is cold and free from all germs [of renewed life], the hero who has conquered all the worlds.'

The Book of the Great Decease, Professor Rhys Davids tells us is the Buddhist representative of what, among Christians is called a Gospel. There is complete ignorance as to the actual authorship; but the *Suttas* contain the beliefs of the earliest Buddhists in India as to what were the original doctrines taught by Gautama. No records of the actual words of the Teacher could have been preserved. The speeches placed in his mouth are only intended to be short summaries of what he said on these occasions.

The four Noble Truths and the Seven Jewels of the Law were probably the teaching of Gautama himself.

The simple Nicene Creed of the Buddhist is:

I take my refuge in the Buddha,
I take my refuge in the *Dhamma*,
I take my refuge in the Order.

EXTRACTS FROM THE MAHAPARINIBBANA-SUTTANTA (THE BOOK OF THE GREAT DECEASE)
TRANSLATED FROM THE PÂLI BY SIR MONIER MONIER WILLIAMS
(*Buddhism*, p. 50)

Shortly before his decease, he (Gautama) said, 'It may be, Ananda, that in some of you this thought may arise: "The

words of our Teacher are ended; we have lost our Master."
But it is not thus. The truths and the rules of the Order, which
I have taught and preached, let these be your teacher, when I
am gone.' (VI, i.)

'Behold now, O monks, I exhort you: Everything that
cometh into being passeth away; work out your own perfection
with diligence.' (III, 66.) (According to the translation by T.
W. Rhys Davids this was the last word of the *Tathagata*, the
Blessed One.)

THE FOUR NOBLE TRUTHS:

1. All existence, whether on earth or in heavenly spheres,
necessarily involves pain and suffering.
2. All suffering is caused by lust, craving or desire for three things
—for sensual pleasure, for wealth, and for existence.
3. Cessation of suffering is simultaneous with extinction of lust,
craving and desire.
4. Extinction of these and cessation of suffering are achieved by
perseverance in the Noble Eightfold Path.

The Noble Eightfold Path consists of right belief or views;
right resolve; right speech; right work; right livelihood; right
exercise or training; right mindfulness; right mental concentration.

TEXT 14 *Extracts from the Koran,*
translated and with notes by J. M. Rodwell

Of the Koran, Bosworth Smith observes that:

'Mohammed and his enemies are quite at one as to the merits of the book. The Arabs said that the *Koran* could not be Mohammed's work because it was too good. Mohammed replied that they were both right and wrong. They were right, for it was too good for Mohammed uninspired: they were wrong, for it was too good to have come originally from any one but the All-Merciful.'[1]

'Strange and graphic accounts have been preserved for us by Ayesha of the physical phenomena attending the Prophet's fits of inspiration. He heard as it were the ringing of a bell; he fell down as one dead; he sobbed like a camel; seemed as though he were being rent in pieces, and when he came to himself he felt as though words had been written on his heart.

'Unlike any other book, the *Koran* lays claim to a verbal, literal, and mechanical inspiration in every part alike and is regarded as such by almost all Mohammedans. In it we have beyond all doubt the exact words of Mohammed.'[2]

Of the word *Sura* Rodwell says:

'It is not easy to determine whether it means a whole

[1] See Bosworth Smith, *op. cit.*, pp. 177-8. [2] *Ibid.*, p. 182.

chapter, or part only of a chapter or is used in the sense of "revelation." It is understood by the Mohammedan commentators to have a primary reference to the succession of subjects or parts, like the *rows* of bricks in a wall.'[1]

The name of each *Sura* is taken from one word occurring in that *Sura*.

In the following extracts, the first number refers to the original arrangement which was according to length, with the short *Suras* at the beginning and the longer ones at the end. The numbers in brackets refer to Rodwell's arrangement which aims to be the chronological order as far as can be ascertained. The notes are by Rodwell.

SURA XCVI—THICK BLOOD, OR CLOTS OF BLOOD (1)
' Recite thou, in the name of the Lord who created:—
    Created man from CLOTS OF BLOOD:—
Recite thou. For thy Lord is the most Beneficent,
    Who hath taught the use of the pen:—
Hath taught Man that which he knoweth not.
Nay, verily, Man is insolent,
Because he seeth himself possessed of riches.
Verily, to thy Lord is the return of all.'

EXTRACT FROM SURA LXXIV. THE ENWRAPPED (II)
' O thou, ENWRAPPED in thy mantle
Arise and warn.
Thy Lord—magnify Him.
Thy raiment—purify it.
The abomination—flee it.
And bestow not favours that thou mayest receive again with
    increase;
And for thy Lord wait thou patiently.'

[1] J. M. Rodwell, *The Koran* (Williams & Norgate, 1861).

SURA I (VIII)

'Praise be to God, Lord of the worlds.
The compassionate, the merciful.
King on the day of reckoning.
Thee only do we worship, and to Thee do we cry for help.
Guide thou us on the straight path,
The path of those to whom Thou hast been gracious;—with
Whom Thou art not angry, and who go not astray.'

(This is recited several times in each of the five daily prayers, and on many other occasions, as in concluding a bargain, etc.)

SURA CXII—THE UNITY (X)

'SAY: He is God alone:
God the eternal.
He begetteth not, and He is not begotten;
And there is none like unto Him.'

EXTRACTS FROM SURA XLIII—ORNAMENTS OF GOLD (LXI)

'And when the son of Mary was set forth as an instance of divine power, lo, thy people cried out for joy thereat:
And they said, "Are our gods or is he the Better?"[1]
They put this forth to thee only in the spirit of dispute. Yea, they are a contentious people.
Jesus is no more than a servant whom we favoured, and proposed as an instance of divine power to the children of Israel.'[2]

EXTRACT FROM SURA XXI—THE PROPHETS (LXV)

'And Zacharias; when he called upon his Lord saying, "O

[1] 'Are our gods or is he the better?' was a captious objection made to Mohammed when he condemned their gods . . . as if they had said, 'Jesus is worshipped as a God by the Christians: does he come under your anathema equally with our idols? We shall be content for our gods to be with him."

[2] That is, as we caused Jesus to be born without a human father.

my Lord, leave me not childless: but there is no better heir than Thyself."

So we heard him, and gave him John, and we made his wife fit for child-bearing. Verily, these vied in goodness, and called upon us with love and fear, and humbled themselves before us:

And her who kept her maidenhood, and into whom we breathed of our spirit, and made her and her son a sign to all creatures.'[1]

EXTRACT FROM SURA XXV—AL FURKAN (LXVI)

' Blessed be He who hath sent down AL FURKAN (the illumination) on his servant, that to all creatures he may be a warner.

His is the Kingdom of the Heavens and of the Earth. No son hath he begotten. No partner hath He in his Empire. All things hath He created, and decreeing hath decreed their destinies. . . .

And the Infidels say, " This Koran is a mere fraud of his own devising, and others have helped him with it . . ."

And they say, " Tales of the ancients that he hath put in writing, and they were dictated to him morn and even." '

EXTRACTS FROM SURA XXXII—ADORATION (LXX)

' This Book is without a doubt a Revelation sent down from the Lord of the Worlds.

Will they say, He hath forged it ? Nay, it is the truth from thy Lord that thou mayest warn a people to whom no warner hath come before thee, that haply they may be guided.'

EXTRACTS FROM SURA II—THE COW (XCI)

' Moreover, to Moses gave we " the Book," and we raised up apostles after him; and to Jesus, son of Mary gave we clear proofs of his mission, and strengthened him by the Holy Spirit.

[1] It is clear from this passage that Mohammed believed in the miraculous conception of Jesus.

And they say, "None but Jews or Christians shall enter Paradise:" This is their wish. SAY: Give your proofs if ye speak the truth.

Moreover, the Jews say, "The Christians lean on nought:" "On nought lean the Jews" say the Christians: Yet both are readers of the Book. So with like words say they who have no knowledge. But on the resurrection day, God shall judge between them as to that in which they differ.

But until thou follow their religion, neither Jews nor Christians will be satisfied with thee.

They say, moreover, "Become Jews or Christians that ye may have the true guidance."

Say ye: We believe in God, and that which hath been sent down to us and that which hath been sent down to Abraham and Ishmael and Isaac and Jacob and the tribes: and that which hath been given to Moses and to Jesus, and that which was given to the prophets from their Lord. No difference do we make between any of them: and to God are we resigned.

God. There is no God but He; the Living, the Eternal; Nor slumber seizeth Him, nor sleep; His, whatsoever is in the Heavens and whatsoever is in the Earth. Who is he that can intercede with Him but by His own permission? He knoweth what hath been before them and what shall be after them; yet nought of His knowledge shall they grasp, save what He willeth. His Throne reacheth over the Heavens and the Earth, and the upholding of both burdeneth Him not; and He is the High, the Great.

Let there be no compulsion in Religion. Now is the right way made distinct from error. Whoever therefore shall deny Thagout and believe in God—he will have taken hold on a strong handle that shall not be broken: and God is He who Heareth, Knoweth.

God is the patron of believers: He shall bring them out of darkness into light. . . .'

EXTRACTS FROM SURA III—THE FAMILY OF IMRAN[1] (XCVII)

'Remember when the wife of Imran[2] said, " O my Lord. I vow to thee what is in my womb, for thy special service. Accept it from me, for thou Hearest, Knowest." And when she had given birth to it, she said, " Oh my Lord. Verily I have brought forth a female."—God knew what she had brought forth; a male is not as a female[3]—"and I have named her Mary, and I take refuge with thee for her and for her offspring, from Satan the stoned."[4]

So with goodly acceptance did her Lord accept her, and with goodly growth did he make her grow.'[5]

EXTRACT FROM SURA LXI—BATTLE ARRAY (XCVIII)

' And remember when Jesus the son of Mary said, " O children of Israel, of a truth I am God's apostle to you to confirm the law

[1] Mohammed supposed Imran or Amran to be the father of the Virgin Mary (see Sura CIX), Mary and Elizabeth to be sisters; who with Jesus, John and Zacharias make up the family of Imran. [Amongst] his Jewish informants . . . the only well-known Mary (Miriam) was the daughter of Imran and the sister of Moses. . . . It is possible that Mohammed believed, as some Muslim writers assert, that Miriam's soul and body were miraculously preserved till the time of Jesus in order to become Mary his mother. Certainly the Talmudists fabled that the Angel of Death and the worm of corruption had no power over Miriam.

[2] The Wife of Imran is Hannah or Anne. . . . Although Mohammed had no direct access to the Apocryphal Gospels, yet these may have influenced, or . . . contained much in common with, the ordinary traditions of S. Syria. And of this the Immaculate Conception of the B. V. Mary, supposed by Gibbon (ch. 50) to have been ' borrowed from the Koran,' probably formed a part.

[3] That is, the female could not become a priest.

[4] That is, accursed. According to the Mohammedan tradition, Abraham drove Satan away with stones when he would have hindered him from sacrificing Ismael. . . .

[5] According to a tradition of Mohammed every new-born child is touched by Satan, with the exception of Mary and her Son, between whom and Satan God interposed a veil . . . Hence this passage may imply the Immaculate Conception of the B. V. Mary.

which was given before me, and to announce an apostle that shall come after me whose name shall be Ahmad. But when he (Ahmad) presented himself with clear proofs of his mission, they said, " This is manifest sorcery." '[1]

EXTRACTS FROM SURA IV—WOMEN (C)

' So, for that they have broken their convenant, and have rejected the signs of God, and have put the prophets to death unjustly, saying the while, " Our hearts are uncircumcised," Nay, but God hath sealed them up for their unbelief, so that but few believe.

And for their unbelief—and for their having spoken against Mary a grievous calumny,—

And for their saying, " Verily we have slain the Messiah, Jesus the son of Mary, an Apostle of God." Yet they slew him not, and they crucified him not, but they had only his likeness.[2] And they who differed about him were in doubt concerning him: No sure knowledge had they about him, but followed only an opinion, and they did not really slay him, but God took him up to Himself. And God is Mighty, Wise.

O ye people of the Book overstep not bounds[3] in your religion:

---

[1] Mohammed had no doubt heard that Jesus had promised a Paracletos. . . . This title, understood by him, probably from the similarity of sound, as equivalent to Periclytos, he applied to himself with reference to his own name Mohammed (i.e., praised, glorified) from the same root and of the same meaning as Ahmad, also one of the Prophet's names. Other passages of Scripture understood by Muslims of their Prophet are Deut, xxxiii, 2, where Paran is said to mean Islam; Isaiah, xxi, 6, where the 'rider on the ass' is Jesus, the 'rider on the camel,' Mohammed; Matt. xx, 1-16, where the morning, noon and even are Judaism, Christianity, and Islam; John iv, 21; 1 John iv, 2, 3, where Mohammed is said to be 'the spirit that is of God,' because he proclaimed that Jesus was a true man and not God.

[2] Lit. one was made to appear to them like [Jesus]. . . . This individual according to the Basilidans was Simon of Cyrene; according to the *Evang, Barnabae*, Judas.

[3] By believing too much, like the Christians who regarded Jesus as God; or too little, like the Jews, who would not believe in Mohammed.

and of God, speak only truth. The Messiah, Jesus, son of Mary, is only an apostle of God, and his Word which he conveyed into Mary, and a spirit[1] proceeding from himself. Believe therefore in God and his apostles, and say not " Three" (There is a Trinity)—Forbear—it will be better for you. God is only one God. Far be it from His glory that he should have a son. His, whatever is in the Heavens, and whatever is in the Earth. And God is a sufficient Guardian. The Messiah disdaineth not to be a servant of God, nor do the angels who are nigh unto Him.

Remember when God said, " Oh Jesus, verily I will cause thee to die[2] and will take thee up to myself and deliver thee from those who believe not; and I will place those who follow thee above those who believe not, until the day of resurrection. Then, to me is your return, and wherein ye differ will I decide between you.

And as to those who believe not, I will chastise them with a terrible chastisement in this world and in the next; and none shall they have to help them."

But as to those who believe, and do the things that are right, He will pay them their recompense. God loveth not the doers of evil. These signs, and this wise warning do we rehearse to thee.

Verily, Jesus is as Adam in the sight of God.[3] He created him of dust: He then said to him, ' Be ' and he was.

Abraham was neither Jew nor Christian; but he was sound in the faith, a Muslim; and not of these who add gods to God.

[1] That is, a Being possessing a Spirit.

[2] Mohammed probably believed that God took the dead body of Jesus to Heaven—for three hours according to some—while the Jews crucified a man who resembled him. (See Sura C.) It would seem from Sura XIX, that Mohammed supposed Jesus to have died a natural death. . . . The Mohammedans believe that Jesus on his return to earth at the end of the world will slay the Antichrist, die, and be raised again. A vacant place is reserved for his body in the Prophet's tomb at Medina.

[3] Neither of them had a human father.

SAY: We believe in God, and in what hath been sent down to us, and what hath been sent down to Abraham, and Ismael, and Isaac, and Jacob and the tribes, and in what was given to Moses, and Jesus, and the Prophets, from their Lord. We make no difference between them. And to Him are we resigned (Muslims).

Whoso desireth any other religion than Islam, that religion shall never be accepted from him, and in the next world he shall be among the lost.

Mohammed is no more than an Apostle; other apostles have already passed away before him. . . .

No one can die except by God's permission, according to the Book that fixeth the term of life. . . .

Every soul shall taste of death: and ye shall only receive your recompenses on the day of resurrection. And whoso shall scape the fire, and be brought to Paradise, shall be happy. And the life of this world is but a cheating fruition.

GENESIS

Now the Lord had said unto Abram, Get thee out of thy country, and from thy kindred, and from thy father's house, unto a land that I will shew thee: And I will make of thee a great nation, and I will bless thee, and make thy name great; and thou shalt be a blessing: And I will bless them that bless thee, and curse him that curseth thee: and in thee shall all families of the earth be blessed.

XII, 1-3.

And Abram said, Behold, to me thou hast given no seed: and, lo, one born in my house is mine heir. And, behold, the word of the Lord came unto him, saying, This shall not be thine heir; but he that shall come forth out of thine own bowels shall be thine heir. And he brought him forth abroad, and said, Look now toward heaven, and tell the stars, if thou be able to number them: and he said unto him, So shall thy seed be. And he believed in the Lord; and he counted it to him for righteousness.

XV, 3-6.

. . . and God talked with him, saying, As for me, behold, my covenant is with thee, and thou shalt be a father of many nations. . . . thy name shall be Abraham; . . . And I will establish my covenant between me and thee and thy seed after thee in their generations for an everlasting covenant, to be a God unto thee, and to thy seed after thee . . .

And God said unto Abraham, Thou shalt keep my covenant therefore, thou, and thy seed after thee in their generations. This is my covenant, . . . Every man child among you shall be circumcised. And ye shall circumcise the flesh of your foreskin; and it shall be a token of the covenant betwixt me and you.

XVII, 3, 5, 7, 9-11.

And the Lord visited Sarah as he had said, and the Lord did unto Sarah as he had spoken. For Sarah conceived, and bare Abraham a son in his old age, . . . And Abraham circumcised his son Isaac being eight days old, as God had commanded him.

XXI, 1-4.

ECCLESIASTICUS

In Isaac also did he establish likewise, for Abraham his father's sake, the blessing of all men, and the covenant; and he made it rest upon the head of Jacob; he acknowledged him in his blessings, and gave to him by inheritance, and divided his portions; among twelve tribes did he part them.

And he brought out of him a man of mercy, which found favour in the sight of all flesh; a man beloved of God and men, even Moses, whose memorial is blessed. He made him like to the glory of the saints, and magnified him in the fear of his enemies. He chose him out of all flesh. He made him to hear his voice, and led him into the thick darkness, and gave him commandments face to face, even the law of life and knowledge that he might teach Jacob the covenant, and Israel his judgments.

XLIV and XLV.

THE ACTS OF THE APOSTLES

. . . Isaac begat Jacob; and Jacob begat the twelve patriarchs. And the patriarchs, moved with envy, sold Joseph into Egypt: but God was with him, and delivered him out of all his afflictions, and gave him favour and wisdom in the sight of Pharaoh king of Egypt; and he made him governor over Egypt and all his house.

. . . But when the time of the promise drew nigh, which God

had sworn to Abraham, the people grew and multiplied in Egypt, till another king arose, which knew not Joseph. The same dealt subtilly with our kindred, and evil entreated our fathers, so that they cast out their young children, to the end they might not live. In which time Moses was born, . . . And when he was cast out, Pharaoh's daughter took him up, and nourished him for her own son. And Moses was learned in all the wisdom of the Egyptians, and was mighty in words and in deeds. VII.

EXODUS

Now Moses kept the flock of Jethro his father in law, the priest of Midian: and he led the flock to . . . the mountain of God, even to Horeb. And the angel of the Lord appeared unto him in a flame of fire out of the midst of a bush: . . .

And Moses said, I will now turn aside, and see this great sight, why the bush is not burnt. And when the Lord saw that he turned aside to see, God called unto him out of the midst of the bush, . . . And he said, Draw not nigh hither: put off thy shoes from off thy feet, for the place whereon thou standest is holy ground. Moreover he said, I am the God of thy father, the God of Abraham, the God of Isaac, and the God of Jacob. And Moses hid his face; for he was afraid to look upon God.

And the Lord said, I have surely seen the affliction of my people which are in Egypt, . . . the cry of the children of Israel is come unto me: . . . Come now therefore, and I will send thee unto Pharaoh, that thou mayest bring forth my people the children of Israel out of Egypt.

. . . Thus shalt thou say unto the children of Israel, I AM hath sent me unto you. . . . And they shall hearken to thy voice:

III, 1-13.

In the third month, when the children of Israel were gone forth out of the land of Egypt, the same day came they into the wilderness of Sinai. . . . and there Israel camped before the mount.

And Moses went up unto God, and the Lord called unto him

out of the mountain, saying, Thus shalt thou say to the house of Jacob, and tell the children of Israel; Ye have seen what I did unto the Egyptians, and how I bare you on eagles' wings, and brought you unto myself. Now therefore, if ye will obey my voice indeed, and keep my covenant, then ye shall be a peculiar treasure unto me above all people: . . . a kingdom of priests, and an holy nation. . . . And Moses . . . called for the elders of the people, and laid before their faces all these words which the Lord commanded him. And all the people answered together, and said, All that the Lord hath spoken we will do. . . .

And the Lord said unto Moses, Lo, I come unto thee in a thick cloud, that the people may hear when I speak with thee, and believe thee for ever. . . . Go unto the people, and sanctify them to day and to morrow, . . . and be ready against the third day: for the third day the Lord will come down in the sight of all the people upon mount Sinai. . . .

And the Lord came down upon mount Sinai, on the top of the mount: and the Lord called Moses up to the top of the mount; and Moses went up. And the Lord said unto Moses, Go down, charge the people, lest they break through unto the Lord to gaze, and many of them perish. . . .   XIX, 1-11, 20 and 21.

And God spake all these words, saying, I am the Lord thy God, which have brought thee out of the land of Egypt, out of the house of bondage.

Thou shalt have no other gods before me.

(*Here follow the rest of the Ten Commandments.*)

And all the people saw the thunderings, and the lightnings, and the noise of the trumpet, and the mountain smoking: and when the people saw it, they removed, and stood afar off. And they said unto Moses, Speak thou with us, and we will hear: but let not God speak with us, lest we die. . . .

And the Lord said unto Moses, Thus thou shalt say unto the children of Israel, Ye have seen that I have talked with you from heaven.   XX, 1-19.

Behold, I sent an Angel before thee, to keep thee in the way, and to bring thee into the place which I have prepared. Beware of him, and obey his voice, provoke him not; for he will not pardon your transgressions: for my name is in him. XXIII, 19-21.

And Moses took the tabernacle, and pitched it without the camp: . . .

And it came to pass, as Moses entered into the tabernacle, the cloudy pillar descended, and stood at the door of the tabernacle, and the Lord talked with Moses. And all the people saw the cloudy pillar stand at the tabernacle door: and all the people rose up and worshipped, every man in his tent door. And the Lord spake unto Moses face to face, as a man speaketh unto his friend. And he turned again into the camp: but his servant Joshua, the son of Nun, a young man, departed not out of the tabernacle.

XXXIII, 7, 9-11.

. . . and Moses rose up early in the morning, and went up unto mount Sinai, as the Lord had commanded him, . . . And the Lord descended in the cloud, and stood with him there, and proclaimed the name of the Lord. And the Lord passed by before him, . . .

And Moses made haste, and bowed his head toward the earth, and worshipped. . . .

And he was there with the Lord forty days and forty nights; he did neither eat bread, nor drink water. . . .

And it came to pass, . . . when he came down from the mount, that Moses wist not that the skin of his face shone while he talked with him. And when Aaron and all the children of Israel saw Moses, behold, the skin of his face shone; and they were afraid to come nigh him.   XXXIV, 4-6, 8, 28-30.

DEUTERONOMY

Hear, O Israel: The Lord our God is one Lord: and thou shalt love the Lord thy God with all thine heart, and with all thy soul, and with all thy might. And these words, which I command thee this day, shall be in thine heart: and thou shalt teach them diligently unto thy children, and shalt talk of them when thou sittest in thine house, and when thou walkest by the way, and when thou liest down, and when thou risest up. And thou shalt bind them for a sign upon thine hand, and they shall be as frontlets between thine eyes. And thou shalt write them upon the posts of thy house, and on thy gates. . . .

And thou shalt do that which is right and good in the sight of the Lord: that it may be well with thee, and that thou mayest go in and possess the good land which the Lord sware unto thy fathers, to cast out all thine enemies from before thee, as the Lord hath spoken.   VI, 4-9, 18,19.

I will raise them up a Prophet from among their brethren, like unto thee, and will put my words in his mouth; and he shall speak unto them all that I shall command him. And . . . whosoever will not hearken unto my words which he shall speak in my name, I will require it of him.   XVIII, 18-19.

So Moses the servant of the Lord died there in the land of Moab, according to the word of the Lord. . . .

And the children of Israel wept for Moses in the plains of Moab thirty days:

. . . And Joshua the son of Nun was full of the spirit of wisdom; for Moses had laid his hands upon him: and the children of Israel hearkened unto him, and did as the Lord commanded Moses.   XXXIV, 5, 8, 9.

ECCLESIASTICUS

Joshua the son of Nun was valiant in war, and was the successor of Moses in prophecies; who according to his name was made great for the saving of God's elect, to take vengeance of the enemies that rose up against them, that he might give Israel their inheritance.

Samuel, the prophet of the Lord, beloved of his Lord, established a kingdom, and anointed princes over his people. By the law of the Lord he judged the congregation, and the Lord visited Jacob. By his faithfulness he was proved to be a prophet, and by his words he was known to be faithful in vision.   XLVI.

And after him rose up Nathan to prophesy in the days of David. As is the fat when it is separated from the peace offering, so was David separated from the children of Israel. . . . In his youth did he not slay a giant, and take away reproach from the people, when he lifted up his hand with a sling stone, and beat down the boasting of Goliath? For he called upon the Most High Lord; and he gave him strength in his right hand, to slay a man mighty in war, to exalt the horn of his people. . . . For he destroyed the enemies on every side, and brought to nought the Philistines his adversaries, brake their horn in pieces unto this day. In every work of his he gave thanks to the Holy One Most High with words of glory: with his whole heart he sang praise and loved him that made him. . . . The Lord took away his sins, and exalted his horn for ever; and gave him a covenant of kings, and a throne of glory in Israel.

After him rose up a son, a man of understanding; and for his sake he dwelt at large. Solomon reigned in days of peace; and to him God gave rest round about, that he might set up a house for his name, and prepare a sanctuary for ever. . . .

Also there arose Elijah the prophet as fire, and his word burned like a torch: who brought a famine upon them, and by his zeal made them few in number. By the word of the Lord he shut up the heaven: thrice did he thus bring down fire. . . . Who did raise up a dead man from death, and from the place of the dead, by the word of the Most High: who brought down kings to destruction, and honourable men from their bed: . . . who was taken up in a tempest of fire, in a chariot of fiery horses. . . .

Elijah it was, who was wrapped in a tempest: and Elisha was filled with his spirit; and in all his days he was not moved by the fear of any ruler, and no one brought him into subjection.

XLVII.

The Texts

JONAH

And the word of the Lord came unto Jonah the second time, saying, Arise, go unto Nineveh, that great city, and preach unto it the preaching that I bid thee.   III, 1 and 2.

[*In his prayer Jonah says:*] '. . . thou art a gracious God, and merciful, slow to anger, and of great kindness, . . .'

JOEL

Therefore also now, saith the Lord, turn ye even to me with all your heart, and with fasting, and with weeping, and with mourning: And rend your heart, and not your garments, . . .
                                                                II, 12 and 13.

AMOS

Seek good, and not evil, that ye may live: and so the Lord, the God of hosts, shall be with you, as ye have spoken. Hate the evil, and love the good, and establish judgment in the gate: it may be that the Lord God of hosts will be gracious unto the remnant of Joseph.   v, 14 and 15.

I hate, I despise your feast days, . . . Though ye offer me burnt offerings and your meat offerings, I will not accept them: neither will I regard the peace offerings of your fat beasts. . . . But let judgment run down as waters, and righteousness as a mighty stream.   v, 21, 22, 24.

ISAIAH

The people that walked in darkness have seen a great light: they that dwell in the land of the shadow of death, upon them hath the light shined.   IX, 2.

For unto us a child is born, unto us a son is given: and the government shall be upon his shoulder: and his name shall be called Wonderful, Counseller, The mighty God, The everlasting Father, The Prince of Peace. Of the increase of his government and peace there shall be no end, upon the throne of David, and upon his kingdom, to order it, and to establish it with judgment and with justice from henceforth even for ever. The zeal of the Lord of hosts will perform this.   IX, 6 and 7.

And it shall come to pass in that day, that the remnant of Israel, and such as are escaped of the house of Jacob, shall no more again stay upon him that smote them; but shall stay upon the Lord, the Holy One of Israel, in truth. The remnant shall return, even the remnant of Jacob, unto the mighty God.   X, 20 and 21.

And there shall come forth a rod out of the stem of Jesse, and a Branch shall grow out of his roots: and the Spirit of the Lord shall rest upon him, the spirit of wisdom and understanding, the spirit of counsel and might, the spirit of knowledge and of the fear of the Lord; And shall make him of quick understanding in the fear of the Lord: and he shall not judge after the sight of his eyes, neither reprove after the hearing of his ears: but with righteousness shall he judge the poor, and reprove with equity for the meek of the earth: and he shall smite the earth with the rod of his mouth, and with the breath of his lips shall he slay the wicked. And righteousness shall be the girdle of his loins, and faithfulness the girdle of his reins.   XI, 1-5.

Who hath believed our report? and to whom is the arm of the Lord revealed? For he shall grow up before him as a tender plant, and as a root out of a dry ground: he hath no form nor comeliness; and when we shall see him, there is no beauty that we should desire him. He is despised and rejected of men; a man of sorrows, and acquainted with grief: and we hid as it were our faces from him; he was despised, and we esteemed him not.

Surely he hath borne our griefs, and carried our sorrows: yet faces from him, he was despised, and we esteemed him not. Surely he hath borne our griefs, and carried our sorrows: yet we did esteem him stricken, smitten of God, and afflicted. But he was wounded for our transgressions, he was bruised for our iniquities: the chastisement of our peace was upon him; and with his stripes we are healed. All we like sheep have gone astray; we have turned every one to his own way; and the Lord hath laid on him the iniquity of us all. . . .

And he made his grave with the wicked, and with the rich in his death; because he had done no violence, neither was any deceit in his mouth.

. . . he hath poured out his soul unto death: and he was numbered with the transgressors; and he bare the sin of many, and made intercession for the transgressors.   LIII, 1-6, 9, 12.

MICAH

But thou, Bethlehem Ephratah, though thou be little among the thousands of Judah, yet out of thee shall he come forth unto me that is to be ruler in Israel; whose goings forth have been from of old, from everlasting.   V, 2.

Who is a God like unto thee, that pardoneth iniquity, and passeth by the transgression of the remnant of his heritage? he retaineth not his anger for ever, because he delighteth in mercy.

VII, 18.

O my people, what have I done unto thee? and wherein have I wearied thee? testify against me. For I brought thee up out of the land of Egypt, and redeemed thee out of the house of servants; and I sent before thee Moses, Aaron and Miriam.   VI, 3 and 4.

Will the Lord be pleased with thousands of rams, or with ten thousands of rivers of oil? shall I give my first-born for my transgression, the fruit of my body for the sin of my soul? He hath showed thee, O man, what is good; and what doth the Lord require of thee, but to do justly, and to love mercy, and to walk humbly with thy God?   VI, 7 and 8.

JEREMIAH

Behold, the days come, saith the Lord, that I will make a new covenant with the house of Israel, and with the house of Judah: not according to the covenant that I made with their fathers in the day that I took them by the hand to bring them out of the land of Egypt; which my covenant they brake, although I was an husband unto them, saith the Lord: but this shall be the covenant that I will make with the house of Israel; After those days, saith the Lord, I will put my law in their inward parts, and write it in their hearts; and will be their God, and they shall be my people. And they shall teach no more every man his neighbour, and every man his brother, saying, Know the Lord: for they shall all know me, from the least of them unto the greatest of them, saith the Lord: for I will forgive their iniquity, and I will remember their sin no more. xxxi, 31-34.

EZEKIEL

And it came to pass at the end of seven days, that the word of the Lord came unto me, saying, Son of man, I have made thee a watchman unto the house of Israel: therefore hear the word at my mouth, and give them warning from me. When I say unto the wicked, Thou shalt surely die; and thou givest him not warning, nor speakest to warn the wicked from his wicked way, to save his life; the same wicked man shall die in his iniquity; but his blood will I require at thine hand. iii, 16-18.

I will feed my flock, and I will cause them to lie down, saith the Lord God. I will seek that which was lost, and bring again that which was driven away, and will bind up that which was broken, and will strengthen that which was sick: but I will destroy the fat and the strong; I will feed them with judgment.
xxxiv, 15 and 16.

DANIEL

I saw in the night visions, and, behold, one like the Son of man came with the clouds of heaven, and came to the Ancient of days, and they brought him near before him. And there was given him dominion, and glory, and a kingdom, that all people, nations, and languages, should serve him: his dominion is an everlasting dominion, which shall not pass away, and his kingdom that which shall not be destroyed. vii, 13 and 14.

And many of them that sleep in the dust of the earth shall awake, some to everlasting life, and some to shame and everlasting contempt. And they that be wise shall shine as the brightness of the firmament; and they that turn many to righteousness as the stars for ever and ever.   XII, 2 and 3.

MALACHI

Behold, I will send my messenger, and he shall prepare the way before me: and the Lord, whom ye seek, shall suddenly come to his temple, even the messenger of the covenant, whom ye delight in: behold, he shall come, saith the Lord of hosts. But who may abide the day of his coming? and who shall stand when he appeareth?[1] . . .   III, 1 and 2.

JEWISH BELIEFS OF THE PRESENT DAY

Moses Maimonides condensed the religious ideas of Judaism into thirteen fundamental principles:

> Belief in God, the Creator; in his unity; his priority and eternity; his non-corporal nature. That he alone is to be worshipped. That he knows the works of men.
> Belief in prophecy; that Moses was the greatest of the prophets.
> Belief that the Law was revealed from heaven; that it will never be annulled or added to.
> Belief in rewards and punishments; in the resurrection of the body.
> Belief in the coming of the Messiah.

These are widely accepted beliefs and fairly representative of opinions in Jewish theology. They are also found in orthodox Jewish prayer books.

[1] All translations are from the Authorised Version except for Ecclesiasticus (R.V.).

There is, too, strict observance not only of the Sabbath, but of four special times in the year:

Rosh Hashanah, the Jewish New Year, celebrated for two days and followed by ten days of self-examination and penitence, leading to

Yom Kippur (Day of Covering) on the tenth day of the New Year when there is strict fasting from sunrise to sunset. There is also a synagogue service. The Jew must make peace with his brethren before he can make peace with God. All wrong-doing must be confessed and forgiveness asked before the final blast of the Shofar which signifies the sealing of the Book.

Pesach, or Passover, a feast of rejoicing in memory of deliverance by Moses. A long ritual has to be observed, involving different foods as symbols.

Hannukah, the Feast of Lights occurring about Christmas time. Candles are lit for eight nights, one being added each night. The youngest child begins by saying the blessing and lighting the candle on the first night.

I. ON WHAT THE CHRISTIAN MUST STRIVE TO BE AND DO:

'God is a Spirit: and they that worship him must worship him in spirit and in truth.'   ST JOHN IV, 24

'Thou shalt love the Lord thy God with all thy heart, and with all thy soul, and with all thy mind. This is the first and great commandment. And the second is like unto it, Thou shalt love thy neighbour as thyself. On these two commandments hang all the law and the prophets.   ST MATT. XXII, 37-40.

'. . . For I was an hungred, and ye gave me meat: I was thirsty, and ye gave me drink: I was a stranger, and ye took me in: naked, and ye clothed me: . . . Inasmuch as ye have done it unto one of the least of these my brethren, ye have done it unto me.'   ST MATT. XXV, 35, 36, 40.

'Ye call me Master and Lord: and ye say well; for so I am. If I then . . . have washed your feet; ye also ought to wash one another's feet. For I have given you an example, that ye should do as I have done to you.'   ST JOHN XIII, 13-15.

'By this shall all men know that ye are my disciples, if ye have love one to another.'   ST JOHN XIII, 35.

'Ye have heard that it hath been said, Thou shalt love thy

neighbour, and hate thine enemy. But I say unto you, Love your enemies, bless them that curse you, do good to them that hate you, and pray for them which despitefully use you, and persecute you; that ye may be the children of your Father which is in heaven: . . .' ST MATT. V, 43-45.

'Take heed to yourselves: If thy brother trespass against thee, rebuke him; and if he repent, forgive him. And if he trespass against thee seven times in a day, and seven times in a day turn again to thee, saying, I repent; thou shalt forgive him.'

ST LUKE XVII, 3-4.

'Judge not, and ye shall not be judged: condemn not, and ye shall not be condemned: forgive, and ye shall be forgiven: Give, and it shall be given unto you; . . .' ST LUKE VI, 37-8.

'And why beholdest thou the mote that is in thy brother's eye, but perceiveth not the beam that is in thine own eye?'

ST LUKE VI, 41.

'Enter ye in at the strait gate: for wide is the gate, and broad is the way, that leadeth to destruction, and many there be which go in thereat: because strait is the gate, and narrow is the way, which leadeth unto life, and few there be that find it.'

ST MATT. VII, 13-14.

'Lay not up for yourselves treasures upon earth, where moth and rust doth corrupt, and where thieves break through and steal: but lay up for yourselves treasures in heaven, where neither moth nor rust doth corrupt, and where thieves do not break through nor steal: For where your treasure is, there will your heart be also.' ST MATT, VI, 19-21.

'No man can serve two masters: . . . Ye cannot serve God and mammon.' ST MATT. VI, 24.

'. . . Take no thought for your life, what ye shall eat, or what ye shall drink; nor yet for your body, what ye shall put on. Is not the life more than meat, and the body than raiment?

ST MATT. VI, 25.

'. . . for your heavenly Father knoweth that ye have need of all these things. But seek ye first the kingdom of God, and his righteousness; and all these things shall be added unto you.'

ST MATT. VI, 32-3.

' Except a corn of wheat fall into the ground and die, it abideth alone: but if it die, it bringeth forth much fruit.'

ST JOHN XII, 24.

'. . . If any man will come after me, let him deny himself, and take up his cross, and follow me. For whosoever will save his life shall lose it: and whosoever will lose his life for my sake, shall find it. For what is a man profited, if he shall gain the whole world, and lose his own soul? or what shall a man give in exchange for his soul?'   ST MATT. XVI, 24-26.

'. . . Except ye be converted, and become as little children, ye shall not enter into the kingdom of heaven. . . . whoso shall offend one of these little ones which believe in me, it were better for him that a millstone were hanged about his neck, and that he were drowned in the depth of the sea.'

ST MATT. XVIII, 3 and 6.

'. . . every tree is known by his own fruit. . . . A good man out of the good treasure of his heart bringeth forth that which is good; and an evil man out of the evil treasure of his heart bringeth forth that which is evil: for of the abundance of the heart his mouth speaketh.'   ST LUKE VI, 44-5.

'. . . It is easier for a camel to go through the eye of a needle, than for a rich man to enter into the kingdom of God. . . . But with God all things are possible.'   ST MATT. XIX, 24, 26.

'. . . whosoever will be great among you, let him be your minister; and whosoever will be chief among you, let him be your servant: even as the Son of man came not to be ministered unto, but to minister, and to give his life a ransom for many.'

ST MATT, XX, 26-8.

' Sell that ye have, and give alms; provide yourselves bags which wax not old, . . .' ST LUKE XII, 33.

' And blessed is he, whosoever shall not be offended in me.'

ST MATT. XI, 6.

' If ye love me, keep my commandments.' ST JOHN XIV, 15.

THE EIGHT BEATITUDES, FROM ST MATT. V, 3-12
' Blessed are the poor in spirit: for theirs is the kingdom of heaven.
Blessed are they that mourn: for they shall be comforted.
Blessed are the meek: for they shall inherit the earth.
Blessed are they which do hunger and thirst after righteousness: for they shall be filled.
Blessed are the merciful: for they shall obtain mercy.
Blessed are the pure in heart: for they shall see God.
Blessed are the peacemakers: for they shall be called the children of God.
Blessed are they which are persecuted for righteousness' sake: for theirs is the kingdom of heaven.
Blessed are ye, when men shall revile you, and persecute you, and shall say all manner of evil against you falsely, for my sake.
Rejoice, and be exceeding glad: for great is your reward in heaven: for so persecuted they the prophets which were before you.'

II. ON WHAT THE CHRISTIAN IS TO EXPECT
IN THE WORLD:

' And ye shall be hated of all men for my name's sake: but he
that endureth to the end shall be saved.' ST MATT. X, 22.

' Think not that I come to send peace on earth: I came not to
send peace, but a sword.' ST MATT. X, 34.

' Behold, I send you forth as sheep in the midst of wolves: be
ye therefore wise as serpents, and harmless as doves.'

ST MATT. X, 16.

III. ON THE ASSURANCES GRANTED TO
THE CHRISTIAN BELIEVER:

' But when they deliver you up, take no thought how or what
ye shall speak: for it shall be given you in that same hour what
ye shall speak. For it is not ye that speak, but the Spirit of your
Father which speaketh in you.' ST MATT. X, 19-20.

' And fear not them which kill the body, but are not able to
kill the soul: but rather fear him which is able to destroy both
soul and body in hell. Are not two sparrows sold for a farthing?
and one of them shall not fall on the ground without your
Father. But the very hairs of your head are all numbered. Fear
ye not therefore, ye are of more value than many sparrows.'

ST MATT. X, 28-31.

' Come unto me, all ye that labour and are heavy laden, and I
will give you rest. Take my yoke upon you, and learn of me;
for I am meek and lowly in heart: and ye shall find rest unto
your souls. For my yoke is easy, and my burden is light.'

ST MATT. XI, 28-30.

'. . . Ask, and it shall be given you; seek, and ye shall find;
knock, and it shall be opened unto you.' ST LUKE XI, 9.

'If ye, then, being evil, know how to give good gifts unto your children, how much more shall your Father which is in heaven give good things to them that ask him?'   ST LUKE XI, 13.

'... If ye continue in my word, then are ye my disciples indeed; and ye shall know the truth, and the truth shall make you free.'
ST JOHN VIII, 31-2.

'And I will pray the Father, and he shall give you another Comforter, that he may abide with you for ever; even the Spirit of truth; ...'   ST JOHN XIV, 16-17.

'... the Comforter ... he shall teach you all things, and bring all things to your remembrance, whatsoever I have said unto you.'
ST JOHN XIV, 26.

'... lo, I am with you alway, even unto the end of the world.'
ST MATT. XVII, 20.

IV. WHAT CHRIST SAID OF HIMSELF:

'Think not that I am come to destroy the law, or the prophets: I am not come to destroy, but to fulfil.'   ST MATT. V, 17.

'I can of mine own self do nothing: ... I seek not mine own will, but the will of the Father which hath sent me.'   ST JOHN V, 30.

'... He that believeth on me hath everlasting life.'
ST JOHN VI, 47.

'... I am the light of the world: he that followeth me shall not walk in darkness, but shall have the light of life.'
ST JOHN VIII, 12.

'I and my Father are one.'   ST JOHN X, 30.

'... I am the resurrection, and the life: he that believeth in me, though he were dead, yet shall he live:'   ST JOHN XI, 25.

'... With desire I have desired to eat this passover with you before I suffer: ... Take this, and divide it among yourselves: ... This is my body which is given for you: this do in remembrance of me.... This cup is the new testament in my blood, which is shed for you.'   ST LUKE XXII, 15, 17, 19, 20.

'... Father save me from this hour: but for this cause came I unto this hour.'   ST JOHN XII, 27.

' And I, if I be lifted up from the earth, will draw all men unto me.'   ST JOHN XII, 32.

' I am the vine, ye are the branches: Abide in me, and I in you. As the branch cannot bear fruit of itself, except it abide in the vine; no more can ye, except ye abide in me.' ST JOHN XV, 5, 4.

' Greater love hath no man than this, that a man lay down his life for his friends.'   ST JOHN XV, 13.

'... In the world ye shall have tribulation: but be of good cheer; I have overcome the world.'   ST JOHN XVI, 33.

INDEX

A

Abelard, 68, 125
Absolutes, 36-41, 67-79, 173
Adam, K., 246
  The Spirit of Catholicism, 243
Agnosticism, 16, 70, 82, 216-17
Alcibiades, 87 n.
Allan, D. J.
  The Philosophy of Aristotle, 81
Anaxagoras, 67-8, 76, 111
Anselm, St, 142, 228
Anthropomorphism, 98, 138
Arianism, 199
Aristotle, 80-8
  De Anima, 84, 283-4
  Eudemian Ethics, 83
  Metaphysics, 80
  Nicomachean Ethics, 84-5, 282-3
Arnold, M., 102, 176
  Literature and Dogma, 225
Atheism, 37, 41-9, 69, 179
Augustine, St, 118, 142, 149, 218, 220, 231, 243 n., 244, 249
  Confessions, 122

B

Babbitt, I.
  The Buddha and the Occident, 176, 178
Bacon, F.
  Idola (from Novum Organum), 99
Balfour, Lord, 54
Baudelaire, 62
Baynes, C., 165
Bell, C.
  Proust, 19
Bendit, L.
  Paranormal Psychology, 55
Bergson, 43, 53, 230, 240, 273-5
Berguer, G., 198
Berkeley, G., 42
Bernanos, G.
  Le Journal d'un Curé de Campagne, 233
Bernard, C., 21
Bevan, E.
  Christianity, 233
Biancani
  Le Mystère de la Vie, 37
Bibby, C.
  T. H. Huxley, 56
Bible, the, 207, 251-2

371

Index

Old Testament, 189, 191, 212, 349-60
New Testament, 195, 362-8
passages quoted (pp. 349-60 [O.T.], 362-8 [N.T.].
Genesis (see also pp. 120, 187, 280)
  XII: 1-3
  XV: 3-6
  XVII: 3, 5, 7, 9-11
  XXI: 1-4
Exodus
  III: 1-13
  XIX: 1-11, 20, 21
  XX: 1-19
  XXIII: 19-21
  XXXIII: 7, 9-11
  XXXIV: 4-6, 8, 28-30
Deuteronomy
  VI: 4-9, 18, 19
  XVIII: 18, 19
  XXXIV: 5, 8, 9
Isaiah
  IX: 2, 6, 7
  X: 20, 21
  XI: 1-5
  LIII: 1-6, 9, 12
Jeremiah
  XXXI: 31-4
Ezekiel
  III: 16-18
  XXXIV: 15, 16
Daniel
  VII: 13, 14

  XII: 2, 3
Joel
  II: 12, 13
Amos
  V: 14, 15, 21, 22, 24
Jonah
  III: 1, 2
Micah
  V: 2
  VI: 3, 4, 7, 8
  VII: 18
Malachi
  III: 1, 2
Ecclesiasticus
  XLIV
  XLV
  XLVI
  XLVII
St Matthew
  V: 3-12, 17, 43-5
  VI: 19-21, 24, 25, 32, 33
  VII: 13, 14
  X: 16, 19, 20, 22, 28-31, 34
  XI: 6, 28-30
  XVI: 24-6
  XVII: 20
  XVIII: 3, 6
  XIX: 24, 26
  XX: 26-8
  XXII: 37-40
St Luke
  VI: 37, 38, 41, 44, 45
  XI: 9, 13

Index

XII: 33
XVII: 3, 4
XXII: 15, 17, 19, 20
St John
IV: 24
V: 30
VI: 47
VIII: 12, 31, 32
X: 30
XI: 25
XII: 24, 27, 32
XIII: 13-15, 35
XIV: 15-17, 26
XV: 4, 5, 13
XVI: 33
Acts of the Apostles
VII
I Corinthians
XII: 26 (see p. 233)
Bonhoeffer, D., 208
Braithwaite, R. B.
An Empiricist's View of the Nature of Religious Belief, 171
Broad, C. D., 47-57, 270-3
Henry Sidgwick and Psychical Research, 51, 57, 273
Human Personality and the Possibility of its Survival, 53 n.
Introduction to McTaggart's ' Some Dogmas of Religion,' 47-8, 125

Mind and its Place in Nature, 50-3, 270-3
Personal Identity and Survival, 53 n.
Brooke, R., 106
Browning, R., 78
Brunner, E., 217
Buddhism, 16, 173-81, 334-9
Anatta, 179
Arhat and Arhatship, 173, 175, 179
Atman, 176-7, 179
Book of the Great Decease, 338-9
Dhamma, 176
Dhammapada, 334-8
Four Noble Truths, 174, 179, 339
Karma, 179
Kwan Yin, 179
Mahayana, 179, 223
Metempsychosis, 179
Nirvana, 173-9
Noble Eightfold Path, 174-6, 179, 339
Parivarta, 179, 223
Skandhas, 179

C

Caird, E.
Evolution of Religion, 67, 128, 189, 219
Hegel, 314 n.

Philosophy of Kant, 300

Cammaerts, E.
Flower of Grass, 219

Camus, A., 15

Carington, W., 230

Carrel, A.
Man the Unknown, 55

Cecil, A.
A House in Bryanston Square, 164, 214

Chaning-Pearce, M.
Sören Kierkegaard, 148, 150, 153, 320-1

Christ, *see* Jesus Christ

Christianity and the Christian Church, 58, 73-4, 76, 87, 98, 103, 112, 138-57, 164, 180 *n.*, 195-257
Apostles, 239, 249
Indulgences, 233
New Testament, *see* Bible
Reformation, 245, 252
Saints, 233-4

Clement XI [Pope], 243 *n.*

Cloud of Unknowing, 320

Coleridge, S. T., 86, 196, 251
Letters, 45
The Friend, 97, 132, 134

Congar, Y.
Christ, Marie et L'Eglise, 248

Connolly, C.
Palinurus, The Unquiet Grave, 18, 131

Corbett, J. P., 254

Cornford, F. M.
Before and After Socrates, 283
Greek Religious Thought, 68, 283

Coulson, C. A.
Science and Christian Belief, 112, 121

Coutourier [Abbé], 246

D

Darwin, C., 58

Davids, T. W. R., 338

De Lubac, H.
Catholicism, 244

De Ruggiero, G., 19

De St Victor, H., 318

Descartes, R., 91-100, 142
Discourse on Method, 91-3, 97, 285
Meditations, 91, 94, 286-7
Olympica (from *Oeuvres Inedités*), 98
Principles of Philosophy, 92

Determinism, 105

Dewey, M. B., 213

Dodd, C. H.
The Bible Today, 107-8, 189, 197, 235, 246, 252

Dogma, 210-27

Dostoievsky, F. M., 12, 218, 249

Drury, M. O'C., 320

Dualism, 42, 101

E

Ehrenwald, 55 *n.*
Einstein, A., 121
Eliot, G., 25
Eliot, T. S., 132
Emerson, R. W., 58, 133
Emmet, D.,
  Nature of Metaphysical Think-ing, 209
Epiphenomenalism, 36, 42, 265-6
Ethics, 50, 214
Evil, 107, 162, 218
Extra-sensory perception, 53-7, 230, 275

F

Farrer, A. (ed.)
  Observations on the book, 'The Origin of Evil', 120
Fechner, 254
Fichte, 132
Flanagan, P.
  Newman, Faith and Belief, 206, 208
Forms (Platonic theory of), 36-41, 68-81, 278-9
France, A., 15
Francis of Sales, St
  Introduction to the Devout Life, 244

Frank, S.
  God with Us, 219
Freud, S., 19, 55, 69-70, 224
Fuller, T.
  Good Thoughts in Bad Times, 235

G

Gandhi, M., 161
Gautama
  Maha-vagga, 173-80
Gibbon, E., 243
Gilson, E., 201
Gnostics, 183-4
God
  absolute Form of Good (Plato), 34, 47, 73-5
  absolute God of a relative universe, 68
  absolute Mind (Spinoza), 101-15, 137
  absolute Person (Hegel), 138-44
  benevolence, 60-1, 68, 133
  Creator, 60, 68, 83, 121, 133, 162
  existence, 35-41, 45-157, 294
  argument from design (Leibniz), 293
  argument from eternal truths (Leibniz), 295
  argument from intuition (Descartes), 94-5

argument from pre-established harmony (Leibniz), 116-26

cosmological proof (Kant), 134, 300-1

ontological proof (Kant), 95, 300

physico-theological proof (Kant), 134, 301-2

Fashioner of an orderly universe (Socrates and Plato), 68

Father-figure (Freud), 69

First Mover, 61, 76

impersonal, 174

inseparable from Nature (Spinoza), 101-15

limited freedom (Leibniz), 117-18

Mind (Anaxagoras), 67

most perfect Being (Spinoza), 101

movement towards the finite (Hegel), 137, 168

Natural Laws support benevolence, 61

prescience, 162

revelation, 24, 45-6, 91-6, 166, 211-13

Self-conscious Reason (Hegel) 137

supreme Monad (Leibniz), 117

theophanies, 21-4

the Trinity, 138-42, 151, 183, 212, 225-6, 311

Unity of God (Mohammed), 342

unmoved Mover (Aristotle), 80-4, 86, 282

whether the unimaginable is credible (Descartes), 98

Goethe, J. W., 99

Gore, C.
Philosophy of the Good Life, 190

Great Decease, Book of, 338-9

Gregory the Great [Pope], 249

Guitton, J.
The Problem of Jesus, 37 *n.,* 200 *n.,* 239-40

H

Hampshire, S.
Spinoza, 98, 117, 289

Hardy, A., 55 *n.*

Heard, G.
Is God in History? 177

Hegel, G. W. F., 136-44, 163, 196-8
Logic, 138
Philosophy of Religion, 136-41, 144, 155, 198, 214, 226, 238, 303-15

Heidegger, 255

Index

Heine, H., 136
Helfferich
Mystik, 318
Hell, 162, 171, 220
Helmholtz, 55
Heraclitus, 107
Heywood, R.
The Sixth Sense, 53-7, 230-1
Hinduism, 16, 161-72, 322-33
Atman, 162
Bhagavadgíta, 167, 169, 171, 326-33
Brahmanism, 173
Brahma-Samaj movement, 170
Castes, 167
Dhamma, 167
Karma, 161-2
Krishna, 168, 326
Metempsychosis, 161, 169
Upanishads, 168-9, 322-6
Vedas, 168
Hobbes, T., 224
Hostie, R.
Religion and the Psychology of Jung, 224, 248
Hume, D., 205, 275
Essay on Immortality, 62
Hunt, L., 59
Huxley, A., 242
Ends and Means, 18-19, 189
Huxley, J.
Evolution in Action, 112

I

Idealism, absolute, 49-50
Iremonger, F.A.
William Temple, 216
Isherwood, C., 171
Islam, 109 *n.*, 182-6, 340-8

J

Jacobi, J., 109-10, 129-30
James, M. R.
Apocryphal New Testament, 183
James, W., 17, 57, 84, 275
Jansenists, 243 *n.*
Jaspers, K., 113
Jeans, J.
The Mysterious Universe, 111-12
Jesus Christ, 108-9, 140, 170, 182-4, 342-7
Atonement, 212, 225, 228-35
Crucifixion, 183-4
Incarnation, 140-1, 145-51, 156, 183-4, 195, 203, 212
Resurrection, 198, 236-41
Trinity, 138-42, 151, 183, 212, 225-6, 311
Joad, C. E. M.
Guide to Philosophy, 274
The Recovery of Belief, 275-7
John the Baptist, St, 87

377

Index

John the Scot, 118
Joseph, H. W. B.
  The Philosophy of Leibniz, 118
Jowett, B., 40-1, 79
  Introduction to Plato's *Laws*,
    76-7, 280
  Introduction to Plato's
    Phaedo, 35
  Introduction to Plato's *Re-*
    public, 74
Judaism, 187-91
  Old Testament, *see* Bible
  Present-day beliefs, 360-1
Jung, C. G., 70, 85, 230, 255
  Answer to Job, 248
  Integration of Personality, 198
  Modern Man in Search of a
    Soul, 223-4
  Psychology and Religion, 56,
    225, 252
  Secret of the Golden Flower,
    165, 180 *n.*

K

Kant, I., 127-35, 299-302
  Critique of Practical Reason,
    128-9, 155
  Critique of Pure Reason, 134
  Enquiry into the Grounds of
    Proof for the Existence of
    God, 301
Keats, J., 37, 132
  Lamia, 88

Letters, 20, 87, 133
Keshab, 170
Kierkegaard, S., 145-57, 165,
  196, 204, 216, 316-21
  Concluding Unscientific Post-
    script, 147-8, 152, 155, 317
  Final Postscript, 318
  For Self-Examination, 148-9,
    154-6, 202, 317-18
  Journals, 148, 316, 318, 320
  Philosophic Fragments, 316
  Point of View, 148, 153, 156
  Sickness unto Death, 148-9, 318
  Supplement to 'On my Work as
    an Author', 317
  That Individual, 153
  Training in Christianity, 148-
    50, 153-4, 156, 316-17, 321
Koran, 109 *n.*, 183-5, 340-8

L

Law, W.
  Christian Regeneration, 223
  Mystical Writings, 152
Lawrence, D. H.
  Apropos of 'Lady Chatterley's
    Lover', 255
Leibniz, G. W., 116-26, 292-8
  Monadology, 117, 124-5, 292-8
  Theodicy, 117-19
Lewis, C. S., 229
  Arthurian Torso, 228
Locke, J., 31, 95, 130, 134

Index

Lotze, 45
Lowrie, W.
  Short Life of Kierkegaard, 148
Luther, M., 86
  Table Talk, 94

M

MacDonald, G.,
  Anthology, 216
Mackinnon, D. M.
  The Resurrection, 237
McTaggart, J. McT. E., 42-9,
  212
  Philosophical Studies, 45, 48
  Some Dogmas of Religion, 42-4,
  253, 267-9
Maimonides, M., 360
Man
  brain, 43, 53, 273-5
  death, 33
  death-wish, 47
  faith, 204-9
  fall, 118-22
  immortality of the soul, 29-
    64, 78, 84, 127-8, 134-5,
    265-9, 312-15
  mind, 52, 271-3
  self, 42, 85, 174-7, 268-9
  self-determination, 118, 128
  sin, 116-26
  soul's self-judgment, 33
  suicide, 31-2
  will, 149-50

Manichees, 284
Marcel, G.
  The Mystery of Being, 114-15,
  201, 233
Maritain, J., 202
Marx, K., 224
Mary, the Virgin, 183, 247-8,
  345
Matter, 42-3
Maurice, F. D.
  The Religions of the World,
  185, 187, 191
Max of Saxony [Prince], 169
Mechanical Theory of Nature,
  36
Mohammed, 109 *n.*, 182-6, 340-
  8
Monads, 116-26, 292-8
Monism, 268
Monotheism, 161, 187
Moore, G. E., 43
Morley, J.
  On Compromise, 214
Morris, W., 192
Mozoomdar, P. C., 170
Muller, M., 322
Murphy, G., 54, 230
Murry, J. M.
  Price of Leadership, 245

N

Narang, G. C.
  Real Hinduism, 163

Nature, Mechanical theory of, 36
— inseparable from God, 101-15
Newman, J. H., 177, 204-8, 213, 222
  Development of Christian Doctrine, 243
  Discourses to Mixed Congregations, 207-8
  Early Journals (from *Autobiographical writings*), 208
  Grammar of Assent, 206
  Loss and Gain, 208
  Sermons on Various Occasions, 207
  Thèses de Fide, 206
  University Sermons, 204, 207
Niebuhr, R., 216
Nietzsche, F., 96

O

O'Malley, L. S. S.
  Popular Hinduism, 161
Origen, 31, 142, 244
Otto, R.
  The Idea of the Holy, 93
Ovid
  Metamorphoses, 123

P

Pantheism, 101-15, 161

Paradise
  earthly, 37-9, 51, 220
  heavenly, 37-9, 162
Pascal, B., 98, 124, 142, 204-5, 235
  Pensées, 96-7, 123, 190-1, 216, 223
Paul, St, 123, 140, 233, 239
Paul III [Pope], 214
Piddington, J. E., 54
Pius XI [Pope]
  Allocution to the Lenten Preachers of Rome, 245
Plato, 29-41, 46, 59, 67-81, 85-6, 95, 162, 200, 223
  Forms, 36-41, 68-81, 278-9
  Laws, 75-7, 265, 279-81
  Meno, 35 n.
  Parmenides, 79, 101
  Phaedo, 21, 32-3, 36, 68, 76, 263-6, 284 n.
  Phaedrus, 30, 35 n., 74
  Republic, 30, 68, 72-4, 93
  Symposium, 30, 74, 87
  Theaetatus, 31
  Timaeus, 74-6
Pliny, 61, 102
Plotinus, 11, 67
Poe, E. A., 22
Pole, R. [Cardinal], 246
Polytheism, 161
Prabhavananda, S., 171
Price, H. H., 53, 55 n., 230-1, 274

Index

Proust, M., 19, 100
Psychical Research, Society for, 51-7, 205
  Proceedings, 51, 54, 55 *n.*
Psychic phenomena, 51-5, 275-7
Purgatory, 221, 250

Q

Quiller-Couch, A.
  On the Art of Reading, 23

R

Radhakrishnan, S., 16
  Hindu View of Life, 161-2
  Idealist View of Life, 163, 168
Ramanuja, 176
  Sayings, 163
Ramsey, A. M.
  The Resurrection of Christ, 236-7, 251
Reid, F., 35
Reminiscence, 35
Rodwell, J. M.
  The Koran, 184-5, 340-8
Roy, R., 170
Russell, B.
  History of Western Philosophy, 43, 68-9, 84-5, 87, 284, 292
  Impact of Science on Society, 253
  Why I am not a Christian, 223
'Rutherford, M.', 22

S

Sanders, J., 236
Santayana, G.
  Winds of Doctrine, 202
Sartre, J.-P., 255
Saurat, D.
  History of Religions, 100
Selwyn, E. G.
  The Resurrection (in *Essays Catholic and Critical*), 237, 239
Sen, K. C., 170
Sherrington, C.
  Man on his Nature, 61-2, 102, 253
Sidgwick, H., 50, 57, 179
Simmias, 21, 36, 41
Smith, R. B.
  Mohammed and Mohammedanism, 182-4, 340
Socrates, 30-3, 68, 72-3, 87, 93, 263-6
Spinoza, 101-15, 288-9
  Cogitata Metaphysica, 107
  Ethics, 109, 290-1
  The Short Treatise, 217
  Tractatus de Emendatione, 111
Stapfer
  The Life of Kant, 134-5
Stern, K.
  The Third Revolution, 224

Sterrett, J. M.
  Studies in Hegel's 'Philosophy of Religion', 136-8, 303-15
Strauss, 239
Swift, J.
  Tale of a Tub, 99, 233
Syncretism, 165-6

T

Tagore, Debendra-nāth, 170
Talleyrand, 164
Taylor, A. E.
  Aristotle, 284
  Plato, the Man and his Work, 265
Taylor, J., 97
  Dissuasive from Popery, 133-4
Telepathy, 53, 276
Temple, W., 197
  Readings in St John, 246
Tennyson, A., 57-8
  In Memoriam, 57
Tertullian, 284
Thomas Aquinas, St, 142, 240
Thomson, G., 55 *n.*
Tomlin, E. W. F.
  Simone Weil, 232, 250
Toynbee, A.
  Christianity among the Religions of the World, 201
Traherne, T.
  Centuries of Meditation, 23, 39-40

Precepts of Felicity, 256-7
The Divine Lover, 253
Truth, 96
Tyrrell, G. N. M., 230

U

Ueberweg, F.
  History of Philosophy, 95, 129-31, 288-9

V

Valéry, P., 37, 132
Van Druten, J.
  Vedanta for the Western World, 18-19
Vann, G.
  St Thomas Aquinas, 169
  The Water and the Fire, 198
Varro, 97
Vaughan, H.
  The Retreat, 77
Voltaire, F. M. A., 134, 254
  Candide, 120
Von Hügel, 251

W

Wallace, W.
  Hegel, 144
Ward, W.
  Life of Cardinal Newman, 206
Wasserman, J., 204

Index

Watts, A.
  Myth and Ritual in Christianity,
  248
Webb, C., 197
Weil, S., 249
  Gravity and Grace, 232
  Notebooks, 113, 162, 178,
  232
Westcott, F.
  The Revelation of the Risen
  Lord, 237
White, V., 198
  God and the Unconscious, 198,
  284
  God the Unknown, 245
White, W. H.
  More Pages from a Journal,
  23
  Spinoza, 111 n., 217 n.
Whitehead, A. N., 121, 125
  Adventures of Ideas, 76 n., 113,
  200, 293
  Nature and Life, 76 n.
  Process and Reality, 76
  Religion in the Making, 223

Willey, B.
  Christianity Past and Present,
  214
  Nineteenth Century Studies, 25
  More Nineteenth Century
  Studies, 23, 57, 58, 214-15
Williams, C.
  He Came Down From Heaven,
  229, 232, 234, 241, 252
Williams, H. A., 226
Williams, M.
  Buddhism, 173, 175, 338-9
  Brahmanism and Hinduism, 170
Willis, R. D.
  Spinoza: Life, Correspondence
  and Ethics, 107-9, 293
Wittgenstein, L., 319-20
Wizenmann, 128
Wycliffe, 178

Z

Zaehner, R. C.
  At Sundry Times, 85, 163, 169,
  175-7, 183-5, 326-7